NUTRITION SURVIVAL KIT

Dedicated to:
    Dr. Hermina Guttmann
        . . . she knew, but no one listened

Nutrition Survival Kit

A Natural Foods Recipe and Reference Guide

Kathy Dinaburg and D'Ann Ausherman Akel

PANJANDRUM PRESS
AND ARIS BOOKS
San Francisco

Panjandrum Press/Aris Books
99 Sanchez Street
San Francisco, California 94114

Editorial and design: Dennis Koran, L. J. Harris, Martin Ilian

Cover design: Elizabeth Delphey, MidPress Productions

Line drawings: Dena McDuffie

First printing: November, 1976
Second printing: February, 1977
Third printing: March, 1978
Fourth printing: September, 1978
Manufactured in the United States of America

Library of Congress catalog card number 76-28772.

Library of Congress Cataloging in Publication Data

Dinaburg, Kathy.
    Nutrition survival kit.
    Includes bibliographical references and indexes.
    1. Cookery (Natural foods). 2. Nutrition. 3. Food, Natural. I. Akel, D'Ann Ausherman, joint author.
II. Title. [DNLM: 1. Nutrition. 2. Cookery. QU145 D538n]
TX741.D56   641.5 63   76-28772
ISBN 0-915572-18-4
ISBN 0-915572-17-6 pbk.

Contents

Foreword

When is a cookbook more than a cookbook? When it gives you the nutritional facts you need to enable you to choose a safe, healthful, economical and ecologically sound diet!

Each shopping day, the average supermarket consumer must face about 10,000 products, many of which are of questionable nutritive value and some of which may be actually harmful. Even conscientious "enlightened" shoppers are affected by hearsay and nutritional misinformation. And unfortunately, when it comes to nutrition and food safety, what appears to be a "common sense" assumption may not be true at all.

What follows is really two books: one provides *facts* culled from respected professional journals and texts; and one translates theory into practice in the form of delicious recipes. In addition, there are extensive references for further study, and most recipes have been analyzed for the major nutrients, making it easier to plan an adequate diet. This is much more than just another cookbook.

* * * * * * * * *

Thanks to all the students whose questions sharpened our thinking and whose enthusiasm carried us through; and special thanks to Jaime Jackson, Pat Johnson, Nancy Loesch, Olga Macomber, Leo Rowe, and Martha Wehrly: for reasons they know best.

I

Politics in the Pantry

Hi and Lois

"Hi and Lois" copyright © King Features Syndicate 1975.

The failure of regulation to insure safe, pure, and nutritious food in the world's largest breadbasket has been in step with each new ingenious technique for manipulating the content of food products.
    —Ralph Nader, Introduction to *The Chemical Feast*, New York, 1970

Food faddism is indeed a serious problem. But . . . the guru of food faddism is not Adelle Davis, but Betty Crocker. The true food faddists are not those who eat raw broccoli, wheat germ and yoghurt, but those who start the day on Breakfast Squares, gulp down bottle after bottle of soda pop, and snack on candies and Twinkies . . . people who eat a junk food diet constitute the norm, while individuals whose diets resemble those of our grandparents are labeled deviants.
    —Michael Jacobson, *Science*, Vol. 188, May 16, 1975

1

Some PEOPLE, in discussing the state of nutrition in America, seem to imply that the boardrooms of the biggest food-producing companies are filled with greedy executives who leer and chuckle at the prospect of malnutrition (American and global) and wring their hands in anticipation of still-greater profits. Hardly.

NEW "FOODS" . . .

But it must be stated that the direction in which food production has gone in the last century, and particularly in the last ten years (when the food industry has become so profitable that it is being taken over by huge conglomerates: Greyhound owns Armour Foods, ITT owns Continental Bakery) has been largely determined by what was most profitable. Or to be more exact, what could be *made* most profitable: the mixed blessing of advertising coupled with an extremely innovative technology and chemical industry has created profitable food areas which did not exist in Grandfather's time (for that matter, neither did the "foods"—Cocacola, non-dairy creamer, instant breakfast, puffed and flaked cereal grains).

. . . NEW PROBLEMS

Adding to consumers' woes is the disturbing if not actually nutrition-robbing tendency toward greater production at the expense of quality and taste: never-ripe fruit (picked too under-ripe, it goes directly from green to rotten), blemish-free, tasteless (but gorgeous) vegetables, and meat that is watery and excessively fatty (if not tainted with hormone and antibiotic residues as well).

Other aspects of American food manufacturing practices have also affected global malnutrition. According to USDA statistics, livestock consume 92% of the enormous American corn crop. In fact, fully three-quarters of the *total* American

2

grain production goes to feed animals.[1] Had it been eaten directly, this grain could have provided ten times as much protein, enough to meet almost the entire globe's protein deficit.

We have also exported some of our worst eating habits along with some of our most questionable foods: refined processed grain products, excessive sugar usage (is there a country in the world in which you cannot find "Coke"?— except China) and artificial feeding of infants. In countries where nutrient intake is already marginal, there's no nutritional room to substitute lower-quality processed or empty-calorie foods. And where literacy is hard to come by, let alone nutritional knowledge, the easily acquired taste for sugar can lead even abysmally poor people to spend what little money they have on essentially nutritionless "foods."

Most tragic is that, as a result of massive international advertising campaigns to expand sales in the face of declining birth-rates in Western countries, formula feeding has lately become a fatal status symbol in developing countries. Because the commercial products are quite expensive in terms of prevailing income, bottle feeding often leads to undernourishment, then progressive emaciation ("marasmus") and often death due to over-dilution.[2] But far worse is the increase in mortality due to gastrointestinal infection which follows the switch to bottle feeding. "The pediatric wards of tropical hospitals are full of babies dying of this man-made disease . . . the single largest cause of infant deaths."[3]

To further complicate the domestic food scene, the science of nutrition has been barely able to keep up with the advances in the industrial aspects of food processing. Witness the fact that it took from the early 1800's to the 1930's to discover that the white flour milled from whole wheat had lost the greatest part of its nutrition. Moreover, trace elements, never heard of twenty years ago, have been found to be essential (and usually lacking) in a heretofore "adequate" diet—to say nothing of intentional or incidental chemical food additives, the dangers of which are often discovered years after "long and uneventful" usage in everyone's food. (More on additives in Chapter XI.)

NOURISHMENT OR PROFIT?

All of which goes to show that the priorities of the profit-oriented food industry do not always emphasize safety, nutrition and ecology over other concerns. There have certainly been some unquestioned successes within the food industry—it's not all cold mashed potatoes. The combination of certain advanced farming techniques, sophisticated methods of preservation, and efficient distribution, has, for the first time in history, assured the populace of an enormous nation a continuous, varied, relatively inexpensive food supply. But that's no longer enough. As our globe shrinks, we have to face the political and moral ramifications of our food choices (more specifically, what we are encouraged to choose from).

THE POLITICS OF PROTEIN

Now that the outmoded classification of protein as "first" and "second" class has been updated, there is no longer any justification for the common American dietary dependence on enormous quantities of meat. Feeding most of America's vast grain production to animals—resulting in a net loss of 90% of the protein (see Chapter VIII: Meat Is Bean Replaced)—stands out as a morally incomprehensible agricultural practice in a world where millions are either malnourished or actually starving. (In addition, excessive meat consumption has been linked to the rising incidence of heart disease and bowel cancer—see Chapter V: Be True To Your Heart Or It Will Attack You.)

But eating less meat, hence more of everything else, only intensifies the domestic side of the food problem. The science of nutrition is finding where many errors were made. Now that enough information exists, it is imperative that we try to correct them—and perhaps learn some sort of lesson for the future. In the case of white flour, for example, there is no longer any justification for refining whole grains. Even after "enrichment" the refined grain is much less nutritious; and its consumption is connected with serious, pervasive "civilized" diseases. (See Chapter VI: You Could End Up With A Semi-Colon.) Storage of whole-grain products, once a problem that refined white flour seemed to solve, no longer presents the same dilemma.

Obviously, it is no more correct to unilaterally ban white flour or grain-fed beef than it is to ban cigarettes or alcohol. But the consumer must have information on which to base

4

an advised, intelligent choice—information which is not readily available.

POLITICS AND THE FDA

In fact, in some cases, nutritional realities are denied by the very governmental agencies whose job it is to see that the principle of honesty in the marketplace is upheld. The FDA calls "faddist" those people who make incontrovertible claims about the nutrition losses which result from food processing including milling and canning, and "alarmist" those people who document the growing world food crisis. They also refuse to open for inspection those laboratory tests upon which the "safety" of proposed food additives are based: you can eat it, but you can't find out what happened to the rats that ate it.

Here again, we are not dealing with evil men reeking of bad intentions: we are dealing with a bureaucracy which of necessity, as it is now constituted, responds primarily to political and economic pressures. Lobbyists for major food-producing corporations and special interest groups legally influence legislation. Ranking policymakers in the FDA have been recruited from the very companies they are required to oversee.[4] It's hard to forget what it was like on the other side of the fence, just because you've crossed over. And, vice versa, the FDA is considered a "stepping-stone" to (much) higher-paying jobs in industry. (It might not pay to be overly rambunctious with your potential next employer.)

So there's a sort of stalemate. As the food industry becomes ever more powerful, it is unlikely that the long overdue re-thinking of the basic purpose of food (nourishment or profit) is likely to come from the top. And the FDA, buffeted between industry demands and "consumerism," tends to pull its head into its shell. So the responsibility finally comes to rest on the people who have the most to gain from seeing basic changes made—you and me.

WHAT YOU BUY IS WHAT YOU'LL EAT

Industry rightly claims that it responds to "consumer demand"; but, what they mostly mean is that they provide the advertising, and, before long, they can drum up the demand. If you can't wait for General Foods, Post, Kellogg,

5

and Quaker (who account for 95% of the market) to decide that over 90 kinds of heavily-advertised, over-sugared, nutritionally-worthless breakfast cereals are not in your best interest, you'll just have to stop buying what you don't really want.

You can say *no*. At present it is a self-limiting choice which has about as much force as not voting for the Russian Premier; yet continued passive, or even resentful, acceptance will not make changes. If you buy it, they'll continue to sell it.

CHOICES

The obvious question then becomes: What's left to eat when you find yourself saying *no* to the foods you used to rely on? You can choose to accept a limited version of what you've always eaten—cut down on meat, avoid the least nutritious or the most overly-chemicalled food products. A more positive choice would be to gradually change your old food patterns to include more of the historically validated foods on which our ancestors thrived: whole grains, fresh fruits and vegetables and other real (not chemical imitation or embalmed) foods that have not been unnecessarily processed. Are you willing to find out how good real food can taste?

CAN YOU STOMACH IT?

Very few of the processes so dear to the heart (and pocket-book) of the food giants are *necessary* for safety or nutrition: like adding humectants, thickeners, flavorings, colorings, bleaches, emulsifiers and sequestrants. Even preservatives aren't as essential as claimed: if some brands of the same foodstuff manage to do without them, why can't they all?[5]

The biggest challenge to this thinking comes, not surprisingly, from the food industry. They claim that (1) they are responding to consumer demand; (2) the additives are safe and the food is nutritious because the FDA says so; (3) these kinds of sweeping changes would endanger the food supply and result in mammoth price increases.

But these arguments don't hold up on closer examination. First, consumer demand is for the most part what the agri-business wants it to be—expensive advertising has created lots of demands that consumers never knew they had. Second, most additives have not been adequately tested, as evidenced by the FDA's more frequent bans and de-listings of once "safe"

6

chemicals (most recently, Red Dye No. 2). As for nutrition, despite official denials to the contrary, the diet of the average American has been deteriorating (qualitatively not quantitatively). According to the most complete government survey to date, half the population is deficient in one or more of the nutrients surveyed. There is increasing evidence that those nutrients which have not, until recently, been thought important enough to be surveyed may be the most seriously deficient.

Finally, it is essential to ask what part of the food supply would be endangered. Although it is true that most of the fabricated foods would either have to be made with ingredients of unquestioned safety (precious few), or they would disappear from the marketplace, it is not at all clear that this would represent a loss *to the consumer*. If artificially flavored, artificially colored and preserved breakfast cereals were banned, people would just have to eat the real thing. It's hard to consider that a net loss.

Price depends more on the whim of the manufacturer and on what the traffic will bear, than it does on the actual cost of ingredients: when General Mills made Total out of Wheaties, by spraying with only ½¢ worth of vitamins per box, the price jumped 20 cents.

It is possible that some prices would legitimately rise. It is more expensive to put blueberries in the muffin mix than to put in a test-tube concoction consisting of sugar, starch, flavors and colors. And there is the additional argument that there wouldn't be enough of the real foods to go around. For example, the synthetic equivalent of six times the actual strawberry crop is needed each year for various products. Again, one must ask, *Go around where?* Strawberry gelatin, strawberry soda, strawberry cakes, jams, tarts. Would the quality of the diet in any way be reduced if the greater part of these "foods" were no longer available? Combining a fraction of a cent's worth of strawberry flavors and (potentially dangerous Red No. 2) with sweetener enables any of the food manufacturers to sell water for over a dollar per gallon. It does not seem that consumers who have been willing to buy potatoes which cost almost $2 per pound (chips) or flour at more than 50 cents per pound (pancake mix) should blanch at spending a few cents more to get nutrition, taste, and safety.

It is even possible that wholly nutritious foods could

7

cost *less*: after all, brown rice requires no expensive milling and enriching machinery; yet at present, since it is a specialty item and not a staple, it costs more.

DON'T FORGET TO VOTE

What has seemed to be a simple enough question, "What's for dinner?" actually has far-reaching ramifications. Only an informed shopper can exert the economic pressures which will improve the overall food picture. Essentially, you as consumer have to decide and vote: if your *no* to non-quality means that certain "foods" don't make the profits they once did, industry response to *real* consumer demand is inevitable.

II

How to Get the Most Out of Your Kitchen or How to Get Out of Your Kitchen the Most

Andy Capp

The consumer needs effective tools in her hands if she is to deal with today's fast-moving, convenience-oriented world. She needs information updated to the minute, to the way things are now, not the way they were 50 years ago.
—Dr. Philip L. White, Council on Foods and Nutrition, American Medical Assn. reported in *School Foodservice Journal*, October, 1973

Typically, food habit changes have been viewed as the result of irresistible social forces produced by 'women's desire for liberation from the kitchen' . . . (but) in a society truly dedicated to time saving, energy conservation, and women's liberation, the pressures that presumably have led to sugar-glazed frozen carrots could have led as well to eating vegetables raw—thus reducing preparation time to zero.
—Jane Gussow, "Evaluating the American Diet", *Journal of Home Economics*, November, 1973

9

THE NEW natural foods cook* is often bewildered, and not a little defensive. With nothing more than his or her faith in the new-found religion, she or he steps off the precipice into the void of new ingredients, new cooking methods, and the likelihood of some negative "consumer" feedback. As with most apprehensions, the reality isn't quite as bad as the fear. But one needs guidance to cushion some of the harder knocks ("Do we have to *eat* it?") and to avoid some others—like walking into the kitchen confident at 4:30 and stumbling out a complete wreck four hours later with the beans still the consistency of soft pebbles.

Nutrition is all well and good (that's what the rest of the book is about): this chapter deals with *essentials*—how, what, and when. ("Why" will have to fend for itself elsewhere.)

TIMESAVERS

One of the critical factors in changing to the natural foods diet is the reorganization of time. Some people who would like to eat differently cling to convenience foods thinking real food might take too long to prepare. And face it, it takes just so long to heat a TV dinner or broil a steak—no matter how well-done you want it. But on the whole, natural foods meals don't take *more* time to prepare, just a different allocation of time. In fact, because there are fewer "courses" in a diet where

---

*The new natural foods cook is not necessarily a *new* cook. However, we have met an increasing number of cooks—with apologies to Men's Lib, more men than women—who've been culturally deprived. They know little about the basics of setting up a kitchen, and they have not yet learned some simple skills that more experienced cooks take for granted. *Some* of the information in this chapter may be more elementary than many cooks will need. If you already know it, skip it.

protein and carbohydrate are usually combined in one dish—or even in one food—well-planned natural foods menus can actually take *less* time to prepare.

At the beginning, when things do not come automatically, it may take longer. But a little planning can avert the major crises. Planning doesn't necessarily imply weekly menus (although, if you decide to do them, you will probably save money as well), but it does require some basic organization. Spend just one minute thinking about today's dinner; if some advance preparation is required, you are forewarned. These advance preparations should not require hours of personal effort; they are usually limited to advance cooking of a bean or some other simple, but time-consuming, job (not time-consuming for you—it takes you only a minute to put the pot on the stove, but the bean is busy for several hours). If there aren't any already-cooked staples in the freezer and you realize you won't have the lead time you need, you can plan a meal to suit the time you have available.

Then, when you're making today's dinner, spend just one more minute to think about tomorrow's. This is when you can put the basic whatsis for tomorrow on another burner. Each day, all you'll have to do is a final assembly or sauce, and salad, while preparing the main time-boggling thing for the next day.

Make in great quantity anything that seems feasible: soups, tomato sauce, pizza, bread, torn greens, cold snacks, granola, yoghurt, hummos, waffles. (See specific recipes for storing or freezing suggestions.) Many entrées can be easily doubled and the extra frozen for a future, harried, there-is-no-time kind of day.

Always make double or even triple beans and grains. You'll be amazed at how easy it is to find a use for them if they glower at you every time you open the refrigerator or freezer door.

MONEYSAVER: BULK BUYING

Aside from the economies suggested on most supermarket handouts (buy produce in season, substitute lower-priced foods where possible, use powdered milk a lot), the best idea we've been able to come up with centers on buying in quantity. Some health foods are admittedly more expensive than their refined counterparts (though not if you stop to consider the difference in nutrition). And even though cutting down your meat and junk consumption offers big savings, more corners to cut are always welcome.

Most health-food stores will give you a discount for buying unbroken sacks of grain (usually 50 lbs.). If you don't live near a natural-food outlet, and you can get enough people together, you can order directly from some companies. Plan to order around 300 pounds—below that, freight charges evaporate potential savings. That may sound like a lot, but 300 pounds (of flour, seeds, and beans) divided among ten adults would probably last a little over a month.

Cooperatives are also usually less expensive to deal with —if you can't find one, start one.

KEEPING FOODS

Canning is great for tomato sauce, fruits, pickles, and preserves, but not for green vegetables. For most vegetables, freezing is easier on the nutrients. If you have a garden, or even if you just take advantage of low in-season supermarket prices for some produce, the freezing section of your refrigerator may not be large enough. You can probably find a second-hand one somewhere, and a separate freezer is exceptionally useful. Don't get a self-defrosting one: they cost more to begin with, use more energy, and, in some instances, food stored in them deteriorates more rapidly. Much better to manually defrost two or three times a year—which is all it will take if you don't open the door every two minutes; or get a chest type so the cold air will stay down inside (with the upright, it spills onto the floor every time the door is opened).

FREEZING

Exhaustive research has been done on the best way to

prepare food for the freezer. Though it seems paradoxical, blanching (a short pre-cooking) of foods to be frozen actually *saves* nutrients. It's true that there is some small loss of water-soluble and heat-labile nutrients during the blanching, but that can be kept to a minimum by carefully following suggested blanching times in up-to-date USDA publications (use a timer with a second hand and a loud buzz), and by using the blanching water over and over. When you're finished, you've practically got soup. Ditto the cooling water, to which you can add ice cubes every so often: the colder it is, the quicker it works and the fewer nutrients you'll leach away.

Despite some unavoidable nutrient loss with blanching, unblanched frozen vegetables suffer even more. Unless their activity is halted by a quick dip in a hot bath, enzymes will continue to act on the vegetable, even in the freezer. In tests, after as little as three months, properly blanched foods had retained twice as much of the nutrients measured as their unblanched vine-mates.

BUGS

Unappetizing as it seems at first, you'll probably have to face the bug problem if you start using natural foods. Even if you get the grain that was sprayed to death, bugs, given the chance, prefer the good food to the other stuff.

Some bugs lay their eggs in the grain before it's harvested. In time, and even in your closed container, they hatch and the grains start walking. These bugs are harmless and I do know some stalwart individuals who murmur "more protein" and keep on eating. For us lily-livers, however, there are other choices.*

At times it has been necessary to examine dinner, grain by grain, before I put it up to cook. But that is no longer necessary—if you freeze grain for two weeks, the eggs don't hatch. It's really as simple as that. You can then store it (in tight jars, there are still creatures that will crawl in if they can find a way) at room temperature until it's used, and nothing will move. Flours, cracked grains, or nuts are different.

---

*There are some books available now that espouse "Insect Cuisine." Many cultures do eat insects, as they are a very good, if obnoxious, protein source.

They should be almost continuously refrigerated or frozen unless you use them quickly—within two months—because once a grain has been broken, as in milling, it is more susceptible to oxidation and rancidity.

If you find you already have small creatures, you don't have to throw the grain away. If you try, you can get them out before you cook. Don't add water and hope they will swim to the top—they won't. Instead they will cling to a grain and drown or scald to death. Put your infested grain on a *low* heat about two or three inches deep in a pan with no water. It may take several minutes, but as the pan and grains get warmer, the beasties will run to where it's coolest —on top of the grain in the middle of the pan. You can scoop them off and proceed with cooking. Larger amounts of grains can be heated in the oven and the little bodies sifted or rinsed away.

One way you can tell you've been invaded, even if nothing actually waves its antennae at you, is to look at the bottom of the jar: if there's lots of powdery stuff, you're looking at bug droppings—they're in there somewhere. A fresh bay leaf or two in a tightly lidded container gets them within a few days, however. Then you can wash the grain just before you use it and they'll float away. You may also notice fine web-like "angel's hair" holding half a dozen grains or a pinch of flour together—in that case, tiny moth larvae have already begun to spin cocoons and you'll either have to eat or run. Freezing is the best prevention.

To foil bugs while storing large amounts of grain, coat the whole grains with a powdery film of pure diatomaceous earth* (made up of the microscopic skeletons of tiny algae called diatoms). Insects scratched by the sharp-edged diatom shells die of dehydration. You can wash the grains before eating if you like, but the material is harmless; test animals even seem to benefit from eating it, perhaps because of the various trace elements it contains.

---

*Perma-Guard D-10 Grain and Seed Storage can be ordered from Bower Industries, Inc., 1601 West Orangewood Ave., Box 1631, Orange, California 92668. Swimming pool diatomaceous earth will not substitute.

Food Storage Chart

- *Flour or cracked grains:* Freeze two weeks. After freezing, flours will keep two to six months or more—depending on the season—in a tightly closed jar. Since rancidity is an ongoing process (oxidation is always happening, even though you may not notice the effects), cracked grains and flours should, optimally, be kept refrigerated or frozen.

- *Whole grains:* Whole grains may keep a year or longer, but freeze first: cracked grains and flours, though, should have first priority for freezing time.

- *Nuts and seeds:* Some nuts may get mushy in only a few weeks at warm temperatures. Rancidity is a definite possibility with raw nuts; ground walnuts from the supermarket usually taste like soap. Whole nuts keep better than chopped, slivered or ground nuts, but keep all nuts as cool as possible. Nuts in the shell keep best of all, but no nut lasts forever.

- *Legumes and seeds for sprouting:* Legumes are excellent keepers and rarely develop bugs even if not frozen. Freezing does not adversely affect sprouting, but long storage at room temperature does.

- *Pasta and noodles:* Bug infestation in pasta is probably introduced after packaging. Try to find a jar or tight-lidded container—a plastic shoebox works well for long noodles. Room temperature is fine for several months.

- *Milk powder:* It will last practically forever *if* you keep it in a tightly closed container. Humidity is ruinous. Riboflavin is probably better preserved if it is kept in the dark, as well.

- *Dried fruit:* The "super dry" fruit (not potassium sorbated, not sulphured) you get at the health-food store doesn't need any special environment other than a tightly capped container. Raisins can sometimes—after months at room temperatures—develop moth larvae: but freezing is not especially recommended because it's so drying.

- *Dried Baking Yeast:* Buy it at the health-food store in bulk packages which are vacuum-sealed and will last forever unopened. Once opened, the yeast may be kept at room temperature if it is not too humid; on general principles I keep mine in a jar in the refrigerator. Moist baking yeast is very

15

perishable and not widely available anymore.

● *Spices and herbs:* Buy in bulk at health food store and keep in tightly closed jars (grow your own, where possible). Date, and throw out after six months or when you no longer notice a pleasantly strong aroma upon opening the jar. There's no point in cooking with stuff that has no taste, and besides, it will throw all your measurements off. You won't believe the difference freshness can make in spices: a home (hand or electric) spice grinder is a delight to use.

● *Honey, molasses, vinegar, and maple syrup:* Never introduce a drop of water into honey—it will "sour." On the other hand, that's just about the only thing that can happen to it; bacteria can't grow in it. It can form crystals ("sugar") in a cold climate—either use it as is or set honey jar in warm water. Molasses, maple syrup, and vinegar can develop a "mother": a thin, harmless scum. Scoop it off for aesthetic reasons, if desired.

● *Oil, peanut butter, sesame butter, and coconut:* At least one major brand of health-food oil is packed with a layer of inert nitrogen; it cannot begin to oxidize (go rancid) until the jar is opened. Open oil (like nuts or cracked grains) is oxidating continuously, but it takes some time before noticable rancidity develops. Optimally, all oils and nut butters should be kept refrigerated (rancidity is retarded by cold). However, if you use them quickly—less than a month—and if you transfer them to smaller jars as you go—for less contact with air—you should have no problem. Natural oils contain natural anti-oxidants, including Vitamin E.

● *Ripened cheese:* Despite official pronouncements, natural cheeses freeze perfectly well. Processed cheese, with its high water content, may not. Although freezing makes for a crumblier texture (swiss-types get a bit dry, cheddar won't slice neatly, but jack and mozzarella seem unaffected), the flavor is not impaired for at least six months. May be thawed and re-frozen, if necessary. We buy cheese in bulk, chop it into usable (1-2 lb.) blocks, wrap them tightly in plastic and freeze individually, thawing blocks as needed. If the change in texture is really objectionable to you, wrapping cheese in vinegar-soaked cloth will usually discourage mold. Also, handle cheese as little as possible: mold usually forms first where you've touched. If some mold appears, the USDA says you can shave it off and eat the rest.

• *Yoghurt:* Official storage times list only about a week for yoghurt. In our experience, however, it keeps perfectly well for up to two months. Boil jars and caps for five minutes before beginning to incubate yoghurt to discourage mold which sometimes develops. It too can merely be scraped off the top.

• *Sprouts:* After desired length of sprout is reached, keep in sprout jar (plastic baggy may take up less room) in refrigerator. If the weather is not too warm, they may even be allowed to keep sprouting; they will develop more leaf and chlorophyll. If left too long (over 1 week) they will "burn" —the edges get slightly brown; they are still delicious.

MENU PLANNING

Things are greatly simplified in the natural-food vegetarian diet: instead of having meat *and* starch *and* dairy *and* vegetable/salad (and probably dessert), you've got a main dish that combines protein and starch (and often dairy), a vegetable or salad, and the simplest of desserts if any. Yet, even though simple, it need never be monotonous. With at least ten grains, ten beans, ten vegetables and ten salads (to say nothing of dairy "accent pieces" and various spices), the number of combinations is staggering. You could probably go at least a year and never have exactly the same meal twice. Let us know if you succeed.

Don't put down four bean recipes in a row, or four rice recipes in a row, either. Every time you pick a main dish, make a note of the ingredients on another sheet. You'll make a shopping list from it, after you've checked your foods on hand. If the main dish is something light, think of a filling salad. If it's an everything-but-the-sink casserole, choose a simple vegetable.

18

Menus

TWO WEEKS OF BALANCED MEALS
(*See Index for Recipe pages)

WEEK No. 1

	BREAKFAST	LUNCH	DINNER
Sunday	Wholewheat waffles* Yoghurt-Fruit topping*	Mrs. Lerch's bean soup* Tabooli with feta*	Rice & Shrimp Barcelona* Basic Braised Vegetables*
Monday	Poached Eggs,* toast, orange sections	Peanut butter sandwich with seeds, milk	Mushroom-barley stew* Kathy Valla's salad* Incredible Cornbread*
Tuesday	Granola* with milk and raisins, ½ grapefruit	Manhattan Clam Chowder* cheese toast	Krautswekel* Parsley-Ginger carrots* Sprout Salad*
Wednesday	Incredible waffles* or Pancakes with fruit	Cheese Surprise Patties* tomato-avacado salad	Broccoli braised with tomato Vegetarian Hash with cheese*
Thursday	Yoghurt Banana split* with Granola* topping	Mulligatawny soup* with cottage cheese cucumber salad	Potato Kugel* John Ree's Cabbage* Celery-olive salad
Friday	Oatmeal* with cinnamon and seeds or nuts dried or fresh fruit	Grainburgers with melted cheese*, Tomato-Onion salad*	Moors & Christians* fried plantains Coleslaw with seeds
Saturday	Spanish Omelette* tropical fruit cup	Sprouted Lentils* with grilled Swiss on Pita*	New England Clam Chowder* raw vegetable salad Peanut Butter-Currant Muffins

WEEK No. 2

Sunday	Yoghurt 'cream cheese'* and lox on wholewheat bagel hot cocoa or Ovaltine	Steamed broccoli with mushroom sauce Bulghur Pilaff*	Soybean Chili with cheese* steamed millet, green salad
Monday	Muesli*, fruit or fruit juice	Melted cheese on corn tortilla* cucumber-tomato slices	Chinese green pepper and mushrooms,* rice* Won Tons*
Tuesday	'Toad-in-a-Hole'* Melon balls	Basque Bisque* raw vegetable slices	Quickest Pasta* Spinach salad with Roquefort*
Wednesday	Yoghurt with fruit compote* Incredible or Biscuit Mix Muffins*	Cous-Cous* Carrifruit-seed salad*	Stuffed Cabbage (Dolmades)* Tabooli*
Thursday	Mixed-grain cereal with fruit and nuts	Kufteh* with Pita* and extra vegetables	Crab Quiche* Tomato-Onion Salad*
Friday	Frittata* with toast juice or fruit	Cottage cheese with raw vegetables, rye crackers	Soybean Curry with condiments* Rice,* Coleslaw*
Saturday	Yoghurt,* fruit, nuts and wheat germ	Sautéed Sprouts* celery/carrots/olives	Cauliflower with cheese sauce* Bulghur* Green-pepper/tomato salad

Note: Some of the above meals will be more balanced with the addition of bread, fruit, or dairy products.

19

International Vegetarian Menus

(See Recipe Index for page numbers)

ORIENTAL

Egg Roll or Won Ton
Stir-fried Vegetables
Brown Rice
Almond Cookies

JEWISH

Mushroom-barley Stew
Blintzes with Yoghurt and Applesauce
Cucumber-tomato Salad
Fruit Compote

MEXICAN

Chiles Rellenos or Enchiladas
Arroz (Brown Rice)
Tossed Green Salad w. Garbanzos
Flan (Caramel Custard)

MEXICAN

Soy Tostadas
with
Lettuce, Cheese, Tomatoes, Cucumber
Tropical Fruit Platter

INDIAN

Vegetable Curry with condiments
Saffron Rice or Steamed Millet
Raita

GREEK

Stuffed Vine Leaves or Spanikopita
Greek Salad or Tabouli
Halvah

MIDDLE EASTERN

Bagdoncia or Hummos
Felafel and Pita
with
Cucumber, Tomato, Sasammaise

FRENCH

Quiche or Soufflé
Braised Vegetables or Ratatouille
Tossed Salad with Lemonette
Strawberries with Kirsch

ABOUT THE RECIPE ANALYSES

Nutrient analyses are, at best, an imperfect measure of the quality of food. If an old bone and some fur were analyzed by current methods, the results would indicate appreciable amounts of calcium and protein; yet that would hardly be useful information in planning a diet. Then, too, the amounts of certain nutrients *as analyzed* may be vastly different from the amounts the body can actually use. A nutrient analysis of cocoa shows that it contains some calcium. But it also contains certain chemical elements which form insoluble complexes with some nutrients. Despite the analysis, cocoa actually "robs" the body of some of the calcium present in the milk with which it is usually drunk. And, of course, any table of presumed nutritional values has to be viewed in light of individual differences in digestion and absorption. With all these cautions, we have chosen to list a partial analysis of most of our recipes. Why? The reasons vary with the category of nutrient.

• *Protein:* For many people, the biggest hurdle to their becoming vegetarians is their insecurity about getting enough protein. We have analyzed for protein, and more importantly for useable protein, so that this myth finally can be dispelled. Our figure shows "grams of useable protein" (GUP); this represents the protein which can be used by the body.

• *Calories:* We are generally a calorie-conscious nation, and with good reason, since so many Americans are moderately to severely overweight. Many people also think that vegetarianism requires more calories for the same nutrition —another myth. Actually, vegetarians tend to be about 10 pounds lighter than age-matched meat-eaters. But calorie-counters can choose recipes they will feel more comfortable with.

• *Carbohydrates:* Another American pastime; for those who count these we have included them as well. We make no claims for a low-carbohydrate diet—all those calories that don't come from meat (if you don't eat meat) have to come from somewhere, and grains are an important source of protein. Many researchers are suggesting that the high-fat, high-protein American diet should be altered in favor of higher (unrefined) carbohydrate intake.

• *Fats:* So much attention has been devoted lately to the fat content of the American diet, it seemed useful to include this information as well. Originally, we planned to list saturated and unsaturated fats separately, but this finally seemed unimportant for two reasons. First, our research led us to the conclusion that the over-emphasis on saturated fats in the diet was misplaced; and secondly, the wholefoods vegetarian diet falls well within the parameters of current recommendations both on total fats and on polyunsaturate to saturate ratio (see Chapter V).

• *Iron and calcium:* These were included because recent government surveys have shown that they are particularly vulnerable areas in American nutrition. We especially wanted to reassure people that iron, which many seem to think is synonymous with meat, can be adequately maintained in the vegetarian diet.

The analyses are for one serving of the particular recipe, except where it is indicated otherwise. We don't necessarily mean all adult portions, however: "serves five" might mean two adults, one teenager and two smaller children. To adjust the figures for your household, multiply the *per serving* by the *yield,* and divide by the number of people who actually dined. Optional ingredients are included only when so stated.

Analysis	Calo- ries	CHO*	Fat	Pro- tein	GUP **	Iron	Cal- cium
Per serving							

*Carbohydrate
**GUP: Grams of useable protein.

Mixes and Make-aheads

BASIC COOKIE MIX

It's nigh onto impossible to make a cookie of less than 75 calories—unless you don't mind hardtack. But most commercial cookies are "empty" calories; the calories in the cookies that follow are practically wall-to-wall nutrition. And, despite the unlikely ingredients, they taste great.

There are enough variations listed below for you to use the whole gallon of Mix without making the same cookie twice. Make up your own variations; the pattern is obvious. We'd love to hear about your favorite creations.

Yield: 1 gallon mix.

2 to 3 c butter	¾ c sesame seeds, ground
2 to 3 c brown sugar	4 Tb brewer's yeast
3 c rolled or steel-cut oats	1 Tb salt
2 c wheat germ (pref. raw)	3 Tb baking powder
2 c milk powder	3 c wholewheat flour
1 c soy powder or flour	

Cream butter and sugar. Mix together all the dry ingredients except the flour; mix the dry ingredients into the creamed mixture thoroughly. Mix in the flour as quickly as possible. The mix will look mealy. Best if refrigerated or frozen, though it may be kept at room temperature for two to three weeks, provided that your kitchen is cool.

If you are addicted to commercial cookies, begin with the larger amounts of butter and sugar. Gradually decrease both. The smaller amount of butter makes a cakey, as opposed to a crisp, cookie. Even with the full amount of both butter and sugar, the nutrient density of these cookies is quite acceptable. But please note: a friend's first-grade class developed some of the following variations using the smaller amounts of butter and sugar—not a crumb was left.

COOKIES FROM COOKIE MIX:

All pans should be buttered. Unless otherwise specified, add everything at once and mix as quickly as possible. Most

variations will make two dozen "drop" cookies. Bake at 350°
for 12-14 minutes.

Almond Cookies:

2 c Cookie Mix, 1 egg, ½ tsp almond ext, 1 tsp vanilla
ext, 1 c ground or chopped almonds. Mix. Chill 1 hour. Roll
out ⅛" thick on lightly floured board—a pastry scraper helps
prevent sticking. Cut in desired shape. Bake about 11 minutes,
until edges are golden.

Carrot-currant Cookies:

2 c Cookie Mix, 1-2 eggs, ½ c currants, 1 tsp vanilla
ext, 1 c grated raw carrot, 2 Tb orange juice. With only one
egg this makes a fine cakey cookie; with two it can be baked
in an 8" square pan and cut into bars. Bake about 15 minutes
as a cookie; 20-25 in a pan.

Fruit-nut Cookies:

2 c Cookie Mix, 1 egg, 1 c chopped dried fruit, 1 c
chopped nuts, 1 tsp vanilla ext; a Tb or two water or milk
if necessary.

Peanut Butter Cookies:

2 c Cookie Mix, 1 egg, ½ to ¾ c peanut butter (or
substitute ¼ c chopped home-roasted peanuts for as much
peanut butter), 1 tsp vanilla ext, sesame (opt.). Combine
ingredients except sesame seeds. Roll in a cylinder. Cut into
12-16 pieces. Roll each into a ball, and, if desired, in sesame
seeds. Press ball lightly onto greased baking sheet with the
tines of a fork in an X pattern. These tend to be crumbly.

Spice Cookies:

2 c Cookie Mix, 1 tsp cinnamon, a couple of dashes each
of your choice of cloves, ginger, nutmeg, allspice, dried mustard, 1 tsp vanilla ext, 1 egg.

Bar Cookies:

2 c Cookie Mix, 1 egg, water or milk to moisten if necessary. Press into an 8" square pan, cover with a fruit filling

and bake. Or use half the dough on the bottom, then the other half of the dough to make a three-layer bar.

BAKING MIX

This is another versatile time-saver, since it will make anything from biscuits to waffles.

8 c wholewheat flour	1½ c milk powder
2 c rolled oats	1½-2 c butter
1½ c wheat germ (pref. raw)	4 Tb brewer's yeast
1½ c soy powder or flour	2 Tb salt
⅓ c baking powder	

Yield: 1 gallon Mix, if you shake down the jar a bit.

Combine dry ingredients. Blend in butter until mealy. If butter is cold but pliable, an electric mixer does the job nicely. Don't over-soften butter, it will lose its shortening effect. Mix may be kept at room temperature, providing you don't live at the equator, for three or four weeks. May be refrigerated or frozen almost indefinitely; use as is, right from refrigerator.

Experiment with Baking Mix on your own: for about 2 c Mix you'll usually need 1 egg, 2-6 Tb sweetening, and ½-1 c liquid. If you use honey as sweetener, or if you want to use 2 eggs, you'll need the smaller amount of liquid. If you want a richer, more cake-like (and more calorific) product, use the larger amount of butter in making the Mix. In our experience, using vanilla extract cuts down on the amount of sweetener needed; as does fresh or dried fruit. The liquid may be any one of several juices; also various milk products: buttermilk, yoghurt, even sweet or sour cream. Each will lend distinction to your finished product. Unless otherwise specified it is best to combine all the liquid ingredients and all the dry ingredients separately; then mix them together quickly. Two cups dry Mix will make an 8" square pan, a 9" round pan or about a dozen muffins or cupcakes. Most cakes will bake at 350° for 30 minutes: exceptions have been noted.

» Biscuits

2 c Baking Mix
1-2 Tb butter
1 tsp sugar (opt)

¾ c milk
½ c grated cheese (opt)

Thoroughly combine dry ingredients. Add cheese, if used. Add milk all at once; stir a scant half-minute. Knead 10 to 15 *times* (not minutes) on a lightly floured board. Pat or roll out dough to about ½" thick or a little less. Cut in square or round 2" diameter shapes. Bake at 450° for 12-15 minutes. Serve *hot*.

» Date-nut Cake

2 c Baking Mix
½ c chopped dates
½ c chopped nuts
2 eggs
3-4 Tb honey

½ c milk *or* ¼ c milk + ¼
   c sour cream
1 tsp vanilla ext.
¼ tsp ground cardamon (opt)

Toss dates and nuts with Mix to coat pieces with flour —otherwise the dates tend to clump. Combine wet and dry ingredients and mix just until blended. Bake about 30 minutes. Set oven at 350°.

» Banana Cake

2 c Baking Mix
½ c dark brown sugar
or ¼ c honey
1 or 2 eggs

1 tsp vanilla ext.
½ tsp cinnamon
½ c applesauce
⅔ c very ripe mashed banana

Combine dry ingredients; combine wet ingredients. Stir quickly together. Bake 8" square pan 40-45 minutes at 350°.

» Cheese Muffins

1 c Baking Mix
4 oz. sharp cheese—1 c grated

1 egg
approx. ⅓ c milk

Beat egg with milk; combine ingredients and stir briefly. Makes ten 2" muffins. Bake at 400° for 20-25 minutes.

» Peanut Butter-Currant Bread

2 c Baking Mix
2 eggs
½ c peanut butter
¼ c peanuts or sunflower
  seeds
¼ c honey

½ c milk
1 Tb molasses
1 tsp vanilla ext
½ c currants or other dried
  fruit
1 Tb crude peanut oil (opt)

Combine everything and beat for less than one minute. Bake at 350° for about 30 minutes. Crude peanut oil intensifies "peanutty" flavor. Use unsalted, dry-roasted peanuts if you can get them; sunflower seeds are an acceptable substitute and have a better nutrient range when combined with the peanut butter. Use a fairly "dry" peanut butter; if it is very oily, use the peanut butter from the *bottom* of the jar.

INCREDIBLE MIX

This mix is *incredibly* nutritious, contains incredible sounding ingredients, and ends up tasting incredibly good!

Yield: 1 gallon Mix.

6 c wholewheat flour
3 c yellow corn meal or corn
  grits
2 c milk powder
2 c soy powder

2 c wheat germ, raw
⅓ c baking powder
1 **Tb salt**
2 Tb brewer's yeast
1½ c butter

Stir dry ingredients together. Blend in butter thoroughly. Best kept refrigerated or frozen, though it may be kept at cool room temperature for three or four weeks. If corn*meal* is used, the following recipes may require an extra Tb or so of liquid.

» Incredible Cornbread

4 c Incredible Mix
2 eggs

2 c water
2 Tb butter (opt)

If desired, simply mix first three ingredients, pour into baking pan; bake at 400° for 20-25 minutes. For a more traditional "crusty" cornbread, melt butter in baking pan in hot oven—preferably a cast-iron skillet or corn-stick pan—when butter is beginning to brown, pour in batter and bake as above. This cornbread is an excellent keeper and may be frozen. Split and toast to re-heat.

» Incredible Waffles

2 c Incredible Mix	*optional ingredients:*
1-2 eggs	vanilla extract, cinnamon,
approx. 1¼ c water	honey, oil or melted butter

Combine. Let sit 5 minutes—while griddle is heating —then stir and add a little liquid if necesary. See directions for texture and baking, page 53.

QUICHE CRUST MIX

6 c wholewheat flour	1½ sticks butter, a bit soft
1 c grated parmesan cheese	paprika, pepper, garlic powder (opt)

Combine flour, cheese and optional spices—as much as a teaspoon of paprika, less garlic powder or pepper—in a bowl. With fingertips, work in butter until whole mixture looks like small crumbs. Work quickly and don't use palms of your hands which are too hot and will melt soft butter unduly. Makes about 2 quarts. Refrigerate or freeze.

To use: for an 8″ or 9″ pie plate, or two 10 oz. custard cups, about 1¼ c Mix and about 1 Tb cold water. Add water to Mix a few drops at a time, wetting Mix as evenly as possible. Press dough into a ball, wrap in plastic and chill at least ½ hour. Crumble dough and press against bottom and sides of pan which must be well-buttered if you plan to unmold quiche. Bake at 350° for about 10 minutes, then proceed with recipe. If you prefer not to pre-bake them, paint the crust with an egg white beaten with 1 Tb of water; this will deter sogginess.

TRIPLE RICH MIX

You can use Triple Rich Mix in bread, biscuits, waffles, cookies, thickening, etc. At this level of "enrichment"—for lack of a better word—the change in taste, if any, will be only for the better. Baked goods will be just a *little* heavier and chewier. As for cakes: on the *rare* occasions when you want to bake a nutritional disaster, you might as well forget the Triple Rich Mix or you'll be lulled into thinking you can have your cake and eat it, too. On the other hand, be *sure* to use this Mix in "quick-bread" cakes which, if you substitute wholewheat for white flour and cut down the excess sugar that most standard recipes call for, can actually become nutritionally acceptable occasional snacks.

Equal parts:

soy powder or flour   wheat germ (pref. raw)
milk powder, either instant
  or non-instant

If you use raw wheat germ, the Mix should be kept cold; otherwise it will keep quite a while at room temperature in a tightly-closed container. The choice of ingredients will make some small difference in analysis: full-fat soy flour, as opposed to lower fat soy powder, will raise the calories and lower the protein of the Mix somewhat. An equal volume of instant milk powder is a little less nutritious than the same amount of non-instant because the non-instant weighs more. Since you're going to use this Mix in foods which will be cooked, it is preferable to use the raw wheat germ: the taste will not be noticeable and the nutrient profile will probably be higher.

But whichever components you finally decide on, *make it and use it*. For example, everywhere you see white or even wheat flour mentioned, decrease the amount of flours called for by about ¼ and put Triple Rich Mix in its place.

If it says 4 c flour, use 3-3¼ c flour + ¾-1 c TRM
3 c	2⅓ c	⅔ c
2½ c*	2 c*	½ c*
2 c	1½ c	½ c
1¼-1½ c	⅞-1¼ c	⅓ c*
1 c	⅔-¾ c	⅓-¼ c*

---

*You can fudge a bit, if it makes the fractions simpler. To simplify a recipe that already calls for soy and/or milk powder: total these ingredients plus flour, then use roughly 3 parts flour to one part Triple Rich Mix.

TOMATO ALL-PURPOSE BASE

a 6-7 qt. soup pot
2-3 Tb oil or butter
4 carrots
4-5 stalks celery
8 cloves garlic
4-5 medium onions

½ c wine or other liquid
tomatoes to fill pot—8-10 lbs.
salt, pepper
herbs, spices (opt)
other vegetables (opt)

Sauté chopped carrots, celery, onions and garlic in oil until slightly browned and beginning to stick to bottom of pan. De-glaze with water or wine. If you have no other preference, use olive oil if you plan to use base primarily for tomato sauce, or butter if you plan to use base primarily for soup. Vine-ripened tomatoes can be peeled without the usual dip in hot water. First scrape the skin all over with the dull edge of the knife blade. Then cut the tomatoes in half and start peeling off the loosened skin from the bottom toward the stem end. Just get off as much as you can: the heat of the sauce will automatically peel them anyway. Add tomatoes until the pot is full within an inch or two of the top—or until you run out of tomatoes. You can use other vegetables: beans, okra, squash, cabbage and so on, especially if this is to be used for soupbase. Strange as it may sound, these vegetables also taste fantastic in tomato sauce, and it helps to round out a pizza or spaghetti dinner. If you add herbs now, they will have been added to every subsequent dish you make out of this base. It may be preferable to add different ones at each cooking to avoid a sameness of flavor. This soupbase may be frozen or canned in glass jars.

To make soup from Tomato Base: add green vegetables, potatoes, leftover vegetables. This is very thick stock, so you can add about half again the volume in water, stock or vegetables cooking water. Adding different vegetables, herbs and spices makes a different soup each time. Clams and potatoes make clam chowder. Many of the soups in Chapter VII can be made from soupbase—omit the canned tomatoes and "aromatic" vegetables; just add everything else.

To make sauce from Tomato Base: Add 3-5 oz. of canned tomato paste for each quart of Base: it will depend on how watery you started and how thick you want the finished product to be. If you object to the vegetables' lumps, whiz the Base in the blender before you add the paste and herbs. Simmer until thickened; season as desired.

» *Sautéed Vegetables—Soupbase*

Yield: about 1 gallon

1 stick butter or ½ c olive oil	1 *head* chopped or pressed garlic
6 c chopped celery	1 c chopped parsnip
6 c sliced carrots	½ c white wine or water
6 c chopped onion	

Choice of butter or oil will depend on which kinds of soup you intend to make from this base: cream soups would probably prefer the delicacy of butter, whereas a hearty tomato soup might do better with an olive-oil base. Sauté vegetables in hot fat, stirring occasionally, until some stick and begin to brown: 5-10 minutes. Divide soupbase among the number of containers you'll use: allow about 1 c of sautéed vegetables per quart of soup. De-glaze pan: pour in water or wine and, with a wooden spoon, scrape up the bits of stuck-on vegetables and the brownish flavor-essence that coats the bottom of the pan. Add to vegetables: label and freeze. Amounts and kinds of vegetables may of course be varied. Potatoes do not freeze well, however. Cabbage, okra, string beans, squash, eggplant and other vegetables may be sautéed with the soupbase, too, though they may limit the kind of soup you will eventually make from the base—cabbage in clam chowder?!

Herb Mixes

» Italian Herb Mix

5 Tb marjoram	5 Tb basil
5 Tb oregano	1 Tb cracked bay leaves

Yield: 1 cup Herb Mix

Use approx. 1 Tb Mix per quart of sauce—more to taste.

» Mexican Herb Mix

1/3 c basil	1/4 c ground cumin
1/4 c oregano	1 tsp cayenne (opt)
2 tsp ground coriander (opt)	3 Tb chili powder

Yield: approximately 1 cup Herb Mix

Use approx. 1 Tb Mix per quart of sauce—more to taste.

» Curry Mix

5 Tb ground coriander	1 Tb cayenne (plus)
4 Tb turmeric	1 Tb cinnamon
2 Tb ground cumin	1 Tb ginger
3 Tb paprika	2 Tb fenugreek (opt)

Yield: approximately 1 cup.

Sauté about 2 Tb in oil for four servings.

You can also mix large quantities of the spices needed in a particular recipe. For example: Soybean Chili or Vegetable Curry call for finding and measuring at least half a dozen spices. Instead, measure out multiples of the spices called for, combine thoroughly, then divide into individual foil or plastic packets—as many as the number of times you multiplied the recipe. Store these in a tightly-capped *labelled* jar. Just pull out a packet when you're ready to cook.

III
Start Your Day a Lot Better

BLONDIE

What is the advantage to society of having thirty or forty different cereals on the grocery shelf which differ in size and shape and not much else? What is the real justification for a two- or three-fold price differential between some of the standard cereals and the new, highly fortified products—most of which results from promotion, packaging, and distribution? As far as we know, most consumers of such products gain nothing from using them. There is something wrong with a system which encourages people to waste their money.

—D. Mark Hegsted, "Food and Nutrition Policy— Now and in the Future," *Journal of the American Dietetics Association*, No. 64 (April, 1974), p. 370

As you stumble bleary-eyed toward that first cup of coffee, you may even be aware, in some of the sleepier recesses of your brain, that breakfast matters. But thinking you only have time for a doughnut and coffee or cold cereal, you grab a bite and leave for work (or school, or shopping). About two hours later starvation sets in and you have nowhere to turn but to that Great American Nutritional Disaster, the coffee break. You get hungry, tired, irritable, your head aches, your muscles may even hurt. You're suffering from a mild case of hypoglycemia—low blood sugar. In order to understand what low blood sugar means, it is necessary to understand something about the major source of sugar in the blood —dietary carbohydrates.

CARBOHYDRATES

"Carbohydrate" (CHO) is the scientific name for the starches and sugars. They come in three main forms: monosaccharides, disaccharides, and polysaccharides. The monosaccharides are the simplest sugars and are most quickly assimilable by the body. They are glucose (also called dextrose or grape sugar), fructose (fruit sugar), and galactose (milk sugar). The disaccharides—sucrose, maltose and lactose—have to be broken down (hydrolized) into simple sugars before they can be used. Polysaccharides include starch, cellulose (a non-nutritive compound), dextrins (formed during seed germination — i.e., sprouting), and glycogen — sometimes called animal starch (the body's own form of instant-replay carbohydrate).

GLYCOGEN

As a general rule, glycogen is formed when there is extra blood glucose; it is broken down, or used, when there is not enough. Once formed, glycogen is stored in the muscles and in the liver. Muscle glycogen can be used only by muscle tissue; liver glycogen is available to provide energy for other

34

body cells. It has been calculated that if the body were to use only the stored liver glycogen, the supply would last no more than four or five hours.

After about twelve hours' fast, your body needs to replenish its energy stores. During the night, the level of glucose in the blood slowly declines. When it falls to a certain level, the appetite regulator mechanism turns on.

Superficially, at least, it would seem that the best breakfast of all would be something chock full of readily absorbed carbohydrates—say, half the sugar bowl or a large chocolate bar? But it doesn't work that way. The body's glucose level is very sensitive to fluctuations (the difference between "low" blood glucose and "high" blood glucose is the carbohydrate equivalent of one teaspoon of sugar).[1]

SUGAR ROLLER COASTER

Table sugar, as its manufacturers are fond of pointing out, is 100% pure sucrose; and with no nutrients, water, or fiber to slow it down, it is speedily absorbed. Too speedily. When the blood glucose level exceeds the maximum, insulin release is triggered (insulin is necessary to "move" the glucose out of the blood) and blood glucose plummets. (The calories haven't disappeared, by the way; they're quietly being used—or stored where you least want them.) In other words, eating sugar is an excellent way to depress the blood glucose level after a short interval of high blood glucose. If you respond to your body's low blood glucose signals with another sugar load, you end up on the sugar roller coaster: Eat sugar —get high; body produces insulin to deal with excess blood sugar—get low; feel low—head for candy bar or coffee break or soft drink; and here we go again, whee! (Some researchers are suggesting that the constant strain placed on the insulin-producing pancreas by the sugar roller coaster may be responsible for pushing genetically sensitive individuals to diabetes.)[2]

Ideally, the breakfast should contain a small amount of readily digestible but not excessively concentrated carbohydrates—whole grains are ideal. Since they will not enter the bloodstream all in a rush, they will not tend to produce the excess insulin that is an integral part of the roller coaster.

For most people, optimal blood glucose level can be maintained with no mid-morning slump if breakfast also contains sufficient protein—and sufficient protein is about one-third the daily requirement, or thirteen to fifteen grams[3] (useable —not total—protein. See Chapter VIII).

COLD CEREAL?

Cold cereal, easily the most commonly eaten "breakfast," provides between 1 and 2½ grams of protein (according to package labels) or between 1/20th and ⅛th of your morning's requirement. Even those cereals that claim to be high in protein contain an additional two grams at most. But the labels do not reflect the fact that turning whole grains into air-filled flakes, puffs, or other fanciful shapes also lessens the protein availability by as much as 75% (and destroys most of the remaining nutrition).[4] In other words, the main source of protein for cold cereal eaters is the milk: each ounce provides just about one gram of high quality protein. So you might be getting six or eight grams of protein out of your breakfast cereal with milk, but your morning's need is twice that.

In addition, packaged cereals average about 25% sugar, according to one estimate. (There are mostly estimates, and few positive answers, because the cereal manufacturers generally refuse to say.) The sugar-coated varieties, many aimed at children, are as high as 50% sugar.[5] Therefore the usual recommended serving of one ounce contains 3½ teaspoons of sugar (1 tsp sugar = 4 gms.)—a massive amount, molecularly speaking.

You may wonder why the nutrient declaration on the side of the cereal box looks so good. Since the time of the Senate testimony on the "nutritional wasteland" of children's breakfast cereals (one wag suggested throwing away the cereal and eating the box with milk for about the same nutrition), these cereals have been consistently "enriched" and "fortified." Today's cereal boxes read more like vitamin pill bottles. (See Chapter VII for a discussion of nutritional labeling.)

As though the nutritional insult weren't enough, cereals —particularly the more outlandish creations that may have been designed to fit an advertising campaign—contain artificial flavorings, artificial colors, and chemical preservatives. Each of these categories has come under fire from consumer advocates and scientists. According to Michael Jacobson: "Repeatedly, colors approved for use in food have been shown to

36

be toxic or carcinogenic and have been banned. The history of approved dyes reads like the guest register in a hotel for transients."[6] (More on additives in Chapter XI.)

It is important to remember that the prime targets for most breakfast cereals are the young, who may be far more vulnerable to the effects of additives. Dr. Ben Feingold, Chief Emeritus of the Allergy Division of Kaiser Permanente Hospital, has suggested that food additives may be a major cause of hyperkinesis in children.

OLD-FASHIONED BREAKFAST

Is the old-fashioned big breakfast the answer? It had a lot to recommend it; too much in fact. Ham 'n eggs, toast 'n coffee ('n butter 'n jelly), cereal 'n cream, and maybe some potatoes or grits. For today's sedentary worker (how many rows did you hoe at the office today?), a breakfast containing as much as 2,000 calories is unrealistic. On the other hand, do not be dismayed by a 500- to 600-calorie breakfast. A breakfast that satisfies your body's protein needs will *prevent* you from consuming excessive, and probably nutritionally-deprived, calories at coffee break. (There's nothing worse for a diet than alternately starving and giving in to destructive food urges: a doughnut and a glass of carbonated beverage provides about 250 to 300 calories of no nutrition whatsoever.)

Years of reading cereal boxes have probably convinced you that the recommended (by whom?) breakfast should contain only 200 calories, especially for weight watchers. Actually, breakfast should contain no less than one-quarter of the day's calories, and up to one-third is fine. One ounce of cereal with one-half cup of milk, a glass of juice, and a cup of coffee does not provide enough of anything; the myriad vitamins and minerals it's "fortified" with are probably poorly absorbed. (See Chapter VII.)

WHAT'S LEFT?

Feel betrayed by Tony the Tiger? Wondering what's left to eat? The following recipes offer just a few of many possibilities. Eggs are still an excellent source of concentrated, easily assimilable, quickly-prepared nutrition. (See Chapter V for the cholesterol controversy.) The hot cereals you may remember abhorring as a child have grown up too, and are quite delicious, suitably spruced up with tasty additions. We even have recipes for cold cereal worth eating. And general favorites like waffles and pancakes can be made nutritious enough to start the day with. Yoghurt for *breakfast?!* Some of our concoctions taste good enough for dessert! Don't be tradition bound: a toasted cheese sandwich is delicious for breakfast; so is last night's cold lasagna, for that matter.

Some mention must be made of people who simply cannot eat early in the morning. Most nutrition authorities tend to discount individual differences by insisting that everyone should have a good breakfast (preferably one-half hour after waking). Since one of us is not so constituted, we have another solution.

If you're hungry enough for a doughnut or some toast, you're not the person we're describing here: you *should* have a sane breakfast. But if you don't snack in the evening (after dinner at six or so) and you still can't face anything but fruit juice or hot beverage in the morning—do as your body tells you—don't eat. *But* when you're ready to eat—whether at nine, ten or later—have the breakfast you missed. Don't have junk and *don't* have a "snack"—take your protein food with you to the office if the vending machine doesn't offer anything sensible.

Studies have shown that the nutrition missed in a skipped breakfast is rarely made up in the rest of the day's eating.[7] Don't be a statistic.

Yoghurt

Yoghurt will not cure dandruff or fallen arches. There's a chance that it may contribute to vigorous longevity, however, which is almost as good. At any rate, Bulgarians, who eat more yoghurt than anyone else in the world (one strain of yoghurt is named *bacillus bulgaricus*) also have one of the highest ratios of centenarians in the world.

Until a few years ago, people who espoused yoghurt for health were immediately suspect. They also touted the virtues of such then esoteric comestibles as granola, molasses, and wheat germ, which didn't improve their credibility.

But yoghurt has come into its own *(viz.* at least twenty varieties on the supermarket shelf). As is the case with most healthful things that are commercially co-opted, excessively sweetened, rainbow-flavored supermarket yoghurt isn't what those health nuts had in mind.

Yoghurt was originally a way of preserving milk. The organisms that make milk unpalatably sour are destroyed by the yoghurt bacteria, which instead make it delightfully tangy. It is this war-like spirit of the yoghurt bacteria that makes yoghurt so healthful for you to ingest. Your intestine harbors millions of bacteria, some beneficial, some not. Yoghurt bacteria help control some of the disease-causing bacteria, just as they did in the milk that would have gone sour. As part of their life process, yoghurt bacteria digest milk sugar (lactose) so some people who cannot tolerate milk because of a lack of the enzyme lactase (which digests lactose) can eat milk in the form of yoghurt.[8]

Doctors are beginning to use yoghurt therapy concomitantly with antibiotic therapy.[9] Antibiotics indiscriminately destroy not only the organisms causing whatever disease you're being treated for, but also the necessary and beneficial intestinal organisms (flora) that aid in digestion. Yoghurt contains good bacteria that, when they get to your gut, crowd out putrefactive bacteria and aid in the assimilation of nutrients from other foods. They also produce extra B-vitamins and vitamin K, which your body can use.

Homemade yoghurt fortified with powdered milk can be twice as nutritious as the store-bought variety and half as expensive. In addition, homemade yoghurt is sweeter (less tangy) than its commercial counterpart; so if you haven't liked it before, make it yourself and try it again.

» Fortified Yoghurt

Analysis	Calories	CHO	Fat	Protein	GUP	Iron	Calcium
Per Cup	115	16g	.2g	11.2g	9g	.2mg	407mg

Yield: 1 quart 1½ strength yoghurt

About 1 quart fluid milk
½c powdered milk or ⅔ instant
(1 c or 1⅓c for "double").

About 4 Tb yoghurt

YOGHURT VARIATIONS:

1. 1 tsp-1 Tb honey, maple syrup, or molasses per quart may be mixed with milk and allowed to incubate.

2. 1-2 Tb carob powder per quart may be mixed with the milk before incubation.

3. 1 tsp-1 Tb preserves may be mixed with finished yoghurt before eating.

4. Fruit, fresh (except pineapple), canned or frozen can be added to the milk mixture before incubation (about ½ cup per quart). The resulting yoghurt will be somewhat more watery, so we prefer to add fresh fruit to plain yoghurt just before eating.

The milk can be whole or skimmed, or even reconstituted from powder. If you live on a farm and have fresh milk or certified raw milk, you may find that the bacteria causing the souring are stronger than the yoghurt bacteria—use a little more yoghurt for "starter," but if that consistently fails, you'll have to start by pasteurizing the milk. (Consult your local agriculture station for details.) There is no reason to scald the milk, despite what other yoghurt recipes may say.

The yoghurt you use as a starter must be *plain,* either commercially made or left over from your last batch. (Actually, using homemade starter sometimes produces a thinner, watery yoghurt—you may want to stick with commercial yoghurt as starter.) Read the label before you buy. Several brands add unnamed "stabilizers" or "inhibitors" that may prevent bacteria from doing their thing in your yoghurt Many health-food stores sell excellent additive-free yoghurt for starter. (If all else fails, the dried bacteria can be ordered through a health-food store or by mail; it is, however, quite expensive.)

Blend the milk with the milk powder and yoghurt briefly. Place this mixture in a heat-conducting container (widemouth jars are ideal). Place that container in another vessel. In the outer container put tap water, as hot as it will run. Leave the yoghurt in the water bath until the water is tepid (or at least one hour). If you change the water hourly you will have yoghurt in about three to five hours. Or do it the lazy person's way—change the water once or twice before

40

going to bed, and once or twice next morning until the desired consistency is reached.

It *is* possible to overdo. Yoghurt bacteria will die at temperatures over 115°. If your yoghurt doesn't yog, try inserting a frying thermometer in the container holding the nascent yoghurt—you may be changing the water too often. If your kitchen is extremely cold and you don't change the water often enough, the souring bacteria may get a head start on the yoghurt bacteria. Both of these eventualities are unlikely, however. The ideal incubation temperature is 90° to 100°—if you are a bit under, that's fine, just don't go too far over.

If you are in a hurry, you can *warm* the milk *(not heat)* until it is just warm to the touch, then proceed as usual. It is imperative that you not overdo on the water bath then, or you'll kill the bacteria.

Homemade yoghurt will never have the slightly rubbery quality of the commercially made product. But it is definitely thick, and will leave a clean edge when cut with a spoon. It also thickens on standing, so don't expect it to look like the supermarket variety before you decide it's finished. If you tip the jar (put the lid on first), done yoghurt will pull away from the sides, like gelatin almost.

If disaster strikes, and you come back to your hoped-for yoghurt to discover that there's a lot of thin, yellowish liquid surrounding a white, curdy mass, all is not lost. You have to start over with all new ingredients; *but* you have made curds and whey, which is eaten by Miss Muffett and many Europeans. Or you can make fresh cheese (frischkase). Pour the curds and whey into a damp cheesecloth-lined drainer and let sit until most of the whey has drained. Save the whey to be used in bread, soups or sauces (it contains protein, minerals, and vitamins—especially riboflavin and B-12). If you drain it to a medium-moist consistency, you've got something like creamed cottage cheese, but tangier. If you drain it quite dry, it approximates high-protein, low-fat cream cheese, also tangier.

The amount of milk powder used determines the degree of nutritional fortification. Each cup of non-instant milk powder (1⅓ c instant) has about the same amount of protein and calcium as a quart of milk (that's good), but not the same amount of fat and calories since skim milk powder is lower in these (that's good too). The more milk powder added to the yoghurt recipe, however, the sweeter it will taste. The above yoghurt recipe is 1½ fortified—it contains half again as much protein and calcium as the same amount of fluid milk contains. If you like a less tangy yoghurt, double the milk powder and you'll have a double strength yoghurt. Yoghurt can easily be made in quantity. See Food Storage Chart, page 15.

» Yoghurt Banana Split

This is so delicious that it could just as easily have been listed in the dessert section, but it seemed a pity not to have all this nutrition to start the day with.

Analysis	Calo-ries	CHO	Fat	Pro-tein	GUP	Iron	Cal-cium
½ recipe	177	34g	1.5g	9.3g	7g	2mg	220mg

Yield: one gorge or two snacks

¾ cup fortified yoghurt
5 lovely strawberries
1 small banana

4 Tb toasted wheat germ (unless you like raw)
1 tsp honey or maple syrup (opt)
½ tsp vanilla extract (opt)

Slice banana and place strips on a plate. Combine yoghurt with choice of fruit and flavor extracts. Plop yoghurt fruit mix in center of split banana, top with one or two reserved berries. Sprinkle wheat germ over, drizzle with honey or syrup if desired. This recipe, halved, makes an excellent, nutritious after-school snack, or low-calorie, high-nutrition dessert.

VARIATIONS:

1. Use ½ cup fresh blueberries or melon balls in place of strawberries.

2. Add 2-4 Tb. chopped nuts or seeds for extra protein, vitamins, minerals, and fiber as well as flavor. Almonds, brazil nuts, walnuts, or sunflower seeds are especially tasty and nutritious—coconut is just tasty.

3. Forget the banana split method, mix everything together and eat plain or use as topping on French toast, pan-

cakes or waffles—increase sweetening if desired.

Cereal

GRANOLA

Granola is definitely one of the better things you can put in your body in the morning. Do not be confused into believing that the latest effort of Madison Avenue to cash in on the natural food market bears any resemblance to *real* granola. Perhaps if sugar were not a prime ingredient (often under different labeling guises) these commercially produced back-to-nature cereals would be edible. As it is, they aren't. Granola is infinitely variable, and it's hard to imagine anyone not liking it, since it can be tailored to taste. But if the sight of an oatmeal cookie makes you gag, you might as well skip this section, because that's basically what granola is like. Unlike most boxed cereals, homemade granola can easily provide the necessary protein with which to start the day.

» *Granola*

Analysis	Calo-ries	CHO	Fat	Pro-tein	GUP	Iron	Cal-cium
Per ½ cup	458	44g	25g	18g	13g	5.6mg	249mg
½ c granola +½c skim milk	502	50.5g	25g	22.5g	16.6g	5.6mg	398mg

Yield: ten ½-cup servings

3 cups rolled oats
½ c sesame seeds
½ c sunflower seeds
½ c soy powder
⅔ c wheat germ
¼ tsp salt
2 tsp vanilla extract

⅓ c unsweetened coconut
⅔ c nuts, chopped roughly
¾ c powdered milk
½ c (or less) sweetening
¼ c oil
1 tsp cinnamon (opt)

Almost everything but the oats, oil, and protein boosters (milk powder, soy powder and wheat germ) are optional and variable. If you don't like it, leave it out. If you do like it, double the quantity.

Combine everything but the oil, sweetening, and vanilla in a large bowl. If your honey is very viscous, heat the sweetening agent slightly, add oil and extract. Otherwise just stir liquids together and pour over grains. Combine thoroughly; you may be able to manage with a wooden spoon, but I always have to get in it up to my elbows. Then spread the mess in a pan (or two) so it isn't more than two inches deep. Leave enough head-room to stir, too. Bake in a 250° oven for an hour or less until desired brownness is obtained. Stir every ten or fifteen minutes to avoid burning on the edges and bottom. Supermarket granola has so much honey in it, it tends to clump in little balls; this granola will be flakier. Makes about five cups that will keep perfectly well for at least three months in a tightly closed jar.

Recipe may easily be doubled or tripled, but it is not necesary to double or triple the oil—merely increase it by half and replace half the oil omitted with water.

VARIATIONS:

● *Grains:* wholewheat, rye, or triticale flakes; barley, millet or buckwheat flours; cornmeal. These provide unrefined carbohydrate, protein (especially when supplemented), some iron and fiber, B-vitamins, Vitamin E, major and trace minerals and polyunsaturated fatty acids (PUFA).

● *Nuts and seeds:* almonds, Brazil nuts, filberts, cashews, peanuts, walnuts, pecans, sesame seeds, sunflower seeds, flax seeds, coconut. These help complement the grain protein, provide trace minerals (varies with nut or seed used), some vitamins, iron, PUFA. Flax seed is a natural, mild laxative due to its content of lubricant oils and fiber. Coconut provides sweetening, but is also a source of saturated fatty acids, as opposed to PUFA.

● *Nutritional additives:* soy powder, wheat germ, rice polishings, brewer's yeast. These provide protein, B-vitamins and iron (except milk). Milk, and to some extent soy powder, add substantial amounts of calcium.

● *Dried fruit:* raisins, dates, apricots, currants, apples, figs, nectarines, pears. These provide simple carbohydrates, fiber. Apricots provide vitamin A. Raisins, apricots and prunes provide some iron.

● *Sweetening and liquids:* honey, molasses, oil, apple sauce, water, and maple syrup provide sweetening and, when granola is toasted, contribute to crunchiness.

- *Taste enhancers:* vanilla extract, cinnamon, salt.

» David's Muesli

This famous Swiss breakfast could be called raw granola. It's much better than that sounds, however. The proportions are entirely variable—just keep changing them till it's irresistible.

Analysis	Calories	CHO	Fat	Protein	GUP	Iron	Calcium
Serving	475	77g	12.4g	18.5g	13g	4.7mg	208mg

Yield: Five 1-cup servings

1 c rolled oats
½ c bulghur wheat
½ c macro-flaked grain
4 Tb wheat germ
4 Tb soy grits
juice of ½ lemon or lime
1½-2 c fresh orange juice

1-1½ c fortified yoghurt
1 or 2 crisp, tart apples
¼-½ c almonds or filberts
¼-½ c Grape-nuts or 100%
Bran
honey (opt)

Mix first five ingredients with enough orange juice to moisten. Add lemon or lime for piquancy, if desired. Refrigerate overnight or until grains are soft. (Using 2 cups of oat flakes in place of the grains listed above will shorten soaking time to the minimum of about one-half hour. But if you don't mind a little crunchiness, experiment with varying cracked or flaked grains and soaking times.) Then grate apples, coarsely chop nuts and add to softened grains. Add enough Grape-nuts or bran to soak up any remaining liquid. (Grape-*nuts*—not the flakes—have the distinction of being the only brand of supermarket cereal now nationally available that contains neither sugar nor preservatives.) Stir in yoghurt. Add honey if necessary (malted barley in the Grape-nuts, or the sugar in the 100% Bran, plus the orange juice, provides a surprising amount of sweetness—taste first). Can be served immediately or refrigerated up to a day and a half.

» Hot Cereal

Then there's always hot cereal. Of course, many people seem to have had a traumatic childhood experience with cooked cereal, but you'd be amazed what a little honey, milk, cinnamon and raisins can do, even to the most offending lumpy mass. Tastes about like rice pudding, if you think imaginatively. Don't bother with de-germinated cereals, though. Stick to whole grain types like Wheatena, oatmeal, bulghur (cracked wheat), and health-food store cracked or flaked grain. Any cracked grain can be cooked to a porridge-like consistency: most grains prefer about four times as much liquid. (If that's too soupy, work your way back towards three.) Soy grits complement missing amino acids and provide a pleasant crunch: use about 2 tablespoons per cup of grain. Leftover cereal (there always seems to be some) is a great moisture-preserving addition to bread. Since most cereal boxes give specific directions, here's just one all-purpose recipe.

Allow about ⅓ cup of raw grain per person. Much will depend on the expansion coefficient of the particular grain as well as the appetite of the individual. That amount with milk will provide almost all the morning protein requirement.

Analysis	Calories	CHO	Fat	Protein	GUP	Iron	Calcium
1 cup	203	30g	4g	15g	12g	1.9mg	225mg

Yield: Four 1-cup servings

1 c oatmeal or other whole-grain
2 Tb soy grits
3 to 4 c water or milk
½ tsp salt

4 Tb wheat germ (optional but especially recommended if a non-wheat grain is used)

Some authorities recommend sprinkling the cereal in rapidly boiling salted liquid—this is supposed to produce fluffier, less gluey texture. I find it simpler to combine the grain, soy grits (which are actually optional, but contribute greatly to the nutrition), salt, and liquid at the beginning. You could put a little sweetening in then, too. Turn it down to a simmer when it boils. Put on a half-cover (that means enough to keep most of the steam from escaping, but not enough to encourage the porridge to climb out of the pan), and cook until done, stirring occasionally. It could be as little as fifteen minutes, or as long as thirty. I prefer a fairly solid consistency, because I like to add cold milk and I don't want gruel.

SERVING VARIATIONS:

1. Sprinkle with toasted wheat germ, chopped nuts, toasted seeds.
2. Use 4 tablespoons sesame seeds in place of soy grits, if desired.
3. Add a dab of preserves.
4. Sprinkle with 2 tablespoons of granola.
5. Pour vanilla milk over ($\frac{1}{2}$ tsp vanilla extract in 4 oz milk).
6. Cook dried fruit with cereal or add after cooking.
7. Add a dash of cinnamon and a teaspoon of honey.

Eggs

Recent research has underscored the fact that there is no single dietary cause of coronary heart disease. Though widely believed, the Saturated Fat Theory of the aetiology of CHD simply doesn't hold up in non-Western countries. Attention is now turning back to the general failings of the American diet such as low fiber and excessive calories, especially from refined and nutrient-poor sources.

Eggs are an excellent protein source, and on a per-calorie basis, they supply considerable amounts of many valuable nutrients. The current recommendation to limit egg consumption must be reviewed against the background of the diet as a whole. If eggs are as bad for you as many Americans have been led to believe, lacto-ovo vegetarians would be prime targets for early heart disease. Exactly the reverse is true. See Chapter V for a discussion of the cholesterol controversy.

» Poached Eggs

Poached eggs are one of the most easily digested forms of cooked egg (second only to soft-boiled), and also have a touch of glamour about them. It is ridiculously easy to poach an egg without a poacher, but for some reason few people realize this. If you follow the directions given below carefully, but you end up with the white in egg-drop soup shreds, and the yolk off sulking by itself in a corner, your egg wasn't fresh. The fresher an egg is, the more the thick albuminous white adheres to the yolk. As the egg ages, the white becomes thin and runny—you'll notice the same thing frying; an old egg white spreads all over the pan. You must, therefore, start with a fresh egg.

Analysis	Calories	CHO	Fat	Protein	GUP	Iron	Calcium
Per Egg	78	.4g	5.5g	6.2g	6g	1.1mg	26mg

Yield: depends on you

Bring water to a rolling boil in a saucepan (at least one quart of water—if you're going to make more than four eggs at one time, you might go to a larger pan). Break the eggs into a dish carefully; if you break a yolk, dig that egg out and save it for scrambled. When the water is at a full rolling boil, remove it from the heat (but don't turn the heat off) and stir for about ten seconds until a whirlpool forms in the center of the pot. Carefully slip the egg(s) into the vortex. If you are doing several eggs, and are very dexterous, it is wise to try to keep the water moving (gently. gently) until all the eggs have been slipped in. The combination of the heat of the water and the circular action (and the freshness of the egg!) tends to hold the egg together while the white sets around the yolk. When all the eggs are in the water, return it to the flame (medium), and let cook two to three minutes. Sometimes it helps to nudge the egg over very tenderly after one minute to cook both sides evenly. As a very finicky egg eater, who demands that the white be almost completely firm, but that the yolk be completely runny, with no dry spots, I have found that poaching is a far superior method to boiling. No matter how many timers I have used, eggs are either over- or under-done when I boil them.

You can also par-poach the eggs (if you're planning breakfast for a crowd, for example) just until set, then remove them to a cool water bath. Just before serving, return them to hot water to finish cooking.

» Basic Omelette

There are three basic approaches to omelettes: the French or "frantic fork" method, which never works for me; the American or puffy omelette, which involves separating the eggs, something I refuse to do before 10:00 a.m., hence never use for breakfast; and my method of choice, the "picking up the edges" method. This last has the added advantage of being simple enough for anybody to manage, which is more than can be said for the first two.

Analysis	Calories	CHO	Fat	Protein	GUP	Iron	Calcium
Per serving	210	.85g	17g	12.8g	12g	2.2mg	65mg

Yield: 2 servings

1 Tb butter
3 to 4 eggs
1 to 2 Tb water or milk (opt)

1 Tb Parmesan cheese (opt)
a grinding of pepper (opt)

Melt the butter in the omelette pan (any evenly heating skillet with other-than-perpendicular sides). The correct sized pan for the number of eggs can make or break you: 3-4 eggs for a 7"-9" pan is about right. Beat the eggs for thirty to forty strokes with a fork—unless you prefer to barely combine the yolk and white as the French do. Adding water, or especially milk, will soften the curd of the cooked egg. It may also make the egg weep so I rarely add either. Do not add salt, no matter what you've heard: it toughens the curd. On the other hand, the Parmesan cheese gives a touch of saltiness without toughening the curd or tasting "cheesy." The pepper is up to you.

When the butter has melted, foamed, and the bubbles

are breaking and disappearing, tip the pan to coat it evenly and quickly pour in the eggs. There should be a satisfying sizzle and the eggs should start bubbling. Wait ten to fifteen seconds, then pick up an edge of the omelette and let some of the uncooked egg run under. (If there is no "edge" —if it is all still soup—the pan wasn't hot enough, and your eggs will probably stick. Be satisfied with scrambled this time, and let the fat get hotter next time.) Repeat this quickly, all around the edge of the omelette until the top is still moist but not sloshy. This should take no more than another thirty seconds or so. Depending on how you like your omelette, let it cook another few seconds. (The French go in for rare, I'm more of a medium fan, well-done is considered barbaric, I'm told.) Then insert a spatula under one side of the omelette and fold the omelette in half (covering any filling). Slide the omelette onto a plate; or if you're chicken, invert the omelette onto a plate. You can even fold it in thirds, once you get the hang of it.

Anything reasonable can be chopped or warmed and sprinkled on the top of the cooking omelette just before it's folded over.

SOME SUGGESTIONS:

2-3 Tb frijoles—warmed (See recipe index); after folding, serve with cheese and/or Mexican tomato sauce (See recipe index).

3 Tb sautéed mushrooms with or without onions.

3 Tb onions sautéed till limp—garnish with chopped parsley.

2-3 Tb cottage cheese to which has been added some chopped parsley and pressed garlic.

Leftover vegetables sautéed with onions and/or mushrooms.

Avocado and tomato slices.

A clump of sprouts—alfalfa are especially nice.

Grated cheese—dust with paprika.

» Frittata

Made with a hearty vegetable filling, this is also a lunch or dinner entrée. On the other hand, it's another approach to the omelette and some people eat big brunches at times.

Analysis	Calories	CHO	Fat	Protein	GUP	Iron	Calcium
Per serving	194	3.3g	17g	9g	7.7g	1.4mg	103mg

Yield: Six servings

2 Tb butter
4 to 6 eggs
3 Tb parmesan cheese
½ c chopped green
   pepper, sautéed

6 slices tomato
¼ c (or more) grated sharp
   cheese

Melt butter in a 9 or 10 inch cast-iron (or other heavy) skillet. Beat eggs; add Parmesan and green pepper, and beat again. Add egg to hot fat, lifting edges until most of the soup is underneath. Off heat, arrange tomato in attractive pattern on top; sprinkle with grated cheese. Put in a preheated broiler for about three minutes or until the cheese is melted. If you prefer, you can let the cheese brown slightly. Cut in pie-shaped wedges to serve.

Some of these variations qualify for dinner:

1. 1 cup zucchini, lightly steamed, with or without sautéed mushrooms and onions.
2. 1 cup leftover braised yellow squash with tomato and basil.
3. Broccoli or cauliflowerets, cooked till just tender.
4. Canned artichoke hearts and chopped olives.
5. Omit 1 or 2 eggs and add about 4 Tb of tofu and 1 tsp soy sauce to beaten eggs. Top with 1 cup celery, water chestnuts and mung sprouts sautéed in peanut oil. Omit cheese; may be served with sweet and sour sauce.

» Bauern Fruhstuk (Farmer's Breakfast)

Another brunch dish. It was originally designed as a pre-dawn tidbit for the German farmer who was going to do a few chores before he came in for a real breakfast at ten or so. If the idea of potatoes so intimately combined with eggs doesn't appeal to you, you could probably cook the eggs separately. Wouldn't be the same thing, though.

51

Analysis	Calories	CHO	Fat	Protein	GUP	Iron	Calcium
¼ recipe	257	13g	19.6g	7.8g	6.8g	1.6mg	37mg

Yield: 4 servings

3 Tb butter or oil
2-3 medium potatoes, cooked and cooled (great place for leftovers)
1 onion
a garlic clove or so

½ tsp (or more) salt
½ tsp pepper
1 tsp paprika
4 eggs
a sprinkling of cheese (opt)

Do not slice or dice potatoes: cut so that pieces are irregular and have some peel on each piece. Chop onion as you will. Heat fat in large, heavy skillet. Add the onion and the minced clove garlic to the hot fat. Let wilt slightly. Add the potatoes, salt, pepper, and paprika; stir occasionally. When the potatoes are uniformly pink and somewhat crusty, arrange them evenly in the pan and break the eggs into the pan, right over the potatoes. Cook about two minutes, or until the bottom of the eggs is opaque and set, then sprinkle with cheese if desired, and run pan under the broiler another minute, or until the tops are done enough for you. With a very sharp spatula, cut under each potato-and-egg portion to serve. If you use an electric fry pan that can't be put under the broiler, add 1 Tb of water, cover pan tightly and let steam until the tops of eggs are done. If there seem to be too many potatoes once they're in the pan, use 6 eggs for 6 servings.

» Leila's "Toad-in-a-Hole"

for each person:

1 slice wholewheat bread
1 egg

½-1 tsp butter
salt, pepper

Make a hole in the center of a slice of bread—about 2½ inches in diameter. Meanwhile heat butter in a large skillet till it bubbles. Put bread slices down and grill, on medium heat, for about 1 minute. Break an egg into each hole and fry until set on bottom and top is no longer translucent. Slip just a bit more butter into the pan and carefully turn each egg-and-bread over to fry tops. At last moment each serving may be garnished with a tsp of grated cheese, fresh chopped parsley or both. Run cheese under a broiler to melt. The bread circles which were removed—a glass works well—may be grilled in the same pan with the eggs and served as "caps."

» Basic Waffles

Waffle making is a simple crowd-pleaser. But most people are so daunted by the prospect, that chains of waffle restaurants abound, charging exorbitant prices for cheap ingredients. In fact, most children are so partial to waffles that you can get sizeable amounts of nutrition in them without their ever knowing. A wholewheat yeast waffle looks a bit darker than a "regular" waffle, but tastes infinitely better.

Analysis	Calo-ries	CHO	Fat	Pro-tein	GUP	Iron	Cal-cium
1 waffle	313	40g	14g	14g	12.3g	4.7mg	221mg

Yield: four 8″ roundish waffles

1 Tb dry (or 1 cake) yeast
1½ c lukewarm water
2 Tb honey or molasses
2 eggs
4 Tb defatted soy powder
4 Tb instant milk powder
¼ c whole cornmeal (not de-germinated)

½ tsp salt
1-1¼ c wholewheat flour
3 Tb sesame seeds
2 tsp primary food yeast (opt)
½ tsp cinnamon (opt)
2 Tb oil or melted butter
1 tsp vanilla extract

Dissolve yeast in water, add sweetening. Separate eggs; add yolks to honey-yeast-water, keep whites in a clean, dry bowl. Mix ingredients. Stir in oil or butter and vanilla. Texture should be "ploppy"—thick enough to mound slightly when lifted on a spoon, but *definitely* runny. If you stir through it with your hands it feels "silky" (except for the grit of the cornmeal). Add more flour or water to achieve this texture. If time permits, let rise one hour (or as long as possible). Then stir down, beat whites until stiff and fold them in thoroughly. Follow waffle-iron manufacturer's directions for baking (but wholewheat takes a little longer—eight to ten minutes).

IV

Bread for Loafers

Beetle Bailey

Instead of being alarmed at the decreased nutritive value of white flour as shown by the inability of insect pests to thrive on it, the production of white flour was hailed as a great forward step.
—Samuel Lepkovsky "The Bread Problem In War and Peace" *Physiology Review*, Vol. 24, 1944

Now if you pushed me into a corner, I'd have to admit that baking your own bread takes more time than just grabbing a loaf from the supermarket shelf while racing through with a shopping cart; in almost no other single food area is the time spent for preparation more richly repaid nutritionally.

Despite constant advertising reminders of how many ways "Plastiloaf" builds your body, bread stopped being the proverbial staff of life just about the same time it turned into cotton. The fascinating thing is that the nutritional wasteland of white bread has been recognized for over thirty years. In the early '40's, milestone research was done on the nutritional value of cereal grains, and particularly bread. Scientists conducted feeding studies in which rats and pigeons sickened and died when fed white bread as the main source of nutrition; yet littermates thrived when fed whole wheat bread. Of course, people don't eat only bread, but a lot of your diet finds its way into your body between two slices of bread. Flour is—in its whole, unrefined state—a good source of many of the nutrients sorely lacking in the Western diet. If we, as a nation, returned to the whole grain standard, dietary levels of B-vitamins, fiber, iron, and trace minerals would be significantly increased. Think of it—the average American eats about seventy-one pounds of bread a year. And some segments of the population—poor people, teenagers, people who tend to "grab" meals—eat even more.

As a palliative measure (in response to the nutritional research done in the '40's), "enrichment" of flour was introduced. "Enrichment" is a euphemism for a process that consists of removing at least twenty-five essential nutrients and replacing four to six of them. (See table, page 77, for comparison—and weep.)

Why then was "enriched" flour accepted as the standard,

despite nutritional studies that clearly showed the superiority of unrefined grains? For several reasons: Thirty-five years ago, the number of essential vitamins and minerals that were known numbered half as many as today; "enrichment" *seemed* to be supplying most of what was lost. The powerful milling and baking lobby also made its contribution. The machines developed to replace costly manpower required certain refinements in the characteristics of the flour: the changes did not make for more nutrition, however. According to a source book for the trade, the highest quality flour has the *lowest* amount of essential nutrients—ash. (After the energy or calorie value of a food is burned off, ash, the total of the non-combustible mineral elements, remains.)

It is also true that, since white bread had once been a status symbol (particularly, perhaps, for recent immigrants from Europe who were astonished to find "fine" instead of "coarse" bread so readily and cheaply available), what was billed as overwhelming consumer preference was allowed to outweigh nutritional realities.

Breadmaking

If you've never made bread, it's probably because most recipes are time-consuming, exacting, and somewhat forbidding. But bread making doesn't have to be any of that. We are going to tell you how to ignore most of the picky instructions, avoid time-consuming steps—in fact, *how to make bread with no recipe at all!*

SPONGE METHOD

Most bread recipes use the "straight dough" method: mix everything, knead, let rise, etc. We will use the "sponge" method, which has several advantages. The sponge method makes lighter bread; especially for initial attempts at whole grain breads, this can mean the difference between success and bricks. In addition, prolonged soaking of whole grains enhances the nutritional value of the finished bread. Bran and wheat germ contain phytic acid, which combines with iron, zinc, and other minerals, making them less available to the body. During fermentation (as in the sponge method) enzyme action releases some of the bound minerals.

Also, by beginning with a huge bowl of sponge, you can make several different kinds of bread on the same day for an additional effort measured in minutes. If you started three different batches of bread by the straight-dough method, you'd be in the kitchen for weeks!

INGREDIENTS

Bread is liquid and flour . . . that's it, basic bread. In India they're called *chappatis*; Arabs make a fairly similar bread cooked on hot stones; Mexicans call theirs *tortillas*. To this base you can start adding ingredients. Most bread we think of as bread includes yeast and salt. After those four ingredients, bread is a matter of infinite possibilities.

• *Flours:* There are dozens of flours you may have never heard of before, or thought of cooking with—almost every grain and even many legumes are ground into flour: millet, barley, soybean, lentil, and chick-pea, to name a few.

Wheat is the most commonly used flour for yeast-leavened breads because of its gluten-forming properties. When the gluten network of well-kneaded bread traps the gases given off by yeast, the dough rises. For bread making, buy high-gluten, wholewheat flour milled from hard winter wheat. It contains about 14% protein—as opposed to soft wheat flours, which may contain as little as 9% protein. (Soft wheat flours are preferable for cakes or wherever elasticity is not desirable; gluten is formed from certain proteins in wheat.) Another alternative is to find a source of gluten flour (actually 30% protein), which looks like dingy white flour. It is not absolutely necessary, but the lighter loaf it produces can mean better consumer acceptance. It also cuts down somewhat on kneading time. Use sparingly: ¼ to ½ cup per loaf. The larger amount is only necessary for very heavy breads high in cracked grains, soy powder, rye flour, and so on.

• *Liquid:* Many liquids are possible—milk, water, boullion, potato water, vegetable water, tomato juice, and some even less probable—pickle juice? But we will stick to water and add milk powder for nutritional fortification if necessary.

• *Yeast:* Dry (granular) and cake (moist) yeast are interchangeable: one tablespoon or one package yeast is equal in rising power to one cube (6/10ths of an ounce) cake yeast. To "prove" yeast of questionable freshness: mix with small quantity (½ cup) lukewarm water and one teaspoon sweetening. If after ten minutes it does not froth, bubble, or at least form blobs, it is too weak to raise bread.

These basic ingredients—water, flour, yeast (and salt)—are all you need to bake bread. French, Italian, Cuban, and Viennese bread and rolls are made from nothing but these four ingredients. There are many wonderful, delicious, and useful additions, however, if you choose to include them: fats and oils, eggs, cheese, nuts, seeds, spices, herbs, onions, sweeteners, and various flours in various proportions. The variety of breads is infinite and limited only by your imagination.

If you follow two simple equations, you can experiment with any combinations you please. It takes roughly three times as much flour as liquid to make bread. That proportion varies with the kind of flour, kind of liquid, age of the flour, density desired in the final loaf, even the weather conditions, but it's a good approximation. And it is necessary to use at least half wholewheat flour (to provide enough gluten).

"RECIPELESS" BREAD

• (For approximate amounts, see table.) Add yeast to lukewarm water: cold water retards rising time, but water over 115° will kill the yeast. If a few drops on the inside of the wrist feel mildly warm, the temperature is ideal. Double the yeast for quicker rising; halve it for a prolonged rise. If you wish, add sweetening to speed yeast action; at 1 or 2 Tb per sponge, the finished bread will *not* taste sweet. If you doubt the efficacy of the yeast, be sure to "prove" it as explained above.

• *Mix the sponge.* Add "first flour" to yeast liquid. The proportion of flour to liquid can vary over a fairly wide range and still be right. An approximate rule of thumb is to add as much flour as you used liquid. Some of that flour can be gluten—shake it with whole wheat before adding to avoid lumps, however. The consistency you're looking for is loose mud pies, but it's not at all critical. If you add too little, you'll just end up having to add more later in order to turn it into a kneadable ball (no one would try to *pour* the dough out for kneading—I hope). On the other hand, if you've dumped too much flour in and it starts to look like setting concrete, you'll either add less flour later or more water now

RECIPELESS BREAD TABLE

No. of loaves	Amount water	Amount first flour	Could incl. gluten flour	Amount yeast	Amount salt	Amount final flour(s)
1*	1¼-1½ c	1½-2 c	¼-½ c†	1-2 Tb	2 tsp	2+ c*
2	2½-3½ c	3-4 c	½-¾ c	1-4 Tb	4 tsp	4-5 c
3	4-5 c	4½-6 c	½-1 c	2-4 Tb	2 Tb	6-8 c
4	6-7 c	7-9 c	1-1½ c	2-6 Tb	2-3 Tb	7-9 c

*Never make just one loaf—it's silly; these measurements are given for reference.

†The higher amount of gluten would be used for heavy breads such as rye, cracked grain or soy; it is not necessary to use any gluten, however—all whole wheat is fine.

*More if eggs, honey or oil are used. The smaller figure is *approximately* what it will take to turn the sponge into a kneadable mass; then knead in more flour as necessary to keep from sticking. When the upper figure is reached, add flour cautiously.

and have an extra loaf.

If you give the gluten a good workout now—about two minutes of enthusiastic beating—your bread will thank you later. I have, upon occasion, done nothing more than try to press some of the more obvious lumps through my fingers before I quit, and the bread was good to the last crumb.

• *Let it rise.* Let the sponge rise about one hour. You can vary this by thirty minutes in either direction, if necessary. Or you can refrigerate the sponge for several hours or overnight. Or you can stir it down two, three, or more times when it doubles (about every hour) if that is more convenient. (Technically, you could eventually exhaust the yeast if you tried; all you'd have to do is add a little more, though, and you'd be off and running again.) One word of warning: refrigerated sponge will rise quickly for the first hour, because of the retained heat from the kitchen. Stir it down or leave enough head room, otherwise you'll find it crawling under the refrigerator door.

• *Dough from sponge:* Whenever you deign to return to the kitchen, stir the sponge down and add, if you want, some of the possible variations: eggs, oil, wheat germ, soy powder, milk powder, or other flours, orange peel, herbs and spices, and so on. Don't forget the salt. Then add the "final" flour. Obviously, the amount needed will vary with whatever other additions you've just made. The approximate guide is: about as much flour as you used in the sponge.

Gradually stir flour into the sponge (gently, so as not to break the gluten strands) until it is no longer runny and it begins to form a ball. On the other hand, it shouldn't have lots of dry lumps. Remember, kneading in more flour will be easier than trying to take some away.

Turn the dough out of the bowl onto a heavy sprinkling of flour on the board, say about ½ cup. The dough should be gooey but have some form. If it spreads out like a pancake, scrape it back into the bowl and add more flour.

• *Kneading:* Flour your hands well (dip them into the flour and shake off the excess) and start kneading. If you've never done it before, try this: Pull the far side of the dough toward you, folding it over the rest of the dough. *Lightly* press the two halves of the dough together; don't try to push it through the table. Then turn folded-over dough ninety degrees and start the whole process over by pulling the far side of the dough toward you again. (See illustration.) If it will help, try to remember "fold, push, turn." Notice that's in alphabetical order.

While kneading you should keep your hands lightly floured; if they build up a layer of stuck-on dough, *don't* wash—rub them together (discard the lumps) and re-flour. You should also scrape the board clean occasionally and re-flour or move to a clean, dry place—dough often sticks to the place where you first turned it out.

It *is* possible to add too much flour at this stage, and hard to explain how to tell if there's enough. Stand-alone loaves like rye need more flour than loaf-pan loaves, however. If they're not stiff enough you'll end up with a very wide, flat loaf. Generally speaking, once the dough has formed a recognizable ball (that will depend on how soupy it was when you turned it out), add flour slowly—half a handful at a time. Sprinkle flour *under* the dough, where it will prevent sticking, not on top, where it may leave dry flour streaks inside the loaf. Be temperate—if you add flour every time the dough threatens to stick, you may well add too much.

Properly kneaded dough is elastic, resilient, and smooth. One test: form the dough into a ball and press the first digit of your finger into the side of the dough. If the impression starts to fill up almost immediately (the dough should feel and look springy), you're done. No one has over-kneaded whole wheat bread except King Kong. You could knead twenty minutes (I doubt it) and things would still be just fine. But eight to ten minutes is adequate.

• *Risings:* You can at this point either let the dough rise in a bowl or go right ahead to shape it and let it rise on the final baking pan. While it is true that two (or more) rises produce a more velvety, professional-looking "tear" and texture, I know of no one who has turned down short-cut, no-rise homemade bread. It's up to your convenience.

For bowl-risings, form the dough into a ball and put it in a bowl large enough to accommodate at least double the volume. If you are using fats or oils in the recipe, oiling the top of the dough and the bowl will help to keep the dough from sticking and drying out. Purists, however, would insist that using oil for French-type breads is unacceptable; just put an oil-less dough in a dry bowl—it won't stick much anyway. In either event, cover the top of the bowl with a well

61

wrung-out damp dish towel, to keep the top of the dough from drying out. Otherwise your dough will develop a hard, scaly surface that will peel leperous patches in the next step. (If that happens, just cut off all the dry parts when you punch it down—they won't bake properly.)

Doubling takes anywhere from 45 minutes to 1½ hours, depending on the weight of the ingredients, amount of yeast, and temperature of the kitchen. With each successive rise the dough doubles more quickly, however. If the first rise took 1½ hours, the second may need only one hour and the third (if there is one) will probably take 45 minutes or less. Most cookbooks call for the bread to rise in a warm place, free from drafts. Literally translated that means in a gas oven with a pilot light, or on top of the water heater unless it's too hot to rest your hand on, or near the automatic dryer. If none of these is available, you could turn your oven on *full* for about three minutes, but be sure to turn it *off* before you put the bread in to rise. A pan of hot water in the bottom of the oven works, too. If your kitchen isn't unusually cold, just a countertop is fine unless you are in a hurry.

Again, if it is more convenient, this step can be stretched almost indefinitely by putting the dough into the refrigerator. Be sure to cover the bowl tightly with a plastic-film wrap. It will not double for several hours or overnight. To finish the bread making process, leave the dough at room temperature until it begins to rise. Then punch it down and continue. (You could freeze the dough if absolutely necessary, but once frozen, it loses some yeast action; it is preferable to freeze after baking.)

• *Punching down:* When the dough "doubles in volume" —when it looks like there's a lot more of it in the bowl than when you left it—punch it down. Press the still bubbly edges toward the center of the depression. This pushes the drier parts to the inside of the loaf, where they can be re-hydrated. (The top of the rising dough will dry out slightly despite all precautions.) Don't worry about hurting it—sock it a few times, if necessary, to get all bubbles out. If you want yet another rise, turn the dough over in the bowl and re-cover with the damp cloth.

• *Shaping:* Most cookbooks give unnecessarily complicated and frustrating directions for shaping loaves. They are also almost guaranteed to leave unsightly holes in the finished loaf that make it difficult to cut, to say nothing of having the sandwich filling fall all over the place. First knead very briefly (five times will do), or pound with flat of hand, to get all the trapped gasses out. If you knead a lot at this point, the gluten will become quite rubbery and difficult to manage. Rising always relaxes the gluten; therefore, if you find when pushing the bread in one direction it is adamantly moving in another direction, let it "rest" for 5-10 min. at room temperature covered with a damp cloth or inverted bowl; then go on. For all but French bread, just push, pummell, and pound the bread into shape. Pat it between your hands, shove it this way and that. In short order it will take on bread-pan shape . . . or any other you want.

Then put the loaf in a well-buttered baking pan—whichever shaped pan you choose—and let it rise again covered with a damp cloth. *This is the most important rising.* This is the only one you cannot fiddle with. When you start this— the *final* rise—plan to be around to bake the bread. If this rise is either over or under the required time, the bread may be dense. A few minutes leeway is still fine, but a half-hour won't do. If you find you can't bake the bread as planned, you cannot just refrigerate the risen bread in the pan and return where you left off. You must punch it down and put it back into a bowl; you may refrigerate if your timing requires it until you have time to re-shape it. You will then have to start the final rise all over. You can, however, punch down and shape already-chilled dough and let it rise, in the bread pans, overnight. It will be ready to bake directly from the refrigerator, though it may take an extra few minutes baking time.

• *Baking:* Whole wheat bread takes longer to bake than white, and the heavier the bread, the longer it takes. Temperatures are not really critical; lower heat will require more time and vice versa. Somewhere between 325° (one hour plus) and 400° (40 minutes or so) is reasonable. The thickness of the crust varies with the heat—suit yourself. For maximum "oven spring" put the loaf in a high oven (400°) and turn it down to 350° after ten minutes.

Some breads are baked at specific temperatures to produce traditional results, but basic all-around bread is fine when baked in a 375° oven. To tell when a loaf is done, tap or thump the bottom of the pan with a knuckle (watch out, the pan is hot!). It should sound hollow. Forty to sixty minutes is a sensible tolerance for most breads, again depending on specific ingredients. If all else fails, and you discover that the middle of the first slice still looks gooey, (don't confuse that with the inevitable pulling that occurs when you slice hot bread), just put it back into the oven for another ten minutes or so. The cut end will harden, but some people like ends—this way you get three per loaf.

When the bread is done, remove it from the pan and let it cool on a rack until quite cold before wrapping. Technically speaking, bread continues cooking for about one-half hour after you remove it from the oven, which might be reason enough for you to wait before cutting into the loaf.

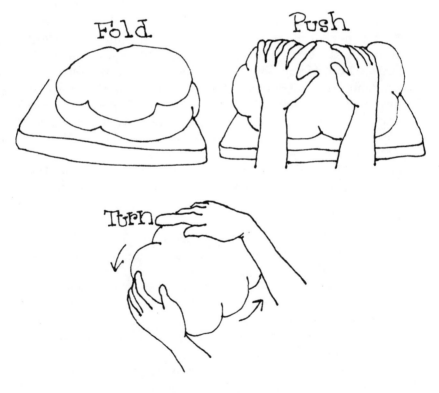

"FOLD, PUSH, TURN"

Breadmaking Outline

1. Mix lukewarm liquid and yeast (and optional sweetening). To "prove" the yeast, let sit 10-15 minutes; if it doesn't form blobs or foam, yeast is dead.
2. To yeast liquid add about half the flour: may be part gluten shaken with equal-to-double the amount of wholewheat . Add enough flour to make a thick, but still liquid, sponge.
3. Let rise from 30 to 90 minutes, as convenient, in a warm place (under 100°).
4. Stir risen sponge down gently; add salt and any other ingredients except final flour.
5. Add flour(s), stir-folding in, until dough begins to form loose ball.
6. Turn dough out of bowl onto a handful of flour on the board; sprinkle another handful on top of dough.
7. Keeping hands and board *lightly* dusted, knead 5-8 minutes (10-15 for very heavy or no-gluten-added doughs).
8. (Optional.) Let dough rise in bowl, covered with damp cloth. If dough is refrigerated during rise, cover with plastic film.
9. (Optional.) If dough has been permitted a bowl rise, punch down when doubled. Repeat steps 8 and 9 once or twice more, if desired. Turn punched-down dough over in bowl between successive rises.
10. Either knead punched down dough five times to press all gases out or let just-kneaded dough sit five minutes to relax gluten. Shape and place on/in well-buttered oiled pan.
11. *Let rise until doubled.* If you cannot, punch down, return to bowl and go back to step 8.
12. (Optional.) Slash tops, glaze, sprinkle with seeds, etc.
13. Bake between 325° and 400° for 35 to 65 minutes.
14. Don't talk, eat first.
15. Cool completely before wrapping tightly for storage.

OTHER BREADS

(Amounts are approximate for two loaves of bread.)

● *Rye:* Use about 4 tablespoons *blackstrap molasses* as sweetening. *Potato water,* though not absolutely necessary, is traditional as the liquid. *Caraway "kummel" seeds* are often used—1 or 2 tablespoons. "Swedish" Rye often uses grated *orange peel*—2 tablespoons and ½ stick of soft *butter,* worked into soft dough before final flour is completely added. Unless you like a very heavy bread, less than half the total flour in the dough is rye; the rest is *whole wheat* with part *gluten.* You may experiment with larger proportions of gluten (up to ¼ of the total flour in recipe) to achieve lighter texture.

● *Pumpernickel:* This is a relative of rye. Not only *potato water,* but also plain *mashed potatoes* are used in the bread (about 1 cup), which should be added to the sponge after it has risen—and before addition of the final flour. Either work in well with your fingers, or better still, use a ricer and rice the slightly cooled potatoes right into the sponge, stirring after every few tablespoons. You could also use *cracked rye* (½ to 1 cup) in place of some whole wheat flour. Other ingredients and instructions are similar to those for rye bread. Dust the buttered baking sheet with *cornmeal* before putting the shaped bread on it. Rye and pumpernickel tend to be very sticky when you start kneading—be forewarned.

● *Onion:* Sauté at least 1 very large *onion* (and some garlic) in 2 or 3 tablespoons of *butter* or other fat. The onions should all be wilted and transparent, and a few should be getting dark brown. When somewhat cooled, add them to the risen sponge. For an onion spice bread strongly reminiscent of "bialys," also add about 1 teaspoon crushed *celery seed* to the risen sponge. One lady suggests that the oniony taste is stronger with raw, unsautéed onions. But melt and add the butter anyway. If you add fresh garlic slivers to the onions while sautéing (do not burn the garlic), rest assured the garlic flavor will be mild. Prolonged cooking of garlic cooks out strong taste.

● *Cornell Triple Rich:* Actually, this should be included in *every* bread recipe, except on those special occasions when you want a completely simple water-type bread (the kind made with the four basic ingredients and no others). In the proportions used, there will be almost no discernible effect on the texture of the loaf, and if no one passes through the kitchen while you're adding offending ingredients, no one will taste the difference either.

The classical method for making triple rich bread is to measure 1 tablespoon soy flour, 1 tablespoon wheat germ and 1 tablespoon milk powder in the bottom of each cup of unbleached white flour being used. That's all right if you're measuring, but who bothers? (To say nothing of the *white* flour!) For each loaf of bread you will need just under ¼ cup of each added ingredient (since most loaves of bread contain between 3 and 4 cups of flour). All you have to do is to shake these ingredients together with 1 cup of final flour to prevent any lumping, then add to the risen sponge. Our method of reserving the final flour until last, and then using only what is necessary for the proper texture, will automatically adjust the rest of the recipe to allow for the changes in absorption or amount. Easy!

● *Cheese:* Add up to 1 cup grated natural *cheese* (could be part *Parmesan)* to risen sponge—could also include ½ cup *cottage cheese.* Brush loaf with melted *butter* or egg white glaze and sprinkle with *Parmesan cheese.*

● *Sprouted grain:* Add 1 cup *chopped sprouted grains* to risen sponge. For added crunch, if your teeth can stand it, add as much as 1 cup cracked wheat, rye, or other grain (unsoaked, or soaked, well-drained if softer texture is desired) to risen sponge.

● *Egg* (sometimes called egg braid—always called "challah"): Add from 2 to 6 *eggs* to the risen sponge. The greater the number of eggs, the more like the real thing it will be. Should be braided.

» *Pita*—(Arabic Bread)

Triple Rich or other dough   sesame seeds (opt)
made with 1-2 Tb oil   wholewheat flour

Kneaded dough may be allowed to rise in a bowl once or twice, but it is not necessary. Form dough into balls between 1-1½″ diameter. They needn't be particularly neat; just rip off a reasonably sized hunk and mash it into slightly spherical shape. Put dough balls on a *well*-floured board and sprinkle more flour on top of balls. It helps to put them in some order so that you can start the next step on the balls which have risen the longest. Let rise 20 to 30 minutes, until about doubled; try to leave enough room between the balls to keep them from touching while they rise. Do *not* cover them to keep them from drying out—you *want* them to dry out. While balls are rising, pre-heat oven to at least 450°.

When first balls have risen, sprinkle more flour on a clean surface—you can also sprinkle with some sesame seeds. With your palm, flatten a ball slightly on the sesame-flour surface, turn over and press down again. Now roll it into a circle 4″ to 7″ in diameter—depending on the size ball you started with—and about ¼″ thick, or slightly less. When the oven is at least 450°, put as many pita as you can fit on an *ungreased* baking pan or cookie sheet—or even tin foil. Bake from 4 to 8 minutes, depending on thickness. The heat of the oven should make the moisture in the pita explode into steam. If you have kept the outside dry, a crust forms quickly and instead of just escaping, the steam "puffs" the pita. They are done when a small spot on the bottom of the pita which is still touching the baking pan is golden brown. Some won't puff or will puff unevenly. As soon as you take these from the oven, open a slit in one side of the rim with a long-bladed knife and split the pita; it's impossible to do when they are cold and you end up with a very thick, flat bread.

68

When the pita are cool, press them flat—don't worry, the pocket will still be there when you want it—put in a tightly closed plastic bag in the refrigerator or freezer. Frozen pita keep well for several weeks. They may be re-warmed just before using—the 4" diameter ones fit neatly into most toasters and don't dry out as much in the re-heating. Fill with any sandwich filling. They are traditionally served with a bean filling like *Felafel*. They also make an excellent walking salad holder.

Pita can be made out of almost any dough—rye are especially delicious—provided that the cooking directions are followed carefully. If your pita chronically don't puff, check your oven thermostat. Below 400° won't work and many ovens can be 50° off.

By adding fat for richness, and sweetening, and even fruits or nuts, ordinary bread dough can be turned into something resembling yeast-raised coffee cake. It's an extra attraction on baking day.

Bread Charts

As you can see from the wide ranges of possible additions to bread in the following chart, the *right* amount of any addition is up to you. Combining different ingredients in the same loaf not only makes interesting bread, it also tends to give a wider nutrient range. Beware of adding several ingredients having the same physical effect on the loaf. If you add soy powder *and* rye flour *and* cracked grains, you might end up with highly nutritious statuary.

If your breadmaking goes smoothly, but the end product isn't the vision you had, consult the Bread Troubleshooting Chart. Although some problems may be traced to various (even conflicting) causes, it will help you find the area of breadmaking that you should pay closer attention to next time. Most importantly: don't worry too much. Even breadmaking "failures" are delicious!

THINGS YOU CAN ADD TO BREAD, AND THE RESULTING NUTRITIONAL AND PHYSICAL CHANGES

(for two 1 lb. loaves)

WHAT TO ADD AND HOW MUCH	NUTRITIONAL CHANGE †	CHANGE IN RESULTING LOAF
⅔-1⅓ c non-fat dry milk powder	increases calcium and riboflavin; supplements wheat protein	softer crumb; less "wheaty" taste
2 tsp to 2 Tb brewer's yeast	some protein; inc. B-vitamins, iron and trace minerals	
1 to 2 c leftover cooked cereals or grains	some iron, B-vitamins	moister bread
1 to 2 c grated cheese	supplements wheat protein; inc. calcium, riboflavin	
2 to 4 eggs	inc. protein, vitamin A; some iron, cholesterol	no change unless 3 or more eggs, then spongier, more voluminous loaf
1 c wheat germ	inc. iron, B-vitamins, trace minerals, PUFA*, vitamin E	more than ½ c could result in denser loaf; sponge method counteracts this tendency

70

WHAT TO ADD AND HOW MUCH	NUTRITIONAL CHANGE	CHANGE IN RESULTING LOAF
½ to 1 c soy powder (low or de-fatted)	supplements wheat protein; inc. B-vitamins, iron, calcium, trace minerals	somewhat denser at higher concentrations
1 c wheat bran (or other polishings)	inc. (fiber, intestinal residue), B-vitamins, trace minerals	same as wheat germ, above
1 to 2 c gluten flour	inc. protein (lowers other nutrients slightly)	lighter loaf
1 c chopped nuts or seeds	inc. calories, protein, PUFA, fiber, B-vitamins, trace minerals (varies with nut or seed used)	crunchy texture
1 c dried fruit	some iron, fiber; vitamin A in apricots	chewy texture; larger amount makes heavier loaf. Soaked fruit adds moisture.
3 c rye flour (in place of as much wheat)	some iron	rye used for more than half total flour makes dense loaf
2 to 8 Tb butter	SatFA**; some vitamin A, D inc. calories	spongier loaf, stays fresh longer

WHAT TO ADD AND HOW MUCH	NUTRITIONAL CHANGE	CHANGE IN RESULTING LOAF
2 to 8 Tb oil	PUFA; some vitamin E	same as butter, above
½ to 2 cup sprouted grains or leg- umes	inc. protein, vitamin C, B-vitamins	chewy texture, moister loaf
2 to 6 Tb molasses	inc. iron, trace minerals, B-vitamins	moister at higher concentrations
2 c chopped onion or 6 to 16 cloves garlic, raw or sautéed		

*PUFA   polyunsaturated fatty acids
**SatFA   saturated fatty acids

† NOTE: Even though there is an increase in certain nutrients, according to analyzed values, the *available* nutrients cannot be precisely determined. Some iron may be unavailable due to the binding action of phytates. Some of the heat-sensitive vitamins (B-complex and C) will be destroyed in baking.

As for moister loaves, the drying and staling is retarded while the tendency to mold is increased.

BREAD TROUBLESHOOTING

IF YOUR LOAF:	YOU MAY HAVE:	THEREFORE:
is dense, heavy	let it rise too long	the gluten strands over-expanded and collapsed.
	not let it rise enough	it wasn't as fully expanded or gas-filled as it should have been. *Remember that the last rising should not be tampered with!*
	not kneaded enough	there wasn't enough gluten network to hold the gases. Knead longer or use gluten flour.
	killed the yeast or it was too old	lukewarm water is warm enough. If the age of the yeast is uncertain, be sure to "prove" it.
	kneaded in too much flour	measure out full amount of flour called for in the recipe. When that is used, add very sparingly. Scrape your hands and the board frequently and keep them *lightly* floured.

IF YOUR LOAF:	YOU MAY HAVE:	THEREFORE:
	not pre-heated the oven enough	the loaf over-rose and fell before the gluten network was baked into place.
	included a large amount of unusual flours or other heavy ingredients	remember that only wheat forms gluten; a light loaf demands at least half whole wheat or whole wheat and gluten flour.
is too moist, gummy	undercooked it	put it back in the oven, with or without a pan, even if you've already cut a slice. It should be golden brown and sound "hollow" when done.
is too moist, gummy	not added enough flour	if the loaf sticks to your hands and the board and is not springy and resilient when kneaded, you should knead in additional flour.
	added too much cooked cereal	either decrease the amount of cereal or increase the amount of flour.

IF YOUR LOAF:	YOU MAY HAVE:	THEREFORE:
has large holes in it when you slice it	shaped it by the old-fashioned roll out and roll up method; especially if the dough was in an oiled bowl (which tends to keep the layers separate)	don't oil the bowl; shape bread by pushing and patting the loaf in-to shape.
is cracked near the base (where it rest-ed on a cookie sheet)	not let it rise sufficiently before putting it in the oven; and probably didn't cover it with a damp towel	the combination of "oven spring" and the dried-out top cracked it at the weakest point. Some heavy breads require a slash in the top to make expansion easier.
does not brown	baked it in too large a pan	use pan in which the unrisen dough comes about halfway up the sides. When doubled, the cen-ter of the loaf should be higher than the sides of the pan and the edges should be almost flush. A glaze might help, too.

IF YOUR LOAF:	YOU MAY HAVE:	THEREFORE:
comes out mushroom-shaped with a large overhanging top lip	baked it in too small a pan	ditto.
is underdone on the inside but crust is too brown	baked it at too high an oven temperature	$400°$ is maximum for most breads. See below.
is done all the way through but not brown on top	baked it at too low an oven temperature	$325°$ is minimum for most breads. Check oven thermostat against a reliable one.

WHOLEWHEAT AND ENRICHED WHITE BREAD
(+2% milk solids) COMPARED
(for standard one pound loaf)

	Wholewheat	Enriched White	% Difference
Calories	1102	1220	+ 10
Carbohydrate gm	216	229	+ 6
Protein gm	48	39	− 19
Fat gm	14	15	+ 7
*Thiamin mg	1.18	1.13	− 5
*Riboflavin mg	.56	.77	+ 37
*Niacin mg	12.9	10.4	− 20
Pantothenic Acid mg	3.45	1.71	− 50
B-6 mg	.82	.24	− 71
Biotin mg	1.99	.018	− 99
Inositol mg	279	212	− 24
Choline mg	290	165	− 43
Folic Acid mg	.127	.054	− 58
Linoleic gm	3	2	− 33
Fiber gm	7	1	− 86
Vitamin E	2	0	− 100
*Calcium mg	449	318	− 29
Phosphorous mg	1034	395	− 62
Magnesium mg	354	100	− 72
*Iron mg	10.4	10.9	+ 5
Potassium mg	1238	386	− 69
Zinc mg	11.8	5.9	− 50
Iodine mcg	59	39	− 33
Lysine mg	1214	924	− 24

There are also significant changes in manganese (−84%), molybedenum, tin, copper (−74%), cobalt, flourine, selenium, chromium, nickel, vanadium, silicon, PABA. Lysine, the limiting essential amino acid in wheat (see Chapter VIII) is listed above. The other EAA's lose from 4% to 31%.

---

*Nutrients so marked are added to enriched flour, accounting for their good showing.

V

Be True to Your Heart
Or It Will Attack You

Hi and Lois

*Changes in the American diet over the last seventy years
. . . do not fit the hypothesis that low ratios of polyunsaturated to saturated fatty acids . . . contribute to the increased
incidence of coronary heart disease in the United States. . . .
The type of dietary carbohydrates, however, may be a factor.*
—Dr. Mohamed A. Antar, et. al., *American Journal
of clinical Nutrition* No. 14, March, 1964

Heart attack! It will scare you to death, if nothing else. Heart disease is the most serious health problem in the United States today, killing one million Americans annually and disabling millions more. As the problem has grown, so has the research. An innovative theory about heart disease concerns the personality of the potential victim. It is claimed that, regardless of diet, the driving, ambitious person—labeled "Type A"—who is also more likely to smoke heavily and drink gallons of coffee—is more prone to heart attack than the less aggressive "Type B."[1] Since, however, we haven't yet developed a diet that can turn Type A into Type B, we'll concentrate on the nutritional theories.

At first glance, the two or three major nutritional theories on the hows and whys of heart disease seem mutually exclusive. And, judging from the cross-fire in their research papers, some of the principal proponents think that the others are guilty of scientific heresy—or worse.

ATHEROSCLEROSIS

Atherosclerosis, a common precursor of coronary heart disease (CHD), is the build-up in the arterial walls of some of the fatty fractions (cholesterol or triglyceride) of the blood (serum). Hence, some doctors are concerned about elevated serum cholesterol levels. Dr. Ancel Keys, a prominent researcher in the field of heart disease, states: "Among adults in the United States, at least, the question is not who has atherosclerosis, but rather who has more and who has less."[2]

It is widely accepted that atherosclerosis is somehow related to diet: three current interpretations of the body of research on CHD are the saturated fat theory, the sugar or refined carbohydrate theory, and the cellular nutrition theory.

SATURATED FAT THEORY

According to the official stand of the American Heart

Association, there is a direct relationship between the consumption of saturated fats and the incidence of CHD. Saturated fats are derived mainly from animal sources: meat, milk, eggs. Except for coconut oil, cocoa butter, and man-made hydrogenated oils, vegetable sources provide mostly unsaturated fats. Studies comparing diets of populations with differing rates of CHD show that as affluence—and therefore per capita consumption of animal fats—increases, so does CHD. The same statistical evidence, however, supports a direct relationship between CHD and animal protein.[3]

P:S RATIO

Research has shown that an increase in the P:S ratio (more *Polyunsaturated fats, less *Saturated fats) can lower serum cholesterol and, theoretically, the potential for arterial plaque formation. If there is also a moderate to marked reduction in the total fat of the diet, the serum cholesterol is lowered to an even greater extent.

The average American diet contains 40%-45% fat, most of it saturated. This is largely traceable to diets that include meat in two or three meals a day. Fast food lunches are particularly high in saturated fats: a typical hamburger, shake, and fries contain about 40% fat, most of it saturated. Although a fried chicken dinner contains less saturated fat, it contains more total fat. Frankfurters and luncheon meats are also prime offenders with 30% (mostly saturated) fat.

Mainly because of research by Dr. Keys and his colleagues, the AHA recommends a substantial reduction in total fat and dietary cholesterol, an increased P:S ratio, calorie restriction as necessary to achieve ideal weight, and a limitation on "empty calories." As a result of the AHA stand, millions of Americans have become cholesterol watchers—sharply cutting their consumption of butter and counting every egg. (Except for brains, eggs have the highest concentration of cholesterol occurring naturally in foods.)

SUGAR OR REFINED CARBOHYDRATE THEORY

Other researchers don't agree, pointing to important exceptions to Dr. Keys' theories. Studies have been made comparing southern Indians who consume diets high in satu-

80

rated fats with northern Indians who consume diets high in polyunsaturated fats. Although the southern Indian diet would be considered cholesterol-raising by AHA standards, the serum cholesterols of both groups do not differ significantly. More interesting still, the polyunsaturated group has a significantly *greater* tendency toward some forms of heart disease.[4]

Dr. John Yudkin is one of the scientists who finds flaws in Dr. Keys' theories. Though there is a connection between saturated fat consumption and heart disease, since populations with relatively high saturated fat intake *often* have correspondingly high CHD rates and vice versa, there is an equally impressive statistical correlation between high sugar intake and CHD.[5] In many cases, fat and sugar consumption vary together; most of the non-meat vehicles of saturated fats are combinations of refined flour, fat and sugar.

The connection between sugar and heart disease has been investigated by Dr. L. Michaels, who surveyed records covering two centuries of British dietary patterns and heart disease statistics. During that time, the percentage of saturated fat in the diet did *not* rise, but the annual sugar consumption made a quantum increase, from 4 to over 110 pounds per person. During the same period, the incidence of angina pectoris (a symptom of heart disease), which had been a medical oddity in 1768, increased astronomically.[6]

American dietary patterns since the turn of the century have shown that while the per capita consumption of saturated fatty acids has remained almost constant, the consumption of sugar has increased more than 100%.[7]

CELLULAR NUTRITION THEORY

Dr. Roger J. Williams, the biochemist who discovered pantothenic acid (part of vitamin B-complex), is the major proponent of the Cellular Malnutrition Theory of heart disease. His basic premise: A healthy organism is one that is healthy at the cellular level; the average American diet lacks many of the 40 or more nutrients necessary to the healthful working of all the cells (including those of the arteries and heart).[8] He indirectly supports the refined carbohydrate theory: he believes that overconsumption of the naked calories in sugar (and alchohol) is a main contributor to the wide-

81

spread American cellular malnutrition. But he is in conflict with the Saturated Fat Theory since he claims that a well-nourished (at the cellular level) organism can properly use cholesterol and saturated fats which therefore need not present a health hazard.

Additional evidence to support both the Cellular Nutrition and Refined Carbohydrate theories has recently come from Dr. Henry Schroeder, the most eminent researcher in the field of micro-nutrients. His studies have shown that the feeding of refined carbohydrates can produce atherosclerotic placques in animals. He states that chromium deficiency (chromium is one of the nutrients lost in refining) is responsible for the increased death rate from heart disease, especially in diabetics.[9, 10] (See Chapter VII.)

YOU WIN!

It is confusing and frustrating for the concerned consumer to hear such conflicting theories about diet. It's not reassuring to a person with incipient heart disease to learn that within twenty years or so the facts of the matter will probably have been decided. How does one tread water meanwhile?

We believe the whole foods vegetarian diet has something for everyone. Whether cholesterol or refined carbohydrates or a combination of both turns out to have been the culprit, our vegetarian diet satisfies the dictates of each. Studies of lacto-ovo-vegetarians (milk and egg eating) have shown lower serum cholesterol levels than typical American diet controls, despite a higher intake of dairy products. And by definition, if you eat the whole-grain, no-junk, high-nutritional-density diet described in this book, you'll not only meet the requirements of the Refined Carbohydrate Theory, but you're bound to be getting more nutrients to your cells as well. No matter who turns out to have been right—you win! And your heart will be much less likely to attack you.

OILS

A study of American market patterns over seventy years has revealed that the consumption of saturated fatty acids has remained remarkably constant, while the intake of polyunsaturated fatty acids (PUFA) has doubled.[7] During the same period, the incidence of CHD has exploded. This fact opens to question the main hypothesis of the Saturated Fat Theory.

Humanity's historically validated fat consumption pattern has until recently been based on greater amounts of saturated than unsaturated fats. The technology for producing large quantities of most oils (olive is an exception) did not exist before this century. There may be undesireable side effects from this major dietary alteration.

At least one follow-up study of the effects of a fat-controlled diet notes that although the death rate due to CHD had fallen significantly, the death rate from all other causes, especially cancer, had risen significantly in the PUFA group. High PUFA intake demands additional alpha-tocopherol intake. Alpha-tocopherol is the most biologically potent form of Vitamin E for humans (see Chapter VII, "Lipid Peroxidation"). If, as is the case with some oils, the Vitamin E present is primarily in forms other than alpha (such as beta, gamma, delta), the safety of increased PUFA intake is questionable.

The lower heat used in processing so called "cold-pressed" oils is probably less detrimental to the natural nutrients of the oil than the commercial methods of solvent extraction followed by steam cleaning at high temperatures for several hours. This refining processs is a series of steps designed to strip the oil of all flavors, odors, and not incidentally, the undesirable breakdown products resulting from the repeated heating. "Crude" oils are even less fractionated than "cold-pressed" and we suggest their use wherever the stronger taste is not objectionable. We feel that neither butter nor oil should be used to the exclusion of the other in a balanced diet.

BUTTER OR MARGARINE

Some people actually claim to prefer the taste of margarine. It's possible that they've only tasted the cheapest butter—which, indeed, often tastes greasy and salty and may be made from reclaimed stale cream or old butter.[13] Just once, buy the best butter available in your area (some of the finest butters available in supermarkets are made in Wisconsin and Minnesota) as well as your usual brand, and see if you can taste a difference.

Butter does have saturated fats and some cholesterol, but it also has nutrients missing in margarine: magnesium, copper, manganese, chromium, cobalt and zinc. Butter is probably colored, although, as with most dairy products, its label doesn't have to tell you that. At least one national brand of unsalted butter is not colored. (The color might be a harmless vegetable derivative or a coal tar dye—perhaps not so harmless.)

If you prefer margarine, be sure to read all the fine print. The less expensive margarines have proportionately more additives. Since there are some brands of unadulterated margarines (particularly those available in health food stores), one wonders why other brands require so many chemicals. Compared with butter, margarine has more Vitamin E (though not necessarily alpha-tocopherol) and a higher P:S ratio; and it is fortified with Vitamin A.

Now comes the question of saturation and hydrogenation, which is a bit tricky. All lipids (fat cells) are composed of both saturated and unsaturated fatty acids. Unsaturated fatty acids are further divided into mono-unsaturates (oleic) and polyunsaturates (arachidonic, linoleic, and linolenic—there are others but these are the prominent ones).

The P:S (polyunsaturate-to-saturate) ratio is based on the comparison of linoleic to the total of all the saturated fractions. The other mono- and polyunsaturates are not taken into consideration since it is the higher proportion of linoleic that is thought to be the active agent in lowering cholesterol in research studies.

Hydrogenation of already highly processed oils results in a "plastic" (hardened) fat. Hydrogen tends to selectively link the most unsaturated fraction of the oil; so most of the valuable polyunsaturate for which health claims are made (linoleic) is changed into a mono-unsaturate (oleic). But any margarine, no matter how thoroughly hydrogenated, may claim to be made from polyunsaturated oil. With the transformation of linoleic to oleic, the P:S ratio has fallen precipitously. Polyunsaturated oil has been turned into mono-unsaturated margarine.

Some margarines are made by mixing an amount of

liquid oil with hardened (hydrogenated) oil until the desired consistency is reached. The AHA suggests this kind of margarine for those following its "prudent" diet. However, if there is more than one hydrogenated oil in the margarine, the total amount of liquid oil may be less than the total amount of hardened. In other words, the oil and margarine manufacturers have been delighted to cash in on the AHA stand, though their cleverly labeled and advertised products may not have the recommended qualities.

If you eat the typical Western diet, no amount or brand of polyunsaturated margarine is going to save you from its long-term effects. Whether butter would be an added insult is open to question. *We conclude that butter is preferable to margarine.* It has fewer objectionable additives and more essential nutrients. Since the total fat and saturated fat of the whole food vegetarian diet tends to be considerably lower than the average Western diet (around which the AHA's dietary recommendations were formulated), we feel there is no problem with using the real thing. A diet high in legumes, nuts, and seeds, and with little or no meat, will have an acceptable P:S ratio, even if butter is consumed in place of margarine.

EGGS

The question of egg consumption is much more controversial. A large egg yolk contains about 300 mg of cholesterol—the maximum suggested by the AHA as the total daily intake. When the other sources of saturated fats and cholesterol in the typical diet are added into the total, someone who eats two eggs (and two slices of bacon or sausage) every morning is likely to be getting a lot more than the current recommendations.

On the other side of the chickenwire, the Egg Council asserts that the egg is one of nature's most perfect foods: very high in nutrients and protein for the number of calories, and easily digested if not overcooked. They also point out that the body produces every day an amount of cholesterol equal to four to six eggs. There is even some suggestion that if cholesterol consumption is too much curtailed, the body will simply produce more.[14]

We do not have the definitive answer to this controversy,

85

but we have managed to completely sidestep it. If it were true that eating more than the recommended number of eggs would lead to a higher CHD rate, then lacto-ovo-vegetarians would have a high incidence of heart disease. Studies on the health profiles of vegetarians find the exact opposite: lacto-ovo-vegetarians have lower serum cholesterol levels (pure vegetarian levels are even lower) and statistically their first heart attack occurs ten years later than the national average.[15] But the catch is—vegetarian.

It is our conclusion that the AHA recommendations are valid primarily for people whose diet can be described as the typical Western diet—high in meat, fat, sugar, and white flour; low in fiber and micronutrients. If you want to eat a meat-based diet, you probably should follow the AHA recommendations for saturated fat and egg restriction. If, on the other hand, you improve your whole diet, not merely patch up a particularly weak aspect of it, you can have your egg and eat it too. We certainly don't recommend eating six eggs a day—but we wouldn't recommend eating six portions of *anything* a day. The best diet is chosen from a wide variety of *different foods*.

From an ecological standpoint, although eggs "cost" more in grain protein than they return, the ratio is much better than meat (4 pounds of grain protein for 1 pound of egg protein vs. 16 to 1 for beef); and their contribution to the diet is great. For vegetarians, they provide one of the two natural sources (dairy products are the other) for essential Vitamin B-12.

CHEESE

Although it is also considered a high-cholesterol food by some, cheese can supply significant amounts of protein: one ounce of most natural cheeses contains about 7 gms (see Chapter VIII), and a substantial amount of calcium—which is potentially marginal in the average adult American's diet. The chances are that people who say they're not fond of cheese have never tasted any—*real* cheese, that is.

PROCESSED CHEESE

In 1912 Joseph Kraft patented something called "processed" cheese, and we haven't seen the end of it. Natural cheeses are made of milk, salt, and usually rennet — an enzyme that starts the curdling action. There are hundreds of varieties of real cheeses, usually lumped into main categories like sweet (dessert), soft ripening, soft, and hard. What category does "American" cheese fit into? None. All "American" cheese is processed cheese: it's a combination of green cheese (that hasn't ripened yet), ripe cheese, water, emulsifiers, flavorings, and colorings. In fact, there are at least 33 non-dairy additives permitted in processed cheeses that don't have to be listed on the label.[16] Even more interesting—and profitable—are the processing variations known as "pasteurized process cheese food," or ". . . spread," or ". . . snack." In each case there are more additives and water, less cheese. In fact, cheese "food" has less than half the protein, calcium, and other nutrients of natural cheese (but it does have more highly-advertised "meltability"). This dilution of nutrients is obviously very profitable. You've seen hundreds of ads for gimmick cheese; how many ads have you seen for natural cheese?

Virtually all cheese made in America (even much "natural" cheese) is bleached with hydrogen peroxide to destroy the uneven yellow color (with it goes the Vitamin A). If they're orange-colored when you buy them—as most "cheddars" are—they have been dyed as well. The dairy industry, incidentally, is unique in not having to list added color. And according to Dr. Jacqueline Verrett, an FDA researcher, processed cheese may be dyed with Red-2.[22]*

Even undyed natural supermarket cheeses have a rubbery texture and no flavor. Look for a cheese store that specializes in international natural cheeses. Though seemingly more expensive, they are so flavorful you'll use less.

FISH

Strict (moral) vegetarians don't eat fish—though they will eat mollusks or bivalves on the theory that anything that doesn't have a central nervous system doesn't mind if

---

*Although Red-2 is now banned, other coloring agents are being used—and they may be just as bad.

you eat it. We're neither that strict nor that moral; besides which, fish have certain redeeming social values. A small amount of fish protein goes a long way toward complementing lower NPU protein; the Japanese rice-fish diet is one of the most efficient in the world (and if CHD statistics mean anything, one of the most healthful). And fish don't graze: they don't eat food which could otherwise have been fed to people, nor do they take up room on land which could grow food. Provided that international restrictions are soon reached (the consistently smaller catches of recent years may be linked to "over-fish") fish are one of our most renewable resources. Fish farms may be the major "meat" source of the future. As currently practiced in China, fish farming gives almost one-to-one protein return as part of an eco-system which also involves sewage disposal and water purification.

FIBER AND SERUM CHOLESTEROL

Although we have explained why the Saturated Fat Theory is probably not particularly pertinent to vegetarians, it may still be difficult for people who have become self-imposed cholesterol-watchers to take our enthusiasm for eggs, butter, and cheese seriously. But we have another ace up our sleeves: fiber. Fiber includes by definition all the indigestible structural plant material in the diet (see Chapter VII). While fiber is improving the intestinal health, it is also helping the heart. The fact that the same countries that have a low incidence of diverticulitis and bowel cancer have a low incidence of CHD is of great significance to many researchers.[17-19]

Numerous studies have shown that besides adding to the bulk of the stool, fiber increases the bile acid content of the stool.[20] Bile acids are formed, in part, from cholesterol. When larger amounts of bile acids are excreted, less is returned to the cholesterol pool. An increase in the bile acid content of the stool, as produced by a high-fiber diet, results in less serum cholesterol.

An unprocessed, unrefined diet as described in this book can be expected to contain from 16 to 24 grams of fiber per day. In some tests with human volunteers, lowering of serum cholesterol, even while on a diet designed to raise it, was accomplished by merely substituting a high-fiber flour for

88

white flour.[21] The typical Western diet contains only trace amounts of fiber per day. Hospital dietitians plan "high" fiber diets of six grams. (For a comparison of the fiber in the Western diet and the whole foods diet, see page 108.)

Despite the AHA's endorsements of the Saturated Fat theories, it is rapidly becoming apparent that *if* heart disease is attributable to a single dietary cause, that cause is not saturated fat. Moreover, research evidence seems to be strongly pointing to several inter-connected reasons for the current epidemic of heart disease, only some of which are diet-related.

Although dietary manipulations such as those proposed by Dr. Keys and others are successful in lowering serum cholesterol, and possibly in lowering the incidence of heart disease, it seems better to attack the root causes, rather than engage in after-the-fact palliative measures. Many researchers have concluded that a low-fat, low-saturated-fat diet should not be considered the total answer to heart disease—though it may be a useful short-term tool in treating existing or incipient heart disease. It is undoubtedly true that the American diet is too high in fats and particularly too high in saturated fats. But merely lowering calories from saturated fats or total fats will not provide the answer if the diet is not also improved in these other ways: lowering the total calories, especially calories provided by sugar and refined carbohydrates; decreasing the total protein where appropriate, especially protein of animal origin; and increasing the fiber and micronutrient content of the diet, especially those trace minerals and vitamins known to be marginal or deficient in the typical Western diet.

The AHA recommendations are built on a faulty base: they accept the basic flaws of the Western diet and then try to work around the disastrous effects by suggesting alterations in fat intake. We prefer to reduce excess consumption of meat and sugar, to increase intake of unrefined carbohydrates (thereby increasing natural fiber as well as trace minerals and vitamins), and to continue eating the amounts and kinds of fat that have been safely consumed for centuries.

» Timbale

A timbale is basically a cheese custard with a delicious vegetable, or fish, addition. It could in fact also be described as a quiche without a crust. It has all the ingredients of a soufflé minus flour, but instead of beating the separated whites and folding them in for leavening, the whole thing is mixed together and baked. It has the smooth, silken quality of well made custard. If you're not sure that your guests will be on time, make timbale and not soufflé. Timbale can be kept for at least an hour in a water bath in a slow oven. It definitely doesn't have the prima donna tendencies of a soufflé.

Yield: 4-6 servings

4 eggs	½ c grated emmenthal
2 c milk	(Swiss) cheese
1 c asparagus (or other vegetable)	nutmeg, savory, salt, pepper
	½ c wine (opt)
½ c mushrooms sautéed with ½ c onion	Parmesan cheese and wheat germ

Barely steam vegetable (in case of asparagus or broccoli, to avoid overcooking tender tips, steam ends and tips separately). If you want to unmold timbale, butter ringmold, sprinkle with cheese and wheat germ. Combine vegetables and other ingredients, pour into mold or oven-proof casserole. Bake at 350° in a *bain marie* until set—about 35 minutes. If unmolded, center may be filled with tuna sauce.

» Broccoli Quiche

A "real" quiche (Lorraine) is made with bacon and cream, neither of which offers much nutrition. But by substituting milk for the cream (forget the bacon), you've got a high-protein, lower-fat dish that is also quick and simple to prepare.

If you would rather use a rolled pie crust, do so. The patted pie crust causes less anxiety for some. (See recipe index for quiche crust.)

6-8 thin stalks broccoli
3 eggs
1½ c milk
1 c mushrooms sautéed in 1
   Tb butter with shallots

salt, pepper, dash nutmeg
2 Tb vermouth (opt)
¾ c grated sharp cheese
1¼ c Quiche Crust Mix (see
   Mixes and Makeaheads)

Follow crust recipe to make 8" or 9" pie plate or quiche pan. Arrange broccoli (chopped if you prefer) or other vegetable in an attractive pattern in crust. Combine rest of ingredients and pour carefully over vegetables. Bake at 350° for 35-40 minutes, until quiche is browned and slightly puffed and a knife inserted in center comes out clean.

» Crab Quiche

4 eggs
2 c milk, or ½ c milk powder
   plus 1¾ c water
salt, pepper, dash paprika
⅓ to ½ lb. crab meat

1 c grated sharp cheese
1 chopped sweet red pepper
2 Tb sherry
2½ c Quiche Crust Mix (see
   Mixes and Makeaheads)

Follow crust recipe to make four 10 oz. custard cups. Combine rest of ingredients, pour into cups. Bake at 350° for 20-25 minutes. Each crab quiche contains over 30 grams available protein, or almost ¾ the Minimum Daily Requirement.

» Spanikopita
(Greek Cheese and Spinach Pie)

2½ c whole wheat flour
½ c grated Parmesan cheese
1 stick butter
⅓ c defatted soy powder
½ tsp salt

½ tsp pepper
½ c water
1 egg white beaten with 1 Tb
   water (opt)

Crumble butter into dry ingredients with fingertips. Add cold water, distributing as evenly as possible. Chill at least 20 min. Pat crust into well-buttered 8"x12" baking dish. Either pre-bake 5 minutes in 350° oven or paint with egg white glaze.

Filling: can be made while crust is chilling or baking.

1 lb chard (or spinach)
1 tsp oil (olive)
3 cloves garlic, chopped
1 small onion, chopped
mushrooms (opt)
2 Tb wine
2 Tb chopped parsley
3 eggs

¾ lb feta (about 2 c crumbled, or substitute cottage cheese-1 lb.)
¾ c milk
juice of 1 lemon
4-5 Tb wholewheat flour
4 oz (1 c) grated cheese

Cut chard stems into ½" pieces. Sauté with oil, onions, mushrooms, and garlic for 2 minutes; then add roughly-cut tops and wine; steam 1 minute. Combine rest of ingredients. Pour into crust and bake at 350° for about 20 minutes.

» Greek Spinach Pastries

This is similar to Spanikopita, but instead of a crust, the filling is enclosed in paper-thin phyllo pastry sheets which make a lighter, melt-in-the-mouth, crisp covering (even if they are made from white flour).

2 Tb olive oil
2 cloves garlic
1 medium onion
1 lb spinach or chard
½ c parsley
1 c grated Swiss cheese
¼ c wine
½ lb mushrooms

1 c grated Romano
1 lb cottage cheese or feta
lg dash nutmeg
½ c wheat germ
¼ c melted butter
5-6 phyllo pastry sheets
salt, pepper

If using chard, cut stems where they join leaves—these are tougher and require a little extra cooking. Sauté mushrooms, onion, garlic in olive oil and chopped chard stems (if used) for about 3 minutes. Then add chard tops (or spinach) and cook for about 2 minutes (4 minutes for chard leaves). Add everything but phyllo and butter. Carefully spread sheet on completely *dry* surface—or it will disintegrate. Brush with melted butter. Cut sheet in 2½" wide strips. Place about 3 Tb of filling in a triangular pattern on one end of sheet and fold up, like a flag, from side to side

in a triangle, until filling is completely enclosed and whole strip is used. Repeat with rest of filling and remaining pastry strips. Place on a lightly-greased baking pan in 350° oven for about 15 minutes until top is golden. These are even better the next day, and delicious cold.

» Broccoli-Cheese Casserole

2 c chopped broccoli
1 pint cottage cheese
2 eggs
½ tsp dill weed
juice of 1 lemon

4 oz grated cheddar cheese
(or more)
2 Tb wholewheat flour
salt and pepper

If whomever you're cooking for likes broccoli, leave the flowerets in recognizable chunks; slice the stems the size of a quarter. If you suspect consumer resistance, however, chop it into oblivion. Steam about 3 minutes in ¼ cup water. Broccoli should be crunchy, tender and vivid jade green. Save water (if any) for soup. Combine rest of ingredients in an oiled casserole. Bake at 350° for 35 minutes.

VARIATIONS:

1. Add ½ c chopped pecans (adds zinc).

2. Make a topping of 2 Tb melted butter, 3 Tb toasted wheat germ and 2 Tb grated dry Parmesan cheese. Sprinkle it on casserole before baking.

3. Eggs may be left out, if desired. Casserole will not hold its shape as well, however.

» Spanish Omelette Filling

½ lg onion, diced
1 canned green chili—about
  2 Tb chopped
5 peeled tomatoes (1 green
  if possible)
1 chopped green pepper

2 Tb fresh chopped parsley
2-3 Tb olive oil
2 cloves garlic
½ tsp each: oregano, paprika,
  marjoram, basil
¼ c vermouth

Sauté onion, chilis, and green pepper in olive oil for 4 min. Squeeze peeled tomato and save juice for soup. Roughly cut tomatoes into skillet and cook until reduced and thick —another 3 minutes or so. Add spices and wine; cook until alcohol has evaporated. Use as a Fritatta filling (see Recipe Index) or for individual omelettes. (Omelette directions in Chapter III.) *Yield: About 4 servings.*

VARIATIONS:

1. Add 1 cup or more sautéed mushrooms.

2. Add 1 cup frozen or fresh (*not* canned) green peas before spices.

» Egg Foo Young

Analysis	Calo-ries	CHO	Fat	Pro-tein	GUP	Iron	Cal-cium
Serving:	167	6g	13g	8g	6.9g	1.7mg	45mg

Yield: 4 servings

1 stalk celery
1 small onion
½ c bamboo shoots or water
  chestnuts, sliced
2 Tb crude peanut oil +

2 cloves garlic, smashed
1″ ginger root, smashed
1 c bean sprouts
1 tsp tamari soy sauce
4 eggs

Sauté garlic and ginger root (which have been smashed with the flat of a knife) in 2 Tb peanut oil until almost smoking: remove and discard (or eat the garlic!). Sauté celery, onion, and bamboo shoots or water chestnuts for 2 minutes. Meanwhile, beat eggs; add sautéed vegetables.

Put ½ tsp oil in wok and pour in a ladle of egg mixture. Cook until done on one side, about a minute; turn to other side. Keep warm in 200° oven until all are done. May be cooked in a flat skillet, but this makes a flatter, wider pancake.

» Chiles Rellenos

Analysis	Calo-ries	CHO	Fat	Pro-tein	GUP	Iron	Cal-cium
Serving:	433	18.6g	27g	19.1g	13.6g	2.9mg	397mg

Yield: 5 servings

8 canned whole chilis
8 oz cheese (Jack or other
   white cheese)
3 eggs, separated

4 Tb wholewheat flour
salt
oil for frying

If desired, fresh bell peppers may be used instead of chilis. Blanch bell peppers for 5 minutes in boiling water, until pliable but not mushy. If using canned chilis, remove seeds and wash under running water. Carefully stuff peppers or chilis with cheese sliver. Beat yolks with flour; beat whites until stiff with large dash salt. Fold whites and yolks together gently. Dip stuffed chilis or peppers in batter, fry in hot oil until browned. Keep warm in 200° oven until all are done. Serve with Mexican Tomato Sauce (see Recipe Index).

» *Basic Cheese Soufflé*

Analysis	Calo-ries	CHO	Fat	Pro-tein	GUP	Iron	Cal-cium
Serving:	327	13g	19g	24.9g	20.1g	2mg	244mg

Yield: 5 servings

4 Tb butter
5-6 Tb wholewheat flour
1½ c milk (approx.)
½ c grated sharp cheese
1 tsp salt
3 Tb vermouth or sherry
½ tsp pepper

¼ tsp dry mustard
dash nutmeg
½ tsp paprika
4 eggs, separated; plus one
  white
2-3 Tb Parmesan cheese

Melt butter; when bubbling, add flour and cook as directed for White Sauce. Add milk, stirring with wire whisk. Add spices; add cheese off heat, stir until melted, let cool slightly. While cooling, beat 5 egg whites until stiff peaks form. Quickly stir egg yolks into cheese sauce mixture, add wine. *Fold* in whites carefully but thoroughly. Turn into straight-sided soufflé dish which has been buttered and sprinkled with grated Parmesan cheese. Bake at 350° for 30-40 minutes. Do not peek until baking time is almost over. *Serve immediately.*

VARIATION: Tuna Soufflé

Follow recipe for Basic Cheese Soufflé; add 1 can drained water pack tuna, flaked, to cheese sauce before whites are folded in.

» Zucchini Pancakes

Analysis	Calories	CHO	Fat	Protein	GUP	Iron	Calcium
Serving:	295	21g	16g	17.7g	13.1g	2.2mg	338mg

Yield: 12 pancakes (6 servings)

4 c grated zucchini (about 5 medium)
1¼ c grated sharp cheese
¾ c grated feta cheese
4 eggs
1 c wholewheat flour

1 Tb grated onion
½ tsp salt
¼ tsp pepper
butter or oil
milk as needed for thinning

It is not necessary to peel well-rinsed zucchini. Combine ingredients. Film heavy frying pan with butter or oil; pour in pancake-sized blobs. Cook over medium heat until bottom is golden; turn and do other side. May be served as vegetable or entrée.

VARIATION:

1. Cut flour to ½ c; bake in well-buttered 8″ square pan for 30 minutes at about 350°.
2. Cut flour to 1 Tb; use as Quiche filling. Makes one deep or two thin 8″ quiches.

» Entrée Crêpes

The essence of a crêpe is its delicate thinness: if you don't achieve that, you've just got an unleavened pancake. It's not at all difficult to manage: the pan must be hot enough to sizzle for about 3 seconds when a drop of water is shaken on it. Then pour the batter *while* turning the pan. Don't pour the batter in the stationary pan and then decide to distribute it: you've already got a pancake. Common errors: (1) Trying to get the crêpe round. It's far preferable to have a thin funny-looking crêpe (I am famous for maps of Africa and centipedes) than a perfectly shaped blob. (2) Tilting the pan in eight directions at one time: the batter never has enough time to run before you move it again and it ends up in the middle. Turn the pan in one or two large arcs. (3) Using too much batter. A quarter cup is usually sufficient for a 7" to 8" diameter crêpe, though it doesn't look that way at first. When the batter is distributed all over the bottom of the pan, pour the excess out; make a note of how much was left over and use that much less next time. Don't be disheartened if the first two or three crêpes stick to the pan. Scrape them out if necessary, wipe with oil, and try again. Adjust the heat so that in 20-30 seconds the edges of the crêpe dry and no longer adhere to the pan. If you look closely a tiny rim will seem to curl up from the edge, asking you to turn the crêpe. If the cooked side is glassy-textured and uniformly brown, the pan is too hot. It should be light amber and not slick.

The Crêpe:

4 eggs	2 c wholewheat flour
1 c milk	1 tsp salt
1 c water	3 Tb melted butter or oil

Whiz first six ingredients in blender until smooth; add butter or oil and whiz again. Refrigerate at least one hour or overnight. Blend again just before using to redistribute heavy particles. To cook: wipe a hot, heavy-bottomed skillet with oil (cast-iron and porcelain-enamel are excellent). Pour about ¼ c batter (for a 7"-8" crêpe) into the pan *while* tilting the pan in a big arc to distribute the batter thinly. Cook about 45 seconds, until the edges dry and begin to shrink up from the pan. Turn and cook the other side *(exception:* cook one side only for blintzes). May be stacked and refrigerated. For freezing, put a piece of wax paper between each crêpe.

The Filling:

Make a thin white sauce out of 2-3 Tb whole wheat flour, 3 Tb butter and 1 c milk. Stir in choice of: ½-¾ c leftover thinly sliced chicken or turkey; or 1 small can tuna (well-drained); or leftover steamed vegetables; or sautéed mushrooms and onions; or a combination of above. Also add 1-2 Tb sherry or vermouth, ½ tsp paprika, a dash of cayenne,

½ c grated cheese (opt), salt and pepper, ½ tsp worcestershire sauce or soy sauce.

Roll 2-3 Tb filling in crêpes, place in buttered bakingdish. Heat in 350° oven until filling is warmed through. May be topped with a few tablespoons of remaining white sauce.

» Crêpe Mound

Analysis	Calories	CHO	Fat	Protein	GUP	Iron	Calcium
Serving:	412	13g	19g	21.5g	15.9g	2.9mg	300mg

Yield: 8 servings

1 recipe Entrée Crêpes
double recipe Cheese Wine
   Sauce (see Recipe Index)
½ lb mushrooms sautéed
   with 1½ c onions

2 c chopped green vegetables
   lightly steamed
1 c cottage cheese
additional grated cheese

Divide Cheese Wine Sauce in three portions. Add mushrooms to one, cottage cheese and green vegetable (spinach, chopped broccoli, well-drained zucchini and/or yellow squash, "frenchcut" green beans) to the second. Hang on to the third. Put a large well-formed crêpe (or overlap two) in the bottom of a baking dish with a lip. Spread with a few Tb of cheese-mushroom mixture; top with a crêpe and spread with some of the cheese-vegetable mixture. Continue the stack, alternating vegetable-cheese and mushroom-cheese until something runs out. Put two overlapping crêpes on the top (by now it should look like Mt. Fujiyama) and "frost" with the reserved cheese sauce. Sprinkle an additional handful of grated cheese on top. Bake at 350° for 20-30 minutes until everything is bubbling hot. Serve in pie-shaped wedges.

» Blintzes

Analysis	Calo-ries	CHO	Fat	Pro-tein	GUP	Iron	Cal-cium
Ea. blintz:	169	16g	6g	12.6g	9.8g	1.1mg	119mg

1 recipe Crêpes, cooked on
one side only
1½-2 lbs. cottage cheese
1 egg
1 Tb butter, softened
½ tsp cinnamon (opt)

grated peel of 1 lemon
1 tsp vanilla extract
1 Tb honey (opt)
raisins (opt)
yoghurt
unsweetened apple sauce

Combine all ingredients but apple sauce and yoghurt. Put 1 to 2 Tb of filling on cooked side of crêpe, fold (envelope style) to enclose filling. Place, seam-side down, in a large frying pan containing a *light film of oil and butter*. Fry until golden and turn to cook other side. Serve with yoghurt and apple sauce (or sour cream instead of yoghurt, if your waistline can stand it).

» Enchiladas

¾ lb cheddar, grated (3 c)
6 oz can pitted black olives,
chopped
1 recipe Enchilada Sauce
(see Recipe Index)
½ tsp salt
1 tsp chili powder
1 tsp cumin, ground

1 tsp basil
1 to 4 canned chilis (opt)
approx. 15 tortillas, commercial or ours (see following
recipe)
1 recipe Mexican Tomato
Sauce (opt)

Combine everything but tortillas and Mexican sauce. Reserve a handful of cheese and a few olives. Soften tortillas by pressing on a slightly oiled pan—just one or two drops for each tortilla; do both sides. Put about two heaping tablespoons of filling on each tortilla, roll and place in slightly oiled baking dish. If you want a moister enchilada, pour Mexican Tomato Sauce over and sprinkle with reserved cheese and olives. Actually, enchiladas in Mexico are a bit drier than the American taste prefers, so if you want them more authentic, omit the second sauce. Bake at 350° for about 20 minutes—until cheese is bubbly—longer if they were frozen first.

» Corn Tortillas

Analysis	Calo- ries	CHO	Fat	Pro- tein	GUP	Iron	Cal- cium
1 tortilla:	66	12g	.4g	3.1g	2.8g	.9mg	20mg

1 c corn grits
½ c soy flour
½ c wholewheat flour
½ tsp salt

½-¾ c water
additional flour—⅓-½ c or more

Combine first four ingredients. Add just enough water to make a soft dough. Knead about 2 minutes, adding flour as necessary to keep from sticking. Form 12 balls about 1″ diameter. Generously sprinkle flour on board, press dough ball flat with hand; turn over and press again, keeping surface well floured. Roll tortillas into about 6″ diameter circle, turning and flouring as necessary to keep from sticking. Bake tortillas on ungreased skillet over medium heat, turning once. May be frozen. They may also be fried in hot oil for dishes that require crisp tortillas.

Kids really like these as snacks, and though deep-fried foods are probably not desirable, these are far preferable to potato chips or corn chips. For snacks, experiment with adding garlic, onion, or chili powder, or paprika to the dry ingredients. You can probably get a good approximation of the flavored chip products.

VI

You Could End Up With a Semi-Colon

ART'S GALLERY

You don't have to put bran in
EVERYTHING!

by Art Finley © San Francisco Chronicle

The removal of cereal fiber from our food . . . may be the most important single factor aside from cigarette smoking, in producing diseases characteristic of Western civilization.
—Dr. Denis Burkitt, "Bran: Nature's Problem Solver," *Life and Health*, March, 1974

As EVIDENCED by the 700 brands of laxatives available,[1] constipation is as American as apple pie—in fact they're probably related. Uncomfortable as they are, constipation and hemorrhoids are only the tip of the iceberg. Current research indicates that diverticulitis and dreaded cancer of the large bowel may both be traceable to the same dietary lack of fiber.[2-7]

MILLING

Of all the ways in which humankind has changed its historically validated diet, none is more striking than the refining of carbohydrates and the removal of fiber. Before the Industrial Revolution, flours were made from the whole grain. What was then considered "white flour" was really carefully sifted whole grain flour. Peasant bread, made from unsieved whole flour, was dark and heavy and full of fiber.

The advent of roller-milling made it possible to remove completely the dark, fibrous bran and germ—for the first time flour could be made entirely from the endosperm (starch) of the wheat. Since "white" flour had been a mark of affluence (and even royalty), this new, truly white flour was widely preferred when available at modest cost. It also kept better: bugs and rodents didn't want it; and without the fat of the germ it couldn't become rancid.

BRAN AND GERM

But two extremely valuable food fractions are lost in milling: the germ and the bran. Wheat germ has long been associated with food-faddists, but one look at a nutritional analysis of wheat germ is enough to make faddists of us all. Wheat germ compares favorably with hamburger for most nutrients—if you don't find that comparison too invidious.

Wheat bran also has respectable amounts of nutrition. It is 16% protein (germ is 25%) but its amino acid pattern

103

—(see Chapter VIII)—is not quite as good as that of wheat germ. Unfortunately, although wheat bran has a high iron content, it also has a high phytic acid content, which binds the iron, making some of it unavailable. ("Binding" describes the action of a chemical molecule that reaches out and grabs other elements, forming insoluble complexes: phytates will bind zinc, iron, and calcium. Fortunately, fermentation of whole grains, as in sponge-type breadmaking, releases some of the bound nutrients.)[8] But bran's major contribution to the diet is its relative indigestibility and capacity to absorb and hold moisture.

The health of the bowel depends on sufficient bulk: completely digested foods leave insufficient residue. Since humans do not produce enzymes for breaking down bran or cellulose, this fiber passes through the intestine virtually unchanged (as opposed to, say, cows, which have four stomachs and can make milk out of hay). After the food of a typical Western meal passes through the small intestine (lots of white bread, sugar, meat, overcooked vegetables, little if any fresh fruits or salad), what's left is hard, compact, and dry. During peristalsis, the muscles of the large bowel must strain to push this pebbly matter along—this raises the normal pressure of the intestinal segments as much as nine times. After years of straining, hernias (diverticulae) can develop along some segments.[3-7]

Anyone with diverticulosis—and that includes four out of five Americans over the age of forty[9]—can tell you it's not much fun. The breakdown products of fecal matter caught in these out-pouchings frequently cause irritation, inflammation, and pain: diverticulitis.*

VARICOSE VEINS AND HEMORRHOIDS

Varicose veins and hemorrhoids, long thought to be

———

*Until quite recently, diverticulitis sufferers were advised to eat a low-roughage diet. Even now, uninformed doctors can be found who recommend as a curative the same diet that caused the disease. If your doctor recommends a low-fiber diet, ask him to read the research papers referenced in this chapter. Or change doctors.

caused by such diverse factors as standing for long periods or the stress of pregnancy, are most probably caused by the same low-fiber diet that leads to diverticulosis.[4, 10, 11] Dr. Denis Burkitt, a prominent researcher in non-infectious bowel disease, has done extensive research in Africa. He points out that Masai tribesmen never sit down, and African women have a threefold higher incidence of pregnancy than Western women. Yet, incidence of diverticular disease, varicosity, and hemorrhoids is practically nil in Africans who consume the high fiber, unrefined carbohydrate diet prevalent in most native areas. But Africans whose diet approaches the low-fiber level of the Western diet, such as urban dwellers and students, have a higher incidence of these diseases.

BOWEL CANCER AND REFINED CARBOHYDRATES

But more serious still is the connection between the incidence of diverticular (and related) diseases and the incidence of cancer of the large bowel. Large bowel cancer, the most common form of cancer in the United States, kills 47,000 Americans a year, second only to lung cancer in men.[7, 9]

There are currently two major theories about the causes of bowel cancer. One points to a relationship between high meat (particularly beef) consumption[12] (see Chapter VIII); the other concerns refined carbohydrates.

Research points to two related factors in the production of bowel cancer that spring from the refining of carbohydrates: alteration of bacterial flora and prolonged intestinal transit time. Along with white flour, sugar is refined carbohydrate, and its pattern of consumption has changed more than that of any other foodstuff (if sugar deserves that name) in the last hundred years. Since the turn of the century, sugar consumption has increased 100% in America.[13] Sugar affects the normal bacterial flora of the intestine. Although the nature of the change is not clear, it seems to be either an alteration of, or an increase in, the flora. In either event, researchers link changed flora to the production of possibly carcinogenic breakdown products in the intestine.[2-4, 9, 10, 14-18]

At the same time, compact stools take longer to pass through the intestine. A number of researchers have used markers to determine how long it takes food to pass entirely through the system (transit time). The consensus is that protracted transit times (as long as 100 hours in some English school boys) are significantly shortened with high-fiber diets.[2-4, 10] Therefore with a high fiber diet, any carcinogenic compounds, whether ingested or produced *within* the bowel by the activity of altered flora, will have less contact with susceptible intestinal mucosa.

The role that refined carbohydrates play is underscored by the fact that when natives of countries with extremely low rates of diverticular disease and bowel cancer adopt a Western diet, the incidence of these diseases rapidly increases. In other words, this is an environmental, not a genetic difference.

WHY WHITE FLOUR?

All these diseases—diverticulosis, large bowel cancer, hemorrhoids, varicose veins, constipation, and even appendicitis—might well be largely prevented by including small amounts of bran (1-4 Tb) in the daily diet. You can easily add bran to prepared foods such as hot cereal or breadstuffs, in which it would be palatable and go almost unnoticed. It would also be possible to add wheat germ in a similar fashion, thus perhaps restoring the original quality of the grain.

But that does seem to be the long way around. Is it necessary to expend the effort and energy to separate these grain fractions, only to combine them later? Whenever the subject of returning to whole grains has come up (as it did during World War II when "enrichment" was decided upon instead), the banners of "consumer acceptance" and "short shelf life" are raised.

"CONSUMER ACCEPTANCE"

Dietary experts usually claim that re-educating the population to prefer more healthful whole grains is practically impossible. Yet the marked change in consumption of fats in recent years has been the result of just such a re-education program. Because of extensive advertising and health information campaigns, the public has changed its consumption of saturated fats. It would seem that an equally enthusiastic campaign could promote whole grains. But unsaturation has the powerful oil and margarine industry behind it—there is no such economic pressure for whole grains—just the reverse.

106

In addition, consumers have responded to other quasi-health claims: note the number of "natural" cereals or "no preservatives" bread on supermarket shelves. Increased consumer awareness plus the astounding proliferation of health food stores and products stressing the importance of whole grains would seem to indicate that the studies done in the '40's (which concluded that re-education was impractical) are sadly out-of-date.

"SHORT SHELF LIFE"

The other main objection, that of shelf life, is equally invalid. There are many foods in an average supermarket that are more perishable than whole grains and whole wheat flour. In fact, many supermarkets now carry both. Properly stored and dried, whole grains can keep for years. Aside from rodents—which sturdy containers can deter—the main problem is insects whose eggs, laid in the grain before it is stored, hatch into larvae that commence to feed on the grain. However, freezing for as little as two weeks kills most of the microscopic eggs and greatly retards the hatching of any that remain. The whole grain can then be stored at room temperature until it is ground.

Flours or other cracked grains should be milled as close to time of consumption as possible—the fresher whole wheat flour is, the better baking qualities it has (as opposed to white flour, which has to be aged—usually chemically—before it will bake properly). Most supermarkets now have elaborate inventory control to distribute foods efficiently according to local consumption patterns. This, combined with refrigeration (and about one sixth of the modern supermarket is devoted to refrigerated and frozen foods) solves the problem of whole grain storage and handling. Of course, there are also differences in storage and handling at home, but flours are not nearly so perishable as fresh produce, and should not pose any greater problem to the consumer.

Since fiber is so important, and since most people have no idea of where to find it, below is a comparative listing of foods: the typical Western diet vs. the whole grain vegetarian diet. After a lifetime of eating what is tantamount to a fiberless diet, a sudden switch to a high fiber diet may cause distress. That doesn't mean you shouldn't eat fiber. Although

107

Comparative Fiber Chart

Traditional American Diet			Whole Foods Diet
BREAKFAST			
(Grams of Crude Fiber)			
1 c Kix or High Pro	.1	3.2	¾ c granola & raisins
1 c Milk	0	0	1 c milk
¾ c orange juice	.2	.8	medium orange
SNACK			
1/6 9″ apple pie	.6	2.3	large apple
LUNCH			
1 serving canned Beef Noodle Soup	.1	1.	Homemade Veg. Soup 1½ c
Bologna or Ham Sandwich	.1	.8	Sandwich—whole-wheat bread (2 sl)
10 Potato Chips	.2	.8	Peanut Butter 2 Tb
2 Butter Cookies	trace	.6	sunflower seeds 2 Tb
		1.2	5 dates
SNACK			
Candybar (chocolate coated type)	0	.5	2 wholegrain sesame cookies
Coke	0	0	½ c milk
DINNER			
Chicken 3 oz.	0	2.4	Soybean chili & cheese soybeans ¾ c
Canned Gr. Beans ½ c	.6	.2	brown rice ¾ c
Jello salad—2 small pear halves	.6	1.	Coleslaw ¾ c
White Roll	.1	1.	Dark bread with Seeds
Chocolate Cake 1 serv.	.1	2.8	Large Pear
Daily Total	2.8	18.6	

a short jog would probably make a sedentary person's heart pound, it would be absurd to conclude that excercise should be avoided.

Some people may have no trouble switching over to all whole foods practically overnight. But people with histories of gastric or intestinal distress may have to soft-pedal a bit. If you've had chronic "funny tummy," introduce whole grains into your diet gradually: toss one-quarter to one-half of your usual flour to the birds and replace with as much whole wheat flour. Use for everything you would have used the old stuff for. (This is also a good method for introducing changes to children who might take umbrage at eating "healthy" foods.)

Beans are another problem: if even canned baked beans give you gas—or worse—don't expect miracles when you sit down to your first mixed-bean casserole. But you *can* work up to it.

It is also true that what some people think of as "peculiar"—having more than one bowel movement a day—may actually be a misunderstood sign of health!

Some authorities suggest adding bran (1-4 Tb a day) to the diet—meaning the average American diet, which is virtually devoid of bran or any other fiber.[11] It is unnecessary for someone eating all whole grains to add more fiber. The only exception to that may be someone who already has diverticulosis. (Four out of five Americans over the age of 40 do.) [9] The problem is you don't know you've got it until the diverticulae inflame. To ask an already suffering intestine to perk up and work right for a change can be a painful insult. But when acute symptoms have passed, it is essential to gradually work fiber into the diet either as whole foods, added fiber, or both. Some doctors claim that patients placed on a high residue (what fiber is called when it passes out of the intestine) diet lose their diverticuli—in other words, fiber may be curative as well as preventative.[4, 6]

Think you might need added bran in your diet? (See Appendix for bran test.) If you decide you do—in *addition* to the whole foods diet—gradually work up to 2 Tb daily. In order to avoid discomfort, take as long as need be to work up to the suggested daily intake.

GRAINS

For most of the world's population, grains are the main

source of protein. We who have access to enormous amounts of animal protein ignore the fact that grains can be an excellent protein source, especially when mutually supplemented amino acid sources are used as well. (See pages 174-179.)

If nothing else, be sure to use 2 Tb of soy granules for every cup (dry measure) grain or grain product you cook. This does not affect the texture or taste but in most cases raises the NPU to a level comparable to or greater than meat.

Adding cheese, eggs, or beans is also good. With so many different and flavorful supplements possible, the whole food vegetarian diet is never dull.

Remember, a grain or other protein source need not be supplemented in the same dish: it is sufficient if the supplementary protein is present in the same meal. Chiles Rellenos with rice is just as good as Rice and Cheese Balls; except for salad, the meal is practically planned for you.

BASIC GRAIN COOKING				
	Regular Cooking		Pressure Cooking	
	Approx.		Approx.	
	Liquid	Time	Liquid	Time
For One Cup Grain	Cups	Mins.	Cups	Mins.
Oatmeal	3-4	15-25	2-3	5
Millet	3+	20-25	2½-3	15
Kasha, buckwheat groats	2-2½	25		
Cracked wheat, Bulghur	2-2½	25-35	2	10
Barley	2½+	30-40	2	10-12
Brown Rice	2-2½	35-45	1½	15
Whole wheatberries			1½-2	15-20
Whole oats			1½-2	15-20
Whole triticale			1½-2	15-20
Whole rye			1½-2	15-20

Begin timing when pressure reaches maximum. Actual times will vary slightly with the length of time grain has been stored, where and in what season it was harvested, and so on. These times represent our preference for a reasonably chewy grain: if you want mush, increase cooking times. *It is essential in all grain and bean pressure cooking to add a small amount of fat or oil to the cooking water to avoid a clogged vent.* Even grains that supposedly should not be pressure-cooked because of their foaming potential will pressure-cook successfully if this rule is followed.

The grains have been listed by increased cooking time; with a pressure cooker, the longest part of meal preparation need never be more than one-half hour.

For grains with widely varying cooking times, cook large quantities separately, then combine and reheat with steam. A pressure cooker is an excellent way to reheat: put grains in a metal bowl, place into the pressure cooker, then pour 1″ of water around the bowl. Pressure-cook 5 to 10 minutes —steam will revive fluffiness without making the grain soggy.

Combining two or more grains makes a better nutrient profile; rice, especially, can use nutrient additions. If you haven't heard of triticale, it was developed as part of the Green Revolution by Dr. Norman Borlaug. It is a hybrid of rye and wheat, has excellent cooking and baking qualities, and is superior in nutrition to either.

"Macro-flake" is a process that "tenderizes" whole grain, allowing it to be cooked in shorter time, but there is some sacrifice of nutrition and flavor. Macro-flaked grains are particularly useful when grains are to be soaked and eaten raw, as in cold cereal.

We have added small amounts of soy grits (or granules) to almost every grain recipe. This is important not only to supplement the protein, but also to improve the nutrient profile. It is not at all noticeable at this level. The analyses have included the grits; if you can't get them or don't want to use them, you will lose some nutrients.

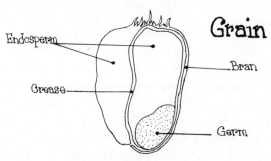

Longitudinal Cross Section

» Basic Steamed Rice

Analysis	Calories	CHO	Fat	Protein	GUP	Iron	Calcium
Serving:	132	19g	4g	5g	3.9g	1.2mg	30mg

Yield: 5 servings

2 c brown rice
4 c water
1 tsp salt

1 Tb butter or oil
4 Tb soy grits (opt, but analyzed)

Do *not* wash rice; simply add water. If a *lot* of pieces of hulls and chaff float to the top, pour off some of the water (measuring what you pour off) and add back the same amount of fresh water. This is not really necessary—they will disappear in the cooking.

Add the rest of the ingredients; cover pan tightly. Put on high flame until boiling, then turn to active simmer. When done (exact time will vary with kind of rice and how you like yours), there will be no liquid left at all—rice will stay firmly in place when you turn the pan sideways, and "clam holes" will show in top. (Clam holes look just like the little bubbling holes that appear at the tide line after a wave has washed over the beach.) Sometimes the rice at the bottom of the pan sticks and gets a little brown (*not* black). Some people think that is the most delicious part.

You might also want to add 1 tsp American saffron or two or three threads Spanish saffron before cooking. Rice should turn yellow.

» Pilaff

Besides steaming (which is obviously a euphemism for boiling), the most popular way of cooking most grains is making pilaff—also called pilau or pilav. It is as international as it sounds. For steaming, all the ingredients are combined at the beginning. For pilaff, the grain is first sautéed in hot oil until slightly golden (rice becomes opaque); then a hot, flavorful liquid is added all at once "exploding" the grain. It is then cooked as for steaming, preferably without lifting the lid. It takes just about the same amount of liquid but a bit more oil. Butter is not recommended, since it burns at

112

such low temperatures, although it may be melted in, just before serving.

» Bulghur Pilaff

Technically, bulghur wheat is a coarse grind of wheat which has been partly cooked and then dried. This has been a nifty way to prolong "shelf life" in countries where insects are a problem and refrigeration has been far from universal. Although *real* bulghur is available here, it is a specialty item and very expensive. What we use and call bulghur is actually cracked wheat. They are almost interchangeable, though *real* bulghur will cook a bit faster since it's already partly cooked.

Analysis	Calories	CHO	Fat	Protein	GUP	Iron	Calcium
Serving:	326	55g	5g	10.4g	6.7g	3.1mg	37mg

Yield: 5 servings

1½ cups bulghur
3 Tb soy grits (opt, but analyzed for)
1 onion, chopped
1 or more cloves garlic,
   chopped (opt)

2 Tb oil
2 c liquid (part wine)
1 tsp oregano
1 tsp paprika
salt and pepper

Sauté onion and garlic briefly in oil. Add bulghur and sauté until it smells nutlike. Add spices and liquid; cover and simmer ½ hour or until all liquid is absorbed.

» Rice Pilaff

Analysis	Calories	CHO	Fat	Protein	GUP	Iron	Calcium
Serving:	215	21g	11g	5.4g	4g	1.3mg	38mg

Yield: 5 servings

2 c brown rice
4 Tb soy grits (opt , but analyzed for)
4 Tb olive oil
1 onion, coarsely chopped
2 cloves garlic, chopped or
   pressed

4 c liquid (may be water,
   stock, vegetable cooking
   water, wine, tomato juice
   or combination)
salt, pepper, paprika
pinch rosemary, thyme

113

Heat oil in heavy skillet. Sauté onion until wilted and golden, add garlic. Cook briefly. Add rice and stir over high heat for about five minutes. When rice is slightly opaque, add *either* boiling stock all at once (or other liquid or combination of liquids), *or* cool liquid slowly to produce furious bubbling and steaming as the cold liquid hits the hot pan. Then cover tightly and let cook about 20 minutes. Add salt, pepper and spices to taste, and more liquid if necessary. Cover again and simmer another 20 minutes until done "al dente."

» *Risotto*

Analysis	Calo- ries	CHO	Fat	Pro- tein	GUP	Iron	Cal- cium
Serving:	227	18g	14g	5.8g	4.3g	1.1mg	72mg

Yield: 6 servings

1 lg onion, chopped
4 Tb butter
2 c brown rice
4 Tb soy grits (opt, but ana-lyzed)

½ c wine
7 c liquid (veg. stock is ideal)
saffron
4 Tb Parmesan cheese
2 Tb butter

Sauté onion in butter; add rice and cook about 5 minutes. Add wine and cook until almost evaporated. Add water, 2 cups at a time, until rice is "al dente." Add saffron while rice is cooking. Add Parmesan cheese and butter; stir in when rice is done.

» *Rice and Cheese Balls*

Yield: 24 balls

Rice (use entire Risotto recipe above)
2 eggs
about 1 cup cheese (Moza-rella)

¼ c each wheat germ, Par-mesan, flour
olive (or other) oil
salt and pepper

Gently combine lightly beaten eggs with warm or cold rice; try not to mash rice. With wet hands or two spoons, form balls of rice, press a cube of cheese in and cover with another ball. Dredge in wheat germ mixture. Refrigerate for about ½ hour. Then deep fry, or bake on oiled sheet, until golden. Balls may be frozen for later use.

» Lemon Barley

Analysis	Calories	CHO	Fat	Protein	GUP	Iron	Calcium
Serving:	395	61g	13g	10.3g	6.5g	3.7mg	46mg

Yield: 5 servings

1½ cups barley
3 c liquid
juice of 2 lemons
1 can tomatoes
½ tsp cayenne
½ tsp turmeric
¼ c oil
½ tsp coriander

2 peeled chilis, may be canned
½ tsp cumin
¼ tsp mustard (powder)
½ tsp fenugreek
1 tsp salt
3 Tb soy grits (opt , but analyzed)

Combine spices (except salt) and chilis and sauté in oil for a minute. Add barley and cook about two minutes over fairly high heat. Add liquid and tomatoes and salt; cover, cook about ½ hour.

» Rice and Shrimp Barcelona

Analysis	Calories	CHO	Fat	Protein	GUP	Iron	Calcium
Serving:	361	6g	29g	20g	15.7g	2.7mg	101mg

(This analysis does not include the rice.)

Yield: 6 servings

2 lbs shrimp
¾ c olive (or other) oil
1 tsp paprika
1 tsp salt
10 (or more) large cloves garlic

½ c large handful fresh parsley
juice of 2 lemons
¼ c dry wine (opt)
2 c brown rice, cooked

This amount of shrimp will feed about six people. It is not necessary to peel shrimp, but do remove legs. If you want to, cut down back (through shell) and remove sand vein. You can peel shrimp (and devein) if you want a less messy dinner, however. Heat oil in a large skillet. Add garlic and heat until it begins to brown. Add shrimp and cook, turning frequently to cook all the shrimp, for about 5 minutes, or until they turn pink and opaque. Add remaining ingredients, saving parsley until just before serving. Serve over rice using garlic oil as a sauce. For a complete meal-in-a-dish, you could also add one or two packages frozen green peas just long enough to heat through. If you don't peel the shrimp before cooking, they don't shrink as much, and the shells make the whole dish a bit more flavorful. On the other hand, some guests won't be delighted about having to peel oily, garlicky shrimp at the table: but that's their hang-up.

» Kufteh

Kufteh is a Middle-Eastern dish which may be made with various grains; some Kuftehs are even sweetened with the addition of dried fruits. It may be served as an appetizer or as a main dish with an accompaniment of a Mediterranean vegetable like Ratatouille.

Analysis	Calories	CHO	Fat	Protein	GUP	Iron	Calcium
Serving:	543	85g	16g	19.6g	13.6g	7.5mg	137mg

Yield: 4 servings (as a main course)

4 Tb butter or olive oil
3 cloves garlic, pressed
1 c chopped onion
4 Tb tomato paste
1 28 oz. can tomatoes and juice
1 tsp paprika
1 tsp cumin, ground

1 tsp salt
¼ tsp cayenne—or less
1½ c bulghur
1 c chopped green pepper
½ c chopped green onion
¼ c chopped parsley, packed
¼ c chopped fresh mint (opt)
1 chopped cucumber

Sauté onion and garlic in oil or butter until golden. Add tomato paste, canned tomatoes and juice, and spices; cook for about a minute, until slightly thickened. Add bulghur and cook, stirring frequently, for about five minutes. Let cool five or ten minutes. Combine the last five ingredients; reserve about 1 cup and stir the rest into the bulghur. Spread kufteh on a plate, sprinkle remaining chopped vegetables on top. Especially nice when served as a filling for hot, fresh pita.

» Cous-Cous

This isn't real cous-cous, which is actually made out of pre-boiled and dried wheat and looks something like non-gluey farina; but it tastes quite similar, and "cous-cous" sounds infinitely better than "millet glop."

Analysis	Calories	CHO	Fat	Protein	GUP	Iron	Calcium
Serving:	302	54g	6g	11.6g	8.5g	5.5mg	145mg

Yield: 4 servings

1 Tb olive oil
3 cloves garlic
1 c millet
2 Tb soy grits (opt, but analyzed)
1 28 oz. can tomatoes
¾ lb green beans cut in 1½" pieces
2 bay leaves
juice of 1 lemon

dash of Tobasco or cayenne
1 tsp salt
½ tsp cumin
¼ c+ wine or other liquid
2 Tb fresh parsley, chopped
1 tsp mint, chopped (opt)
several dashes cinnamon (opt)
½ c yoghurt

Press or finely mince garlic into hot oil. Add millet and cook, stirring frequently, about 2 minutes. Add tomatoes all at once—they will sputter mightily. Add next 6 ingredients. Cover tightly. Cook on med.-high heat, 20-25 min., stirring as necessary to keep millet from sticking. Check for liquid and add, a few tablespoons at a time. Just before serving, stir in parsley and, for more authentic Middle Eastern flavor, the cinnamon and mint. For a soupier texture, add more canned tomatoes. Best served with a dollop of yoghurt.

» Kasha Varnishkes

Analysis	Calories	CHO	Fat	Protein	GUP	Iron	Calcium
Serving:	373	50g	16g	12.5g	8.5g	3.1mg	108mg

Yield: 6 servings

2 c kasha
4 Tb soy grits (opt, but analyzed)
2 eggs

4 c liquid
2 large onions
4-6 Tb butter
mushrooms

Combine raw egg and kasha. Cook over medium heat in dry pan until egg is absorbed and each grain is separate. Add liquid. Steam (covered) for about 25 minutes. May be served as-is with salt and pepper. Or, sauté onions and mushrooms and stir into kasha. May be served on bed of noodles with dollop of yoghurt or sour cream.

» Wheat Berry Cheese Rice

Yield: 5 servings

1 c wheat berries	1 c or more grated sharp
1 c brown rice	cheese
2½ c water	1 tsp salt
4 Tb soy grits (opt, but analyzed)	½ tsp freshly ground pepper

Combine grains and water; pressure cook 40 minutes at 15 lbs. Run water over pressure-cooker lid. When pressure subsides, lift lid; liquid should be absorbed. Add at least 1 c of sharp cheese, salt and pepper and stir to melt cheese slightly.

» Dolmades (Stuffed Vine or Cabbage-Leaves)

1½ c raw rice, cooked	3 Tb chopped fresh mint
3 Tb soy grits (opt, but analyzed for)	1 tsp paprika
3 Tb olive oil	salt, pepper
1 lg onion, chopped (or use leftover *Risotto* for first four ingredients)	⅔ c sunflower seeds
	⅓ c sesame seeds
	2 Tb tomato paste
½ c raisins or currants	1 tsp cinnamon
½ c raw bulghur soaked in	30 to 40 vine or cabbage leaves
¼ c lemon juice + water to cover	

Cook rice and grits until barely tender. Sauté onions in oil and add to grain—or use leftover rice or *Risotto*. Increase spices, if need be, for a slightly sweet, slightly tart filling. If using cabbage leaves, bring pot of water to full boil. Without splitting cabbage, cut out core. Insert heavy two-tined fork in hole and submerge cabbage for one minute.

118

Carefully peel off outer layer of leaves and repeat. When small inner leaves are reached, save them for another use. Bottled vine leaves need only to have the excess brine washed off. Using about 1½ Tb of filling, roll each leaf into a neat envelope-shaped package. You may need to cut the hard center spine out of the cabbage leaves. Place dolma, seam-side down, in oiled baking pan large enough to hold them in one layer. Pour over broth, Avgolemono Sauce, or a light tomato sauce. Put in 350° oven until dolma heat through.

» Avgolemono Sauce

3 eggs
juice of 1 lemon

1½ c hot, flavorful broth
dash paprika, salt, pepper

Beat eggs until frothy, beat in lemon. Whisk in hot broth. Pour over dolmas. Bake until egg sauce is slightly thickened. Serve dolmades with Greek Salad made with feta cheese and ripe olives. Traditionally, dolma are also served with homemade yoghurt.

» Grainburgers

Analysis	Calo-ries	CHO	Fat	Pro-tein	GUP	Iron	Cal-cium
Serving:	103	15g	3g	5.9g	4.3g	2.3mg	32mg

Yield: 10 "burgers"

½ c soy grits or granules
½ c bulghur wheat
water to cover—about 2 c
½ c chopped onion
2 cloves garlic, pressed
1 Tb tamari sauce

¼ c oats
1 egg
1-2 Tb whole wheat flour
½ tsp salt
¼ tsp pepper
cheese slices (opt)

Soak grits and bulghur in hot tap water for at least one hour. If all the water is not absorbed, invert in a colander lined with cheese cloth for a few minutes, squeeze out extra moisture; then turn into a bowl. Stir in remaining ingredients except for cheese. Taste for seasoning; you may wish to add paprika, a few grains of cayenne, an herb, or some freshly chopped parsley. Form one patty and sauté in a lightly oiled skillet. If it tends to disintegrate when you turn it over, add

119

a little more flour to the mixture. When underside of patties are golden brown, turn and place a slice of cheese on each. If you cover the skillet the cheese melts better. Children love these with a glob of ketchup.

VARIATION:

If you can't seem to get the patties to cohere, sauté the whole mess in 1-2 Tb hot oil until golden brown and crunchy. At the last moment, add about ½ c grated cheese: voilà—vegetarian hash!

Pasta

Kids, of course, are the world's original noodle-lovers. Show me a kid and I'll show you a creature who would cheerfully eat macaroni and cheese for breakfast, lasagna for lunch, and spaghetti for dinner. Not the least of its charm is that pasta is the base for quick, relatively cheap meals. But most noodles are nutritionally slight. They're gluey, starchy, low in nutrients (except the few with which they're "enriched"), and tasteless.

There are a few good-tasting noodles around, but most of them are not yet available in the average supermarkets. The tastiest of them all—from a poll taken at our dinner table—is the artichoke noodle. It's made from a tuber, similar to a potato, called the Jerusalem artichoke. Its advantage is that it's higher in protein and lower in available carbohydrates than some other starches, and also higher in iron.

The noodle itself is formulated from a combination of Jerusalem artichoke powder and soy powder as well as other more typical noodle ingredients. Because the first two are not included in the Federal Standards of Identity for noodles, these delicious, high-protein noodles must be officially listed as "imitation." Don't let that fool you. They come in a kind of dingy white that, when cooked, most closely resembles whatever you usually get at the supermarket. They also come in spinach noodles, which are made with dehydrated spinach powder and are a lovely green. (Our family's favorite.)

Another delicious and somewhat unusual pasta is buckwheat noodles, called "soba" by the Japanese. You can also find soy-wheat noodles and whole wheat noodles at some supermarkets. When they first came out, some brands of whole wheat noodles were thick and doughy when cooked. Try several kinds if need be.

» Macaroni and Cheese

Analysis	Calo- ries	CHO	Fat	Pro- tein	GUP	Iron	Cal- cium
Serving:	346	26g	21g	14.3g	10.2g	1.7mg	281mg

1 c elbow or shell whole wheat macaroni
3 Tb wholewheat flour
3 Tb butter
1 cup milk
½ tsp salt
pepper
½ tsp Worcestershire sauce

2 Tb vermouth (opt)
1 c grated cheese
½ tsp mustard (opt)
Topping:
2 Tb Parmesan cheese
2 Tb butter
3 Tb wheat germ

Boil macaroni until tender; drain. Make a roux of fat and flour; make white sauce with milk. Add spices and optional wine. Turn off heat, stir in cheese. Melt some additional butter in a skillet, add a few tablespoons Parmesan and wheat germ; cook just until warmed. Combine pasta and cheese sauce in casserole dish, sprinkle with topping. Broil until bubbly.

VARIATION:

Add 2 Tb soy grits—soak them in a little warm water while everything else is going on, then throw them in the sauce. This will improve the protein value of this dish.

» Noodles Stroganoff

Analysis	Calo-ries	CHO	Fat	Pro-tein	GUP	Iron	Cal-cium
Serving:	305	47g	8.3g	11.4g	8.3g	2.2mg	136mg

2 Tb butter
1 cup chopped onion
3 cloves garlic
½ lb mushrooms sliced
1 tsp paprika
2 Tb sherry
1 Tb tomato paste
1½ cup yoghurt
½ cup sour cream
½ tsp Worcestershire sauce

½ tsp salt
dash nutmeg
juice of ½ lemon
3 Tb chopped parsley
2 drops Tabasco or a few
  grains cayenne
2 Tb sherry
1 lb noodles, cooked and
  drained

Sauté onions and garlic in butter; add paprika and mushrooms, sauté briefly. Add sherry and let alcohol boil off for a few seconds. Stir in tomato paste, yoghurt, and sour cream. Heat gently—if you boil the sauce, the yoghurt may "crack." Add the flavorings. Just before serving, stir in the additional 2 Tb sherry. Pour over noodles, garnish with additional parsley, if desired.

» Krautswekel

Analysis	Calo-ries	CHO	Fat	Pro-tein	GUP	Iron	Cal-cium
Serving:	30	49g	8g	9.6g	6.5g	2.4mg	84mg

Yield: 6 servings

1 medium head cabbage:
  2-3 lbs.
1 tsp salt+
2 Tb oil
¼-½ c water

¾ lb noodles, cooked and
  drained
¼-½ tsp pepper
poppy or caraway seeds—1-2
  Tb

Slice cabbage in fairly thin shreds, then chop crossways too. There will be about 16 cups chopped cabbage. Heat oil in a large, heavy skillet. Put cabbage in skillet, add salt, and cover tightly—I usually have to push down on the lid to get it all in. After a few minutes, stir the bottom to the top and cover again. This should be done on high heat; while you want the cabbage to soften and brown in spots, you don't want it to burn, so take care. If it threatens to burn, add water by spoonfuls; not too much or you'll have stew. It may take 15 minutes or so, but the cabbage will reduce and begin to smell heavenly sweet. This is one of the rare times that crunchy-tender vegetables are not desireable—it should be soft and golden. The caraway or poppy seeds are traditional European accompaniment: sauté them for a brief minute with the cabbage to bring out the flavor. Stir the noodles and cabbage mixture together. Add salt and pepper to taste. For best results, use bow-tie, shell, or macaroni noodles: long noodles like linguini or spaghettini refuse to combine properly with the cabbage. May be served with yoghurt.

» Lasagna

Analysis	Calo-ries	CHO	Fat	Pro-tein	GUP	Iron	Cal-cium
Serving:	589	59g	24g	34g	23g	4.9mg	523mg

Yield: 12 servings

1 lb lasagna noodles
¾ c unflavored burger-like
  soy granules
2 28-oz. cans tomatoes
3 6-oz. cans tomato paste
3 Tb olive oil +
1 onion, coarsely chopped
celery, carrot, green pepper
  (opt)
5-6 cloves garlic
wine (opt)

1-1½ lb Mozarella (or
  other cheese)
4 oz grated Parmesan
2 lb cottage cheese (or pot
  cheese + yoghurt)
½ cup chopped fresh parsley
cooked drained spinach (opt)
herbs: oregano, basil, thyme,
  marjoram, bay
salt, pepper
hardboiled eggs (opt)

Cook noodles in a large amount of salted boiling water, with a little oil added. When barely tender, drain, rinse, separate, and let sit. Meanwhile, make tomato sauce: sauté olive (or other) oil in a large skillet. Add onion, garlic, and other chopped vegetables if desired. When they become aromatic, add tomatoes, tomato paste, and wine. Add *at least* 1 Tb of your choice of herbs; add salt and pepper to taste. While that is simmering, grate Mozarella cheese. Combine cottage cheese with Parmesan cheese and chopped parsley.

To layer lasagna, oil bottom of large baking dish. Put down a slightly overlapping layer of noodles, then a layer of cottage cheese, then noodles, then tomato sauce, then Mozarella, then noodles, etc. End with a layer of tomato sauce and Mozarella. You may drizzle over the top 1 Tb of olive oil and sprinkle with more combined herbs. Bake at 350° for 20 minutes if ingredients were warm; 40 minutes if it was first refrigerated.

» Quickest Pasta

Yield: 5 servings

1 lb. your favorite noodle, cooked
2 oz. fresh grated Parmesan or Romano cheese
1-2 Tb butter or olive oil
¼ c or more freshly chopped parsley

1 tsp freshly chopped basil if you can get it
1-2 cloves pressed garlic (opt)
salt and pepper

As soon as the noodles are cooked, drain and toss with oil or butter to keep from sticking. Then toss with everything else and serve immediately.

VARIATION:

Cottage cheese—at least ½ pound may be added, too, or substituted for Parmesan.

» Whole Wheat Spaghetti

Yield: 6 servings

3 Tb olive oil
3 Tb butter
1 large onion
5 cloves garlic
½ lb mushrooms
salt, pepper
3-4 peeled tomatoes (1 green)

½ tsp marjoram
½ tsp oregano
3-4 Tb fresh parsley, chopped
1 can tuna (10 oz. water pack)
⅓ c vermouth
1 lb noodles, cooked & drained

Melt butter in large skillet, add olive (or other) oil. Add coarsely chopped onion and stir until slightly wilted, then add garlic, finely minced or pressed. Add sliced (or whole, small) mushrooms, then peeled tomatoes. When they have exuded most of their liquid and become somewhat soft, add the spices and undrained tuna. Add the salt and pepper and wine; cook until the alcohol evaporates. Just before serving, stir in the fresh chopped parsley. Serve over whole wheat, soy, or artichoke "imitation" noodles.

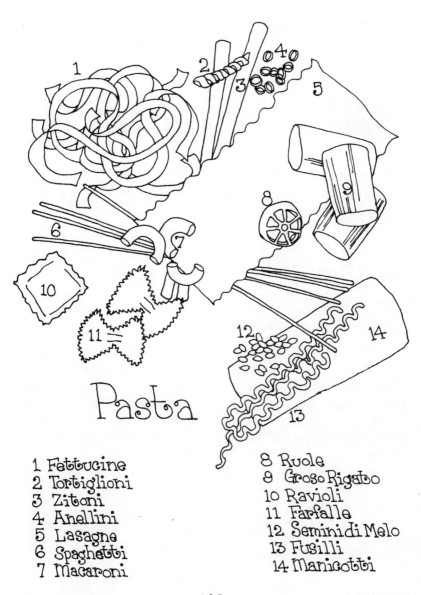

Pasta

1 Fettucine
2 Tortiglioni
3 Zitoni
4 Anellini
5 Lasagne
6 Spaghetti
7 Macaroni
8 Ruole
9 Groso Rigato
10 Ravioli
11 Farfalle
12 Semini di Melo
13 Fusilli
14 Manicotti

VII
Where Have All the Nutrients Gone?

HÄGAR the Horrible

"Hagar the Horrible" copyright © King Features Syndicate 1975

We are not certain we shall ever know enough to keep man alive . . . on sawdust (plus) vitamins and minerals. . . . While we know that . . . ordinary foods got mankind into the 20th century, we have no evidence at all that . . . colas, sugary cereals, snack cakes, and mock fruit juices—even if they are fortified—will take our children safely into the 21st century.

> —J. Gussow, "Evaluating the American Diet," *Journal of Home Economics*, November, 1973

Protein, fats, and carbohydrates have been around for a long time, but vitamins and minerals are relative newcomers to the science of nutrition. The first vitamin so designated (Vitamin B-1 or thiamin) was discovered by a Dutch doctor named Eijkman, who recognized the cause of—and ultimately the cure for—beri-beri. In the sixty years since Eijkman's discovery, at least forty micronutrients (vitamins and minerals) have been recognized as essential for man, and reams of research have been published on their activity in the body.

DIETARY DEFICIENCY

An analysis of the nutrients available to the American population on a per capita basis shows that there is enough nutrition available to meet everyone's Recommended Dietary Allowance (RDA). Yet the Ten-State Survey found evidence of iron, protein, calcium, riboflavin, and Vitamin A deficiency, from mild to severe, in both blacks and whites of high and low socioeconomic status.[5] In addition, the prestigious National Academy of Sciences/National Research Council (NAS/NRC —the people who set the RDAs) has stated that there is also risk of thiamin, niacin, Vitamin B-6, folacin, magnesium, and zinc deficiency among significant segments of the population. Numerous surveys have found everything from "zinc deficiency in children from middle and upper socioeconomic families in Denver, Colorado," to "evidence that 10 to 60 per cent of various populations . . . have anemia."[1]

As research on trace elements in the diet continues, scientists are suggesting that even this list is not exhaustive. A diet relying heavily on fats and oils, refined carbohydrates and meat is low in several important nutrients. This is not surprising when you consider that "in the last century sugar intake has reached the level of 25% of our calories [and] we have increased fat intake to 45% of the calories."[2] As a further complication, the average Western diet may actually increase the need for certain already marginal nutrients.

CHANGING FOOD PATTERNS: THE MODERN FOUR

Remember the glowing pictures of the Basic Four (or Basic Seven, if you go back to Methuselah) that graced the walls of your school room? There was a cornucopia of fruits and vegetables, wind-blown grains (with an obviously just-baked loaf of bread in the foreground), glistening steaks, and glasses of foamy milk beside a platter of cheeses that would have pleased an epicure. Following the recommendations for choosing foods from this magnificent assortment assured an adequate diet.

Unfortunately, the modern consumption of the Basic Four hardly resembles its traditional form (see Modern Four illustration on page 130 and compare it to our suggested diet based on Structural Integrity).

Obviously, no amount of juggling could produce an adequate diet from these choices. Despite the addition of certain minerals and synthetic vitamins to the refined, processed, and artificial foods, they do not provide adequate amounts of all necessary micronutrients.

People often *think* they're eating the Basic Four when they're actually choosing from the Modern Four. Objective diaries revealed that members of some families averaged 22 food contacts a day—most of them with low nutritional density (junk) foods, while in subjective questionnaires the food preparers indicated that their families were getting "three square meals" a day. These surveys also showed that "mealtime" practically no longer exists: everyone's social schedules —Girl Scouts to P.T.A. meetings—encourages snacking and instant meals.

In addition, labor saving devices (from cars to vacuum cleaners) and generally, the mechanization of heavy labor, have greatly curtailed people's energy expenditures. Our nutrient needs have not declined as sharply as our energy needs have, yet we now must obtain these nutrients while consuming half as many calories as we once required. Therefore, we have even less room for empty calories—derived from foods lacking sufficient nutrients for their own metabolism, although empty calories form an ever larger part of our diet. Nutrients are not only necessary for cellular nutrition, but they are also required—frequently as co-factors—for enzymes that aid in digestion. When micronutrients are missing, as in most processed foods, the body must call on ever-depleting stores.

Since 1942, the per capita consumption of dairy products has dropped 21%; that of vegetables has dropped 23%; that of fruits has dropped 25%. Soft drink consumption is up 300%; pies, cookies, desserts, up 70%, and consumption of snacks is up 85%.

"ENRICHMENT" AND "FORTIFICATION"

It would seem that the problem of widespread nutrient deficiency might be solved by adding the missing nutrients to the foods that everyone is actually eating—the Modern Four. In fact, the NAS/NRC is suggesting something similar to that. They are proposing that cereal grains—wheat, corn, rice—be used as the vehicles for "fortification" with ten nutrients now thought to be at risk for a significant segment of the population.[1] This would be an extension of the "enrichment" program begun during World War II, after widespread iron and B-vitamin deficiencies—exacerbated by flour refining—were discovered.

In 1941, when "enrichment" was first proposed, the complicated interrelationships of micronutrients were not well understood. Even at that time, the FDA declared, oddly enough, in its policy statement encouraging "enrichment" of bread and flour: "Adequate nutrition could be better assured through the choice of natural foods than through reliance on enrichment."[1] Since then the FDA has forgotten they ever said that and accuses anyone else who says it of being a food faddist.

RECOMMENDED DIETARY ALLOWANCE (RDA)

Also during World War II, the NAS/NRC was working out RDAs. Since adequate food supplies were part of the defense effort, it was useful to establish whether whole population groups were likely to get enough of certain basic nutrients from a given amount of food. The groups for which RDAs are set have since been redefined: the differences in

129

Modern Four

Most of the foods of the Modern Four do *not* provide the nutrition they seem to: non-dairy creamer does not supply calcium; refined grains lack the trace elements removed in processing; fiber and nutrients have been cooked out of canned fruits and vegetables. And many of these "foods", from bacon to peanut butter, contain added sugar which dilutes whatever nutrients they do provide.

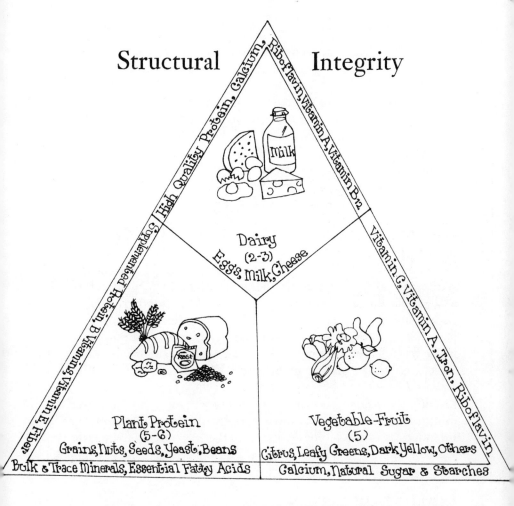

Structural Integrity

Supplemented Protein, Vitamin B, Vitamins, Vitamin E, Fiber

High Quality Protein, Calcium, Riboflavin, Vitamin A, Vitamin B₁₂

Vitamin C, Vitamin A, Iron, Riboflavin

Dairy
(2-3)
Eggs, Milk, Cheese

Plant Protein
(5-6)
Grains, Nuts, Seeds, Yeast, Beans
Bulk & Trace Minerals, Essential Fatty Acids

Vegetable-Fruit
(5)
Citrus, Leafy Greens, Dark Yellow, Others
Calcium, Natural Sugar & Starches

There are two reasons for a three- rather than four-way division of food groups: 1) For a vegetarian, a *Meat Group* makes no sense; but more importantly, 2) *Grains* are the protein source for most of the world's population. In a four-way division, they are relegated to the *Cereals Group* with no mention of their important protein contribution. Only recently has the *Meat Group* been reclassified into the *Protein Group*, and even so, alternate protein sources like legumes or nuts are not given much prominence.

As a rough guide to the construction of an adequate vegetarian diet, use the numbers in parentheses as the suggested daily servings for each group. Much will depend however on what constitutes a "serving".

nutritional needs between children, pregnant and lactating women, adult males, and older Americans have been calculated. The method for arriving at RDAs purports to take into account the nutritional needs of 97% of the population.[3] But it makes no allowance, nor does it claim to, for fluctuating needs caused by catching a cold, smoking, drinking, breathing polluted air, recovering from infections or trauma, being overweight, or taking contraceptives, or any of the dozens of other drugs most Americans take much of the time. It also makes no allowance for the very important criteria of heredity and individual variability of absorption: some tests have shown as much as a fivefold difference in the needs of individuals for certain nutrients.[31]

The NAS/NRC says of its own standards: "Such general statements as 'RDA includes a large safety factor; therefore a diet that meets two-thirds of the RDA standard should be adequate' have no validity. It will be adequate for some, inadequate for others and—without elaborate studies—there is no way of knowing who falls into which category."[3] Contrast this with a statement by the FDA in its *Guide to Nutrition Labeling:* "Set at generous levels, [these allowances] provide a considerable margin of safety for most people above minimum body needs for most nutrients."[4] RDAs were never intended as a guide for evaluating the adequacy of an individual's diet, yet that is precisely how they are now being used by the FDA in its nutritional labeling program.

NUTRITIONAL LABELING

Ever looked closely at the nutritional panel on your favorite "fortified" food? The column headed "US RDA" has been extrapolated to a single standard from the 17 age-sex divisions listed by the NAS/NRC. But whether RDA or USRDA is being used, the drawbacks to using average statistical standards are the same.

First, RDAs have been established for only about one-third of the essential nutrients. Second, "fortified" foods can be made to appear superior to natural foods. And third, the RDAs have come to be used as the *basis* for a sound diet.

Although over 40 nutrients have been recognized and described as essential, for most of them there is not yet sufficient information on which to base dietary recommendations, hence no minimum is required. Although the nutrition labels give no hint of the problem, according to an NAS/NRC publication, "increasing consumption of highly refined or fabricated foods substantially reduces the intake of essential micronutrients, unless these foods are fortified to concentrations at least equal to those naturally occurring in the products that they replace."[3] The current practice is to fortify and enrich *some* products (notably cereals) with only those nutrients *for which standards have been established*. The other —equally important—nutrients that were also removed in the processing, but for which no statistical standards have yet been devised, are still missing. Also, rather than using an amount of a nutrient that would approximate the original balance of nature, some convenient-to-list per cent of the USRDA standard (often 33% or 100%) has been added to most fortified foods. This has made it possible for some manufacturers to claim that their highly processed, refined product is actually *superior* to a natural product. Actually, micronutrients are usually distributed in small amounts in natural foods; the body needs only limited amounts at a time and over-kill "fortification" is probably poorly utilized.

Assimilation of micronutrients is not simply a matter of stuffing them in the body and having them obediently absorbed. For example, one of the nutrients already used in "enrichment," iron, has not produced the expected benefits.[6] Large segments of the population, including those who are eating considerable quantities of enriched grain products, are still exhibiting moderate to severe iron deficiency. This may be due, in part, to the varying absorbability of the form in which the nutrient is added (the one that bakes best is poorly absorbed). Even more important is the recognized but largely ignored matter of synergistic relationship.

SYNERGISTIC EFFECT

Before one micronutrient can perform all its functions in the body, other micronutrients (its synergists) must also be present.[7] For the production of red blood cells, not only iron, but Vitamins C, E, B-12, folic acid, and copper must be available, too. While a portion of the nutrients added to "fortified" or "enriched" foods is undoubtedly utilized by the body, much will be wasted unless the synergists that have

133

been removed are provided by other foods.

If a diet is based on the Modern Four, many micronutrients are going to be lacking. Proponents of synthetic and devitalized foods are always claiming that it's all right if a particular food doesn't have much nutrition in it. They say you have to consider the diet as a whole. Okay, go back to Modern Four and consider.

Even if all the *known* synergistically related micronutrients were added to foods, we have not yet discovered *all* the necessary nutrients or the *proper proportions* for best biological effect. Besides, by this point, it must seem a bit absurd to strip perfectly good foods—e.g., whole grains—of almost all their nutrition, feed the best part to livestock, and then spend the earth's vanishing energy to add back synthetic forms of everything that was removed! This reconstructed food might be so like the original, the bugs would start to eat it again . . .

SYNTHETIC VITAMINS

It is not clear that added synthetics are utilized as well by the body as those occurring naturally in food. Although chemists recoil in horror at the suggestion that synthetic vitamins are different from their natural counterparts—a molecule is a molecule!—there does seem to be a difference in effect. Whether because other micronutrients present in natural sources play an unexpectedly large role in using vitamins to maximum effect, or whether some as yet unrecognized difference actually exists, significant differences in effect have been demonstrated. In a study done at the University of South Wales, young guinea pigs fed equal ascorbic acid strengths of black-currant juice concentrate, dried acerola powder, and synthetic Vitamin C, utilized the natural sources significantly better, as evidenced by greater growth rate and superior retention of the vitamin.[8] Another study has shown that bioflavonoids (vitamin P—a compound that occurs naturally where vitamin C does) increase utilization of synthetic vitamin C to a level that approximates natural vitamin C.[9] The "purity" of synthetics may be their undoing. To sum up, in the words of two nutrition authorities, Mark Hegsted and Ruth Leverton:

A common fallacy is to assume that if a diet provides the recommended allowances, the needs for all nutrients

134

have been met. . . . Of great concern . . . is the use of the Recommended Dietary Allowances as the basis for fabricated, contrived or synthetic foods. Such products may not be reliable replacements for traditional foods if only the nutrients for which there are allowances have been added.[11]

ABOUT MICRONUTRIENTS

The lack of certain vitamins and minerals is connected with specific diseases—Vitamin C and scurvy, Vitamin B-1 and beri-beri, iron and anemia. Other micronutrients have been discovered so recently, or occur in the body in such minute amounts, that their role is less well understood. And some, like Vitamin E, have been exhaustively studied with confusing and conflicting results.

For information about all the known vitamins and minerals, you can go to any elementary nutrition text. Below is a discussion of some that are likely to be deficient in the refined Western diet, or have been thought to be at risk in the vegetarian diet, or are "new" but merit close attention in light of current research.

Wonderful cures have been claimed by various researchers who use vitamins as therapeutic agents in massive doses ("mega-vitamins") for everything from heart disease to the common cold. Whether mega-doses of vitamins are or are not of benefit in certain disease conditions is irrelevant to the study of dietary requirements of specific nutrients in the healthy human. In the discussion that follows we are interested in vitamins as nutrients rather than as pharmaceuticals.

• *Vitamin B-12* (cyanocobalamin, hydroxocobalamin): This is the only vitamin that could be at risk in the well-chosen vegetarian diet, and then *only* in the pure vegetarian diet. Pure vegetarians (those who eat no animal products) have to take supplemental Vitamin B-12 (as did George Bernard Shaw, who had the good grace to live to 94 as a fruitarian, thus earning himself a place in vegetarian tracts forever).

Vitamin B-12 is unique in that it seems to be made exclusively by microorganisms—bacteria and molds; all other vitamins are made by plants. Bacteria also make Vitamin B-12 in the human intestine, but not where it can be readily ab-

135

sorbed. Japanese Buddhists, who eat neither meat, eggs, nor dairy products, may be getting Vitamin B-12 produced by microorganisms on the fronds of seaweed—one of the only known "vegetable" sources.

In people who have been consuming adequate amounts of Vitamin B-12, the liver can store as much as a five-year supply;[12] however, some people develop deficiency symptoms after only three months on a pure vegetarian diet not supplemented by Vitamin B-12. Left untreated, Vitamin B-12 deficiency can lead to pernicious anemia and death. Folic acid (found abundantly in vegetables) taken in large amounts can mask Vitamin B-12 deficiency symptoms. Lacto-ovo-vegetarians with ordinary intakes of these animal products will have no trouble meeting their needs.[15]

• *Vitamin B-6* (pyrodoxine): This is a key factor in normal fat and protein metabolism. Requirements for Vitamin B-6 increase whenever the consumption of fats and protein increases (Western diet again). But the Western diet is potentially low in this vitamin: canned foods lose from 57% to 77% of their Vitamin B-6; refined grains lose 70% of their Vitamin B-6 and milk processed at high temperatures (particularly canned milk) loses almost 100% of its Vitamin B-6.[18]

Dr. Henry A. Schroeder says in his study of vitamin and trace mineral losses in the processing of foods:

> The major sources of calories in this country are flour and cereal products, sugar, potatoes and fats, making up approximately . . . 80 per cent or more of the calories . . . A diet consisting of these foods would be deficient (in Vitamin B-6).[18]

In monkeys, deficiency of Vitamin B-6 has caused atherosclerosis; in rats (a species resistant to atherosclerosis), hypertension.[19] Since individual variability may be so high, and since the average diet might be quite poor in Vitamin B-6, people may wish to have themselves tested for possible deficiency with a simple urine test. Good sources of B-6 are seeds, nuts, wheat germ and bran, yeast, and bananas.

• *Vitamin E:* This vitamin might just as well stand for enigma. Though it was discovered in 1922, Vitamin E has eluded the efforts of researchers to find a simple deficiency state in man. At first it seemed that Vitamin E would provide the cure for many diseases. Animal studies had shown

Vitamin E to be necessary in various species for prevention of sterility, muscular dystrophy, brain disease, heart damage, and other illnesses. Unfortunately, subsequent clinical studies in humans have not shown equivalent benefits.

This is not to say that it has no uses, but they are less miraculous than had been hoped. Vitamin E is useful in intermittent claudication (a vascular condition in which blood flow to lower limbs is reduced and walking becomes painful). Its deficiency has definitely been linked to hemolytic anemia in premature babies (whose formulas were deficient — see Chapter XI). Success has been claimed for the use of Vitamin E (both oral and topical) in severe skin problems such as burns and ulcerated bedsores.[13]

Vitamin E's chief function in the body is as an antioxidant. Since it quickly absorbs oxygen molecules, it prevents other oxygen-susceptible elements from being adversely affected as in lipid peroxidation (a process that can disrupt enzyme systems, and destroy cells: Vitamin E interrupts this activity). Some researchers believe that peroxidation may be the "main-spring of the aging process."[14]

Vitamin E is actually a complex of six components called tocopherols. Alpha-tocopherol is the most biologically active in humans. Different natural sources of Vitamin E have different ratios of the various tocopherols. Alpha-tocopherol is not necessarily high in polyunsaturated fats (though Vitamin E may be). Wheat germ oil has the highest concentration of alpha-tocopherol, corn oil has one of the lowest. Particularly if the intake of polyunsaturates is increased, the intake of *alpha*-tocopherol must also be increased.

• *Iron:* Some nutritionists claim that one reason for the national tendency toward anemia stems from modern cooking practices. When we used lots of cast-iron pots, some of the iron found its way into the food and then into us. It has been calculated that as much as one-third of the dietary iron may have been lost when we switched to non-iron cookware.

Whatever the reasons, after thirty years of "enrichment" (to a level approximating that of the grain before refining), the levels of iron added to flour and bread products have been increased threefold. Despite the high levels of meat and "enriched" bread products in the diet, Americans—particularly women and children—seem prone to anemia. One prob-

137

lem may stem from the chemical forms of iron used in "enrichment"; not all forms are equally useable and much is left to industry discretion.

It is too early to evaluate the benefits, if any, from the new threefold increase in iron "fortification." It is our contention, however, that a contributing cause in anemia is the absence in refined grain products of the other nutrients (synergists) necessary for building red blood cells.

The population of vegetarians is neither more nor less anemic than the population as a whole:[15] useful non-meat iron sources include whole grains, legumes, and leafy green vegetables. It is known that iron absorption increases with protein value and in the presence of Vitamin C.[16, 17] Therefore a vegetarian diet based on supplemented proteins should have an acceptable level of iron absorption.

Two high-iron foods that can be included in the vegetarian diet, but which are not often discussed in standard nutrition texts, are molasses (blackstrap or third extraction) and brewer's yeast.

• *Chromium:* At one time, chromium was considered a contaminant—something harmful in the environment—like cadmium and lead. Now, however, the role of chromium as an essential nutrient has been expanded to include a possible role in the prevention of heart disease and diabetes. It may have been thought of as a contaminant at first because tissue concentration of chromium in Americans is so small. In fact, it is highest in babies and begins to fall throughout life (13% of American children tested had no detectable chromium at all). This is in contrast to Africans and people from the Near and Far East, who had relatively constant chromium levels after the first decade of life. The only exceptions were foreigners dying of heart disease: both this group and Americans dying of heart disease had significantly lower levels of chromium in their aortas. Only a few of the Americans suffering from heart disease had *any* detectable chromium in their aortas.[20] Dr. Henry A. Schroeder, noted researcher in trace elements, has stated: "Chromium deficiency is a causal factor in atherosclerosis."[21]

In animal and human research, chromium has been found to normalize glucose tolerance; it is required for the action of insulin and helps to lower serum cholesterol.[22-3] It is deficient in the refined diet, however. What's worse is that the little chromium you have in your tissues may be excreted when the diet is also high in refined sugar.[21]

The Western diet—high in sugars and fats—probably increases the *need* for chromium while, at the same time, *supplying less* of this essential nutrient. The best natural source of useable chromium is brewer's yeast. (If you want it in solution, drink the sediment of homemade beer.) Dark brown sugar, molasses (refinery or blackstrap), and butter are foods with relatively high chromium content.[20, 23]

• *Magnesium:* Some researchers are investigating a possible connection between adequate magnesium intake and a healthy heart. Animal tests indicate that rats given three times their normal intake of magnesium showed lessened heart damage from cardio-toxic agents. Dogs on a magnesium-deficient diet developed hardening of the aortas, and their increased serum cholesterol was markedly greater when the cholesterol was given in a diet lacking in magnesium. This substance has also been used successfully in the treatment of persons with hypertension and angina pectoris.[24]

Researchers who have been trying to explain the low CHD incidence of people living on diets common to the Orient are now pointing to the relatively high magnesium content of that diet as a possible factor. The Western diet based on meat, eggs, and dairy products—all relatively low in magnesium—could lead to substantial magnesium deficit.[25]

Dr. Willard Krehl says: "Dietary magnesium deficiency is far more prevalent than we suspected. In our opinion, it can be said to have become one of the common nutritional deficiencies in clinical medicine."[25] Adult males seem to be under greater risk. Even more magnesium is required when the diet is high in calcium, sodium, sugar, and fat (the Western diet again) and low in Vitamin B-6.

Rich dietary sources of magnesium are vegetables, cereals (unrefined, natch), and nuts. If you choose a diet of natural foods adequate in trace minerals, you will be getting plenty of magnesium.

• *Zinc:* Zinc is "in" now: a lot of attention has been devoted to it lately. It's also another of those nutritional elements vegetarian diets are supposed to be deficient in. A few areas of the world do have clinical zinc deficiency. Cases of hypo-

139

gonadism, which were alleviated by zinc supplements, have occurred in poverty areas of Iran and Egypt. Milder deficiency can cause growth failure, lack of taste acuity, and slow wound healing.[28]

Aside from its role in the synthesis of nucleic acids (RNA) and protein, adequate amounts of zinc in the diet may protect against cadmium-induced hypertension.[29] Cadmium is an environmental contaminant found in "soft water" (especially water that's been standing in galvanized pipes) and many foods—refined grains have proportionately more cadmium than whole grains. In laboratory tests, cadmium has caused hypertension in some animals; cadmium consumption can also be statistically linked to hypertension in humans. Since zinc and cadmium compete for the same repositories in the body, an adequate amount of zinc can prevent excess cadmium retention.[30] (Incidently, refining whole grains results in a greater loss of zinc than of cadmium because the zinc is concentrated in the bran and germ but the cadmium is distributed throughout the grain.)

Although meats are an excellent source, nuts (especially pecans and Brazil nuts) have a higher concentration than most meat. Egg yolks are also a good source. Whole grains and legumes have a lot of zinc, but there is a question whether and to what extent it's bound by the phytic acid also present. (See Chapter VI for a discussion of phytase and fiber). And for those who have Tom Jones tendencies, oysters have the highest zinc concentration of any food. One oyster can supply the RDA for zinc; but it has a high cadmium concentration, too.

PRESERVING NUTRIENTS

To maintain our fantastically healthful, nutrient-rich diet, you have to try to keep the vitamins and minerals from slipping away. While it's absurdly easy to lose 60%, 85%, or even 100% of some nutrients through careless handling and cooking, it's also quite simple to keep losses to a minimum. The five basic things to consider are solubility, light, heat, oxygen, and acidity-alkalinity (pH). *Solubility:* Most vitamins are water-soluble, which means they dissolve in water. Not just cooking water, but rinsing water; you can lose an enormous amount of nutrition by soaking your green vegetables clean. As to *light,* keep the pot covered, don't use glass.

140

Instability to light is often exacerbated by heat and oxygen, although some vitamins are stable to one but not the other. *Heat* is easily the most punishing factor: jade green vegetables are properly cooked; "pea-green" (actually olive drab but named after the color of *canned* peas) vegetables are *overcooked* and have lost most of the heat-labile nutrients. Milder heats matter, too: don't leave your vegetables in a hot parked car, or on the kitchen counter. Even the *pH factor* is important: most nutrients are more stable in a slightly acid medium (add a little lemon juice, or wine, or tomato juice to cooking water).

Generally speaking:

1. Wash vegetables as briefly as possible—don't soak.
2. Keep them refrigerated.
3. Use minimal amounts of water to cook, unless you plan to drink the water.
4. Make cooking liquid slightly acid with either lemon juice or vinegar.
5. Cover pot tightly to eliminate air and light.
6. Cook only until crunchy-tender.

Vegetable Cooking

Even in this age of nutritional enlightenment, one can still find suggested vegetable cooking methods that are guaranteed to destroy as much nutrition as possible. One nationally syndicated columnist recently claimed that canned green beans could be made to taste fresh—doubtful enough—by throwing away all the canning liquid (where the nutrients are) and drenching the beans in lots of cold running water! Another oft-repeated suggestion to add a pinch of soda to vegetable cooking water ("to preserve the color") is a fine way to destroy most of the B-vitamins, which are more sensitive to heat in an alkaline solution.

CHINESE STIR-FRY

There is a definite relationship between how good vegetables look—and taste—and how nutritious they are. No one who has been delighted with the taste and appearance of crisp, crunchy-tender, vivid-colored vegetables prepared in the Oriental manner is surprised to discover that they retain most nutrients as well.

This is due both to the shortness of cooking time and to the use of small amounts of oil, which tends to keep water-soluble nutrients—the ones most vegetables have most of—from being leached away. The Oriental stir-fry pan, the wok, keeps cooking time to a minimum. It has a large cooking area, and the shape makes it possible to cook foods at high heat without burning them, since they can be vigorously stirred and turned. A large, heavy frying pan can substitute, but it takes a bit more caution to keep dinner off the floor.

To stir-fry successfully, you have to cut vegetables in the proper size for rapid cooking; enormous, thick chunks won't be done in the middle when the outside is cooked. You also have to cook the vegetables in the proper order. Longer-cooking vegetables, like onion, celery, or green pepper, have to be put in the pan first and partially cooked before adding shorter-cooking vegetables, like sprouts or bok choy which only need to be heated through. Otherwise you'll end up with limp sprouts and raw onion.

Non-Oriental vegetables can be stir-fried too: carrots, squash, and tomatoes, while not traditional in the East, may be used as long as the rules outlined above are followed.

The first few times you stir-fry, have all the vegetables pre-cut and the ingredients for the sauce, if any, combined. As you get the hang of it, you'll be able to stir with one hand while chopping with the other.

Cut along dotted lines

» Ginger Asparagus

Analysis	Calo-ries	CHO	Fat	Pro-tein	GUP	Iron	Cal-cium
Serving:	131	8g	11g	1.9g	1.1g	.7mg	18mg

Yield: 4 servings

1 lb asparagus
2 Tb oil
3 cloves garlic
1 Tb ginger "matchsticks"

½ c orange juice
2 tsp cornstarch
1 Tb toasted sesame oil
1 tsp Tamari sauce

Snap asparagus, save tough lower stems for soup. Cut asparagus on sharp diagonal; set aside tips. Heat oil in wok or large skillet. Add garlic (smash first with flat of cleaver) and cook until it turns golden; then remove with slotted spoon and discard (into your mouth, if you like). Add ginger, cut in long, thin "matchsticks," and sauté about 1 minute, until aromatic. Add asparagus bottoms and sauté about 2 minutes. Meanwhile, combine remaining ingredients for sauce. Add asparagus tips to wok and stir-fry about 1 minute. Stir sauce just before pouring into wok—lower heat and cook until sauce thickens slightly.

» Chinese Green Pepper and Mushrooms

Analysis	Calo-ries	CHO	Fat	Pro-tein	GUP	Iron	Cal-cium
Serving:	156	15g	10g	3.7g	2g	1.4mg	28mg

Yield: 6 servings

1 Tb dark sesame oil
1 Tb sherry wine
1 Tb soy sauce
1" ginger root, crushed
1 clove garlic, crushed
½ lb or more sliced mush-rooms
2 Tb peanut oil
½ Tb corn starch

3 to 4 large green peppers, sliced
1 red pepper, sliced
water chestnuts or bamboo shoots (opt)
2 c bok choy, sliced
1 onion, cut in wedges
1 Tb water

143

Make marinade of first five ingredients; marinate mushrooms for about ½ hour. Heat oil in wok or large skillet; sauté onions until slightly wilted. Add pepper and sauté another minute or two. Drain mushrooms, reserving marinade; add mushrooms to wok. Stir other vegetables into wok. Combine reserved marinade, water, and cornstarch. After about one minute, push cooked vegetables to one side and spoon vegetable liquid from wok into cornstarch sauce. Then return sauce to wok, stirring over a low flame to keep cornstarch from thickening unevenly. Stir vegetables into sauce and cook about one minute more, until sauce is slightly thickened. Other vegetables may be substituted for part of the green pepper. Oriental dried mushrooms may be substituted for all or part of the mushrooms.

» Chinese Sweet and Sour Stir-Fried Vegetables

Analysis	Calories	CHO	Fat	Protein	GUP	Iron	Calcium
Serving:	131	24g	6g	2.3g	1.2g	1.3mg	39mg

Yield: 4-6 servings

1 can (approx. 8 oz.) unsweetened pineapple chunks, drained; reserve liquid
2 Tb cornstarch
2 Tb soy sauce
2 Tb dry wine
2 Tb vinegar
2 Tb dark brown sugar
½ to ¾ c reserved pineapple liquid

2 cloves garlic
1" ginger root (opt)
1 large onion, wedged
2 large ribs celery, sliced
1 tomato (opt)
2 green peppers or 2 c bok choy, sliced
2 Tb peanut oil

Mix sauce ingredients: cornstarch, soy sauce, wine, vinegar, sugar, and pineapple juice; let stand. Sauté garlic and ginger in hot oil; remove after about 1 minute. Add onion, celery, and green pepper; if bok choy is used, add it after other vegetables have cooked about 2 minutes. Add tomato and pineapple chunks. Stir sauce and taste for balance—it should be slightly sweet with a sour bite; add a bit more sugar or vinegar as necessary. If you can get it, rice vinegar is traditional and more flavorful than ordinary distilled vinegar. When vegetables are just tender, lower heat and add sauce to wok. Stir and cook until sauce is thick and glazed.

The sweet and sour sauce may be made for use on other dishes such as Fried Won Tons: just combine all the ingredients and heat slowly in a small pan until sauce is clear and thickened.

» Szechuan Shrimp

Analysis	Calo-ries	CHO	Fat	Pro-tein	GUP	Iron	Cal-cium
Serving:	156	7g	8g	14.9g	11.7g	1.5mg	62mg

Yield: 4 servings

1 tsp grated fresh ginger
3 cloves garlic, pressed
2 Tb oil
1 lb shrimp
2 Tb hot bean sauce*
2 stalks celery, chopped
hot pepper flakes (opt)

1 green pepper, sliced
3 Tb white wine
1 Tb soy sauce
2 Tb water
1 Tb cornstarch
sprouts (opt)

---

*Available in Chinese delicatessens or some supermarkets.

Add garlic and ginger to hot oil; sauté shrimp about 3 minutes until just pink. Remove shrimp. Add celery and green pepper to wok, sauté about 1 minute. Add bean sauce, wine, soy sauce. Stir cornstarch and water until there are no lumps. Return shrimps to wok, sauté briefly. Stir some of wok liquid into water and cornstarch, then stir thickening back into wok. Add sprouts at the last minute and just heat through. If desired, sprinkle with hot pepper flakes. More vegetables can be added to "stretch" the shrimp: cook them with the peppers and celery.

» Basic Braised Vegetables

Braising vegetables is like a less hectic form of stir-fry. It, too, sears vegetables in hot fat and uses just a little liquid that then becomes a sauce, but it doesn't require the fairly constant attention that wok cooking does. It's easier on the cook, who can be off somewhere else getting the rest of dinner ready, yet braising has about the same nutritional advantages. And, as with stir-frying, many vegetables can be cooked by the basic method with only minor alterations in spices or cooking times.

Yield: 6 servings

1 Tb oil
1 Tb butter
1 large onion, wedged thinly
2 cloves garlic (opt)
1 small head cabbage, or
    other vegetable

¼ c liquid
salt and pepper
savory or oregano or sage
    or other herb

Sauté onions and garlic in hot fat in heavy skillet. Cut cabbage in wedges; try to keep a piece of core on each wedge to hold layers together. When onions are wilted, put cabbage wedges in one layer in skillet. Add herbs and other spices. Cover tightly for 1 minute. Add liquid and cover tightly again. Let steam 5-7 minutes, depending on thickness of vegetable. Turn once and steam other side. Add more liquid only if necessary. Liquid may be water, wine, tomato juice, stock, or combination.

» Parsley-Ginger Carrots

Analysis	Calories	CHO	Fat	Protein	GUP	Iron	Calcium
Serving:	95	10g	6g	1.5g	.8g	1.2mg	54mg

Yield: 4 servings

4-6 carrots, cut in ovals
parsnips, cut in ovals (opt)
2-3 Tb butter
2-3 Tb liquid

3 Tb fresh parsley
salt, pepper, ¼ tsp powdered
    ginger

Melt butter in heavy saucepan. Add carrots, and parsnips, if used. Add liquid and cover tightly. Cook over medium heat about 15 minutes. When barely tender, add fresh parsley and other spices to taste.

»Almost Southern Cabbage

Southern-cooked vegetables—with a piece of fat-back—have a distinctive, pleasing flavor. But they also tend to be over-cooked, which is not so pleasing. Here is a vegetarian recipe that tastes quite like the traditional Southern dish—provided you don't have them side by side for comparison.

Yield: 6 servings

4 Tb butter
1 lg head cabbage, cut in
  large shreds
¼ tsp freshly ground black
  pepper

½ tsp salt
1 tsp yeast extract
1 Tb wine, white
½ tsp Worcestershire sauce

Melt butter in heavy saucepan. Add cabbage and cook, stirring fairly constantly for about five minutes. As leaves become more tender, add rest of ingredients. You may not need additional salt since yeast extract is already salty. The "meaty" yeast taste is as close as a vegetarian is going to come to the smoky pork fat taste. Entire cooking time is less than ten minutes. Other vegetables like yellow squash, turnip and mustard greens may be cooked this way with varying cooking times.

»Jon Ree's Sweet-Sour Red Cabbage

Analysis	Calories	CHO	Fat	Protein	GUP	Iron	Calcium
Serving:	100	19g	2.6g	2.2g	1.1g	.9mg	78mg

Yield: 6 servings

1 Tb butter
¾ c chopped onion
2 lbs red cabbage, sliced
  thinly
1 lb apples, cored and thin
  sliced

1½ tsp salt
4 Tb red wine vinegar
2 Tb wine
¼ tsp pepper
1 tsp brown sugar (opt)

Sauté onion in oil until golden and soft—about 2 minutes. If you want your cabbage al dente, sauté the apple slices next until they are soft; then add the other ingredients, cover, and cook on medium heat until cabbage is the way you like it. But this dish takes kindly to long, slow cooking—almost ½ hour—in which case you can just put the apples in with everything else. If your apples are not sweet enough to offset the vinegar, you may need a pinch or two of brown sugar— no more than a teaspoon, certainly.

VARIATIONS:

1. Add 1-3 tsp caraway seeds
2. Add 1-3 tsp poppy seeds

Either of these variations makes a dish with decidedly European flavor. You could also serve with a dollop of yoghurt or sour cream.

» Ratatouille

Analysis	Calo-ries	CHO	Fat	Pro-tein	GUP	Iron	Cal-cium
Serving:	297	23g	19g	11.1g	8.3g	3.2mg	271mg

Yield: 5 servings

1 medium eggplant	olive (or other) oil
2-3 zucchini	garlic
2 medium onions	parsley, large handful
2 medium green peppers	*greenery:*
4-5 tomatoes or 1 lb can tomatoes, drained	thyme, sage, rosemary, basil salt, pepper
wine	1 c grated cheese

Pare and slice eggplant; slice zucchini; slice onions thinly (do not chop); slice peppers in slivers. Peel tomatoes if using fresh. Puckery eggplant should be salted to "draw" astringency. Sauté eggplant and zucchini one layer deep (so they don't steam) in hot olive oil until slightly browned. Add garlic to the olive oil, too. When they are sautéed, remove to a separate dish. Sauté onions and peppers until slightly wilted, add tomatoes, and let steam until juicy. Raise heat and evaporate most liquid. Add some greenery to cooking zucchini and eggplant, different greenery to cooking tomatoes and onions. Layer in a top-of-the-stove casserole, sprinkling cheese between layers. Add a little wine, salt, and pepper. Cook, basting with liquid, about 5 minutes. Raise heat and evaporate liquid. May be served hot or cold.

» Curried Vegetables

Analysis	Calories	CHO	Fat	Protein	GUP	Iron	Calcium
Serving:	273	27g	12g	11.4g	8.4g	1.3mg	341mg

Yield: 6 servings

½ stick butter (or equivalent oil)
1 lg onion, diced
2 cloves garlic, minced or pressed
1" ginger in "matchsticks" (opt)
1 tsp turmeric
2 tsp ground coriander
½ tsp ground cumin

1 tsp paprika*
¼ tsp cayenne, cinnamon, fenugreek (opt)
2 tsp salt
1 lg eggplant, diced
3 zucchini, diced
3-4 tomatoes, peeled
½ cup water or wine
1 quart yoghurt
yeast extract, (opt)

*You can substitute 1-2 Tb curry powder for the turmeric, coriander, cumin, paprika and cayenne.

Melt butter; sauté onion, garlic, and optional ginger. Add all spices except salt and cook about 2 minutes. Add eggplant and zucchini and sauté about 3 minutes, or until mingled with spices. Add tomatoes and enough liquid to steam vegetables slightly. Cover and cook about 10-15 minutes or until vegetables are crispy tender. Add yoghurt, salt, and optional yeast extract. Simmer another 2 minutes, until everything is well combined. Serve over Saffron Rice.

» Saffron Rice

Yield: 4-6 servings

2 c brown rice
1 Tb butter or oil
5 c water or broth

2 tsp American or lg pinch
Spanish saffron
1 tsp salt

Combine in covered saucepan. When boiling, reduce heat to simmer for 35 minutes, or until all water is evaporated. Serve with Curry Condiments.

CURRY CONDIMENTS:

raita (see below)
peanuts or cashews
currants or raisins
banana or apple or pear

chutney
chopped green pepper
chopped hard-boiled egg

To make raita:

Mix *1 c yoghurt* with *1 peeled chopped cucumber,* add *lg dash cayenne, ¼ tsp cumin, ¼ tsp salt.* Let stand 15 minutes for flavors to develop; adjust seasoning if necessary.

» Chinese Spring (Egg) Rolls

Analysis	Calories	CHO	Fat	Protein	GUP	Iron	Calcium
Serving:	96	7g	5g	6.4g	4.6g	1mg	30mg

Yield: 12 egg rolls

one dozen 8″ egg-roll leaves
2 Tb peanut oil
2 tsp dark sesame oil
1 c chopped celery
1 c chopped onion
½ c chopped green or red pepper
1 c chopped water chestnuts (about 12)
½ c chopped mushrooms
2 cans (4½ oz drained) tiny shrimp

3 c (packed) lentil or mung sprouts
2 tsp soy sauce
2 tsp grated ginger root
1 egg
1 Tb whole wheat or rice flour or cornstarch
¼ c dry white wine (sherry)
English mustard powder (about 2 Tb)

Sauté vegetables in oils until wilted. Barely chop sprouts and add soy sauce, ginger, and shrimp (or other leftover meat—about one cup diced). Five minutes should be enough to cook cook it. Off heat, stir in egg and thickener. Put cigar-shaped filling on spring-roll sheet and roll up. Be sure to wet edges of eggroll leaf and seal the ends so filling does not run out. Store rolls on counter, seam side down, while the rest are being formed. Heat ½ inch of cooking oil and fry eggrolls over high heat until they are brown, turning once (about one minute on each side). Or lightly oil a baking dish and bake eggrolls in 400° oven, turning so they brown evenly. Mix mustard powder and wine; serve as condiment to hot eggrolls: this is Oriental Mustard.

VARIATION:

Won Tons: Cut each eggroll leaf in 4 pieces. Make egg-roll filling with half the bean sprouts and finely chopped ingredients. Put a rounded teaspoon of filling on each quartered wrapper. Paint edge with water or egg white and cover with a second wrapper, pressing down around lump of filling. Let dry about 10 minutes. May be boiled in soup or deep fried and served plain or with a sweet-and-sour sauce.

»Vegetarian Moussaka

Analysis	Calo-ries	CHO	Fat	Pro-tein	GUP	Iron	Cal-cium
Serving:	257	15g	19g	7g	5.5g	2.5mg	43mg

5 lg eggplants
1 lg onion
1 lb mushrooms
2 Tb butter
olive oil (approx ½ c)
About 1 c thick white sauce
    made with wine and stock

thyme, sage, rosemary (approx. ½ tsp)
salt and pepper
4 eggs
3 Tb tomato paste
2 cloves garlic

Slice eggplants in half; score flesh deeply. Salt heavily and let rest 15 minutes, wash and dry. Oil and place, cuts up, on shallow baking pan; add ½" water; bake at 400° about ½ hour until tender. Carefully (hands are best) remove flesh from skin, reserve skins intact if possible. While eggplants are baking, sauté mushrooms and chopped onions in butter. Chop the eggplant flesh and combine with mushrooms. Add white sauce and other ingredients. Oil mold—heavy pot with lid will do—and line with skins flesh side up. Patch holes with pieces of skin as necessary. Pour eggplant mixture into mold, press flat and cover with leftover skin, if any. Cover tightly. Set mold in a pan of boiling water in 375° oven for about 1½ hours. Let cool in pan about 15 minutes. To unmold: run knife around outside of moussaka, put serving platter upside down on mold. Quickly invert — moussaka should drop down. If it sticks, cover ugly places with sauce. Serve with a light tomato sauce made with lots of vegetables. If you prefer, discard skins and bake moussaka in an ordinary casserole; spoon out to serve. *Yield: 8 servings.*

»*Potato Kugel*

Analysis	Calories	CHO	Fat	Protein	GUP	Iron	Calcium
Serving:	161	19g	7.6g	4.8g	3.5g	9.8mg	27mg

2½-3 lb grated unpeeled potatoes
4 eggs
1 med onion, grated
4 cloves garlic, crushed

1 c chopped fresh parsley
1 tsp salt +
¼ tsp freshly ground pepper
4-6 Tb butter, could be part oil

Grate potatoes quickly on coarse shredder—they will darken if left too long. It is not absolutely necessary to separate eggs, but it makes a more delicate Kugel if the whites are beaten stiffly and folded in last. Otherwise, combine everything but butter. Melt butter in 8x12 pan in 350° oven. When butter is very hot, almost ready to turn brown, pour in batter. Bake for 25-35 minutes. Serve with unsweetened applesauce. *Yield: 6 servings.*

VARIATION:

Potato Latkes (potato pancakes)

Drain potatoes thoroughly through doubled cheesecloth. Separate eggs, beat whites until stiff, fold into mixture of potato, onion and spices. Barely film bottom of skillet with half butter and half oil. Using wet hands, press a very thin pancake and drop on hot fat. When one side is golden, turn and cook other side. Add more fat as necessary. Serve with applesauce and/or yoghurt. Pancakes should be thin and lacy, not thick and globby.

Stock and Soup Making

Soup making is one of the simplest of the kitchen arts, yet a generation of can openers (human, not metal) has made it almost extinct. One wonders whether what's *in* the famous can is a Warhol creation as well.

While it is true that most soups improve with a little aging (flavors have time to blend), the indistinguishable chunks of wet cardboard vegetables in what passes for soups these days must have been aging since Noah docked the Ark. Especially with vegetables, freshness makes the soup. It also saves a lot of nutrients.

Soup's great nutritional advantage is that all the water-soluble vitamins and minerals that would ordinarily disappear in the cooking liquid (to be fed to the drain) are incorporated into, and are eaten with, the final product. Even otherwise unuseable ends and bits of vegetables can provide extra nutrition before they are consigned to the compost heap.

As opposed to most vegetable cooking, in which you're trying to keep all the nutrition *in* the vegetable, stock-making means you're trying to get it out of the vegetable and into the liquid. You're using things like tough outer leaves of cabbage or cauliflower, unattractive pieces of lettuce, wilted carrots and celery, mushrooms that are turning brown, fibrous ends of broccoli and asparagus stalks, over-soft tomatoes, spotty beans, or any other discarded but edible piece of vegetable. You won't leave them in to be eaten, so you want as much of their nutrition as possible to remain behind.

» Basque Bisque

Analysis	Calo- ries	CHO	Fat	Pro- tein	GUP	Iron	Cal- cium
Serving:	281	36g	10g	15g	10.1g	3.3mg	245mg

Yield: 10 servings

4 c cooked white and red beans (or 2 c beans pressure cooked in 5 c water or stock)
1-2 tsp salt
3 Tb butter
4 Tb wholewheat flour
1 c chopped pepper
1½ c chopped onion
2 cloves minced garlic

2 c milk + (to desired consistency)
28-oz. canned tomatoes
2 c corn (1 10-oz. pkg frozen)
1 tsp each: paprika, chili powder, celery salt, marjoram
2 bay leaves
6 oz. cheese

Melt butter, sauté vegetables. Add flour, cook 2 minutes. Add milk; stir until slightly thickened. Add everything else except cheese. Just before serving, grate cheese and stir into soup. This is a great place for leftover beans of any kind.

VARIATION:

Add 1 or 2 diced potatoes and cook until tender before adding cheese.

»Mulligatawny (Lentil) Soup

Analysis	Calories	CHO	Fat	Protein	CUP	Iron	Calcium
Serving:	431	56g	13g	25g	16g	5.1mg	403mg

Yield: 6 servings

2 c lentils
8 c liquid (approx.)
3-4 Tb butter
3 ribs celery
1-2 carrots
1 lg onion
3-4 cloves garlic
(or use 3 c Soupbase for
    last five ingredients)

½ tsp chili powder
2 tsp curry powder
juice of ½ lemon (or some
    wine)
1 tsp salt
1 chopped apple
Parmesan cheese
yoghurt

Cover lentils with liquid (water, vegetable water, tomato juice, wine, or comb.). Let cook about 25 minutes or until not quite tender. Add sautéed diced vegetables or Soupbase to lentils. Add spices, lemon, salt, and chopped apple. If possible, let soup sit 1 hour or longer to blend flavors. Serve with a dollop of yoghurt and a sprinkling of Parmesan cheese for greatest protein supplementarity. Instead of curry powder, you may use about ¼ tsp turmeric, 1 tsp coriander, ¼ tsp cumin, large dash ginger, and ¼ tsp paprika.

»Shortcut Lentil Soup

2 c lentils
4 c soup stock or vegetable
    cooking water
2 c water
1 lg carrot, cut in slices
1 lg stalk celery, sliced
2 Tb oil

½ tsp garlic powder
½ tsp onion powder
2 Tb tamari soy sauce
1 tsp salt
½ tsp pepper
1 tsp paprika

Combine everything. (See what we mean about shortcut? Using the garlic and onion powders means no sautéeing of vegetables first—one less pot to wash and a preparation even a child could manage.) Pressure cook 15 minutes.

» Mrs. Lerch's Green Bean Soup

Yield: about 5 servings

1 lb green beans
1 lg onion, chopped—2 c
2 potatoes diced—3 c
1 tsp salt
6 c water or vegetable stock
1 Tb yeast extract

1 Tb oil or butter
2 Tb fresh parsley or ½ tsp
dried
¼ tsp pepper
sour cream

Sauté vegetables in fat until onions are wilted and golden and beans are bright green. Add everything—simmer until beans and potatoes are tender, 20-30 minutes. Delicious served with a dollop of sour cream.

» Clam Chowder (Manhattan)

Analysis	Calories	CHO	Fat	Protein	GUP	Iron	Calcium
Serving:	186	24g	8g	6.3g	4.2g	2.9mg	62mg

Yield: 6 servings

3 stalks celery
3 carrots
1-2 onions
4 cloves garlic
1 parsnip (opt)
3-4 Tb butter
(Or use 3 c Soupbase instead
of above ingredients; see
Soupbase in Recipe Index)

2 cans (6-8 oz. ea) clams
2-3 medium potatoes
1 28-oz. can tomatoes +
salt, pepper, yeast extract,
basil
lemon juice, and/or wine

Sauté aromatic vegetables in butter until slightly browned, or use Soupbase. Drain clams, pour juice into vegetables. Add canned tomatoes, juice and all. Dice potatoes and add to soup; cook until tender, 20 to 30 minutes, depending on size. Taste for seasoning. Add clams just before serving since prolonged heat makes them tough. This makes a fairly thick soup; you may add another can of tomatoes, if desired.

VARIATION:

New England Clam Chowder

Omit tomatoes. Instead use double Basic White Sauce recipe plus 2-3 cups milk. Pre-cook potatoes as well; if you try to cook them in the white sauce, the prolonged heating will tend to toughen the milk protein and the sauce will "crack." But you may simmer ingredients together to allow flavors to blend. (See Recipe Index under White Sauce.)

»Mushroom-Barley Stew

Analysis	Calo-ries	CHO	Fat	Pro-tein	GUP	Iron	Cal-cium
Serving:	351	51g	9g	16.5g	11.6g	2.6mg	245mg

Yield: 8 servings

3 stalks celery
2 carrots
1 parsnip (opt)
2 medium onions
3-4 cloves garlic
2-3 Tb fat or oil
(or use 3 c Soupbase for
  above six ingredients)
1 c lentils
1 c barley (or millet)
1-2 tsp Worcestershire sauce

1-2 tsp soy sauce
8 c water +
1 bay leaf
1 Tb yeast extract
⅓ c or more red wine
1 tsp ea salt, paprika
½ tsp ea pepper, thyme
¼ tsp ea cumin, cayenne
juice of 1 lemon
½ lb, or more, mushrooms

Sauté chopped vegetables or use Soupbase. Add everything and simmer, covered, about 1 hour. Add more water for thinner consistency, if desired. Be sure to serve with some milk product for full supplementation. Serve with: grated cheese or yoghurt.

» Gumbo

Analysis	Calories	CHO	Fat	Protein	GUP	Iron	Calcium
Serving:	130	11g	6g	9.7g	7.1g	1.7mg	101mg

Yield: 8 servings

5-6 cloves garlic
3-4 Tb olive oil
1 lg onion, coarsely chopped
2 stalks celery with leaves
1 large green pepper
1 lb okra
1 lb shelled shrimp
1 qt fish stock or bottled clam
  juice and water

28 oz can tomatoes
1 tsp salt, ½ tsp pepper
2 Tb each lemon juice, white
  wine
¼ c fresh chopped parsley
few threads saffron
1 Tb gumbo file

Sauté garlic in olive oil. If you prefer less slimy okra, slice and sauté it immediately. Otherwise, sauté the other fresh vegetables first. When everything smells wonderful, add the stock, tomatoes, etc.—but not the gumbo file. When shrimp are done, stir in the file just before serving. Gumbo may be stew-like and served on a plate, or you may choose to have it soupy and serve over rice. This dish can be stretched by adding another 28 oz. can of tomatoes.

THE FISH STOCK

fish trimmings
shellfish shells
piece of bay leaf

1 onion
½ cup white wine
water to cover

Combine ingredients. Simmer ½ to 1 hour. Strain, reserve juice.

Outline for Do-It-Yourself Soup

1. The *brunoise:* your choice of a combination of the "aromatic" vegetables: carrots, parsnips, onions, garlic, celery, cabbage. Sauté in a choice of butter, for cream-style soups, or olive oil, for tomato-based soups. However, now that you know that rule you can ignore it, and sauté in whatever fat you choose at the moment. You would want no less than three cups chopped vegetables for a soup to serve four to six people. Sauté about five minutes on medium-high heat, stirring occasionally. Let the edges of the vegetables brown—not burn—slightly.

2. Deglaze the *brunoise* with some liquid other than milk: wine, vegetable-cooking water, tomato juice, water. Use just enough to make a thick syrupy base into which you scrape as much of the stuck-on bits of sautéed vegetables as you can without endangering the pan—use a wooden spoon.

3. Optional—the thickening: usually a few tablespoons of flour; about 2-4 per quart of soup. Sprinkle over the sautéed vegetables and cook about two minutes. (Or use *beurre manie* near the end of the soup-making: see Step 7 below.)

4. The liquid: For cream (milk) soups, you can save money and enhance the flavor by using all or part vegetable-cooking water and then adding instant powdered milk near the end of the cooking. You can use vegetable-cooking water, reserved juices from canned—perish the thought—vegetables, canned tomatoes and juice, clam juice, stock. Be careful in adding yoghurt—excess heat tends to make it "crack" (curdle) —it will be edible, but unsightly.

5. The main character: it may be beans (in which case the bean liquid may have already been added), potatoes or other vegetables, clams, or mushrooms.

6. Herbs and spices: You'll have to experiment. Try reading the suggested uses on the labels. Check other recipes for ideas.

7. The thickening: If it wasn't added in step four, this is another optional place for it. To make *beurre manie,* rub together butter and roughly twice as much flour until com-

pletely creamed. Whisk about ½ cup of the hot soup into a few tablespoons of the *beurre manie* until smooth; then whisk this combination back into the main pot. Bring to a simmer to thicken. Some soups are thickened with the addition of a potato, which is allowed to cook until it is completely soft. A small amount of pasta, cooked right in the soup, will also provide starch for a little thickening. Soft-cooked beans usually don't require extra thickening.

8. The final adjustments: salt and the suggestions that follow.

SUGGESTIONS:

To avoid having meatless soups that taste like insipid water-logged vegetables, you can take advantage of some "taste enhancers."

• *Yeast extract:* this is not to be confused with either nutritional yeast or baking yeast, though it is a derivative of the former. In England it goes under the trade name Marmite, and they spread it—very, very thinly—on buttered toast. It looks like old axle grease: it's dark brown and scudgy. It tastes like essence of gravy; and in fact so-called gravy-starters are based partly on hydrolized yeast. It's also quite salty, so add salt *after* you add the yeast. An acceptable range in almost any soup is 1 teaspoon to 1 tablespoon per quart. It imparts a meaty taste and generally intensifies flavors.

• *Vegetarian boullion cubes:* several good brands are available. While they often consist of a large measure of plain salt, they also contain ½ dozen or more dehydrated vegetables. Without having to chop and add more celery, onions, tomatoes and so forth, the essence of their flavors enhances your soup. It is certainly not a substitute for real sautéed vegetables, but it's a good addition to soup that seems to be missing that certain something.

• *Lemon juice, wine, vinegar:* while they are obviously not completely interchangeable, any of these, added in the last few minutes of cooking, gives soup a little tang. Using wine for deglazing sautéed vegetables is especially recommended. By the way, all the alcohol evaporates; all that's left is the taste.

160

• *Fresh ground black pepper:* a few grindings of a fresh pepper into a slightly blah soup can give it the lift it needs.

• *Cheese, yoghurt, cottage cheese:*—or sour cream if your waistline can afford it—any of these, either stirred into soup at the last minute, or added at the table, gives the soup's morale a great boost. And all—with the exception of the sour cream—also add protein and calcium, and may improve the overall protein quality of the dish.

• *Chopped fresh parsley or other herbs:* no matter how much dried parsley you use, it doesn't do for soup—or anything else for that matter—what a healthy sprig of freshly-chopped parsley does.

• *Two tablespoons of butter:* stirred into "cream-style" soups, just before serving, adds a velvety richness.

Salads

Salads can and should be crunchy, plentiful, raw, and varied. With a dressing based on yoghurt or cottage cheese (instead of mayonnaise), they are a dieter's delight—filling, high-protein, low calorie. Besides containing micronutrients, salads provide fiber. And they can easily be turned into a quick meal-in-a-bowl.

If your life-long exposure to lettuce has been limited to iceberg (so named because of the similarity of flavor), you may be forgiven for a lack of enthusiasm at the mention of salad. If you're over the age of consent, however, you have no valid excuse—there are other types of greenery available—one has but to choose. Since different salad greens have different nutrient profiles, you can maximize your salad nutrition by mixing the kinds of greens. Aesthetically, too, salads are enhanced by the variations upon the theme of "green."

We're not going to analyze most of the salads because the nutrients they supply aren't among those we're analyzing for, and because most of the calories come from the dressings, which are analyzed elsewhere.

» Kathy Valla's Salad

Analysis	Calo-ries	CHO	Fat	Pro-tein	GUP	Iron	Cal-cium
Serving:	158	29g	5g	1.6g	1.1g	.8mg	73mg

Yield: 6 servings

3 c sliced celery
1 20-oz. can unsweetened
   pineapple, drained
2 pears or apples

1 c cauliflowerets
¾ c Basic Mayonnaise Dressing
½ c slivered almonds (opt)

Slice, chop, core, mix.

» Carrifruit-Seed Salad

Yield: 8 1-cup servings

7 large carrots
7 medium apples
1 c raisins

1 c sunflower seeds
1 c Basic Mayonnaise Dressing
lemon juice

Grate carrots; core and slice apples—it's not necessary to peel. Toss everything together.

SUGGESTIONS:

1. Substitute dates or currants for all or part of raisins.
2. Substitute raw cashews for all or part of seeds.
3. Substitute diced celery for part of carrots.

» Tomato-Onion Salad

Analysis	Calo-ries	CHO	Fat	Pro-tein	GUP	Iron	Cal-cium
Serving:	123	15g	7g	3.5g	1.7g	2.4mg	76mg

Yield: 4 servings

5 medium tomatoes
2 small bermuda onions
½ c fresh chopped parsley

2-3 Tb fresh chopped basil
salt and pepper
6-8 Tb Lemonette

To slice tomatoes so that they "bleed" less, put tomato on cutting board stem side down. Layer sliced tomatoes in bottom of dish, cover with very thin slices of onion; sprinkle with salt, pepper and herbs. After everything is done, drench with Lemonette (see Recipe Index) and let sit 10 minutes.

» Greek Salad

1 lg head romaine lettuce, about 5 c, torn
½ to 1 c Greek brined olives —no substitute
½ lb feta cheese +
½ c chopped fresh parsley
6-8 Tb Lemonette Dressing made with opt anchovy paste

(See Recipe Index for Lemonette Dressing.)

Toss together.

» Tabooli

Analysis	Calories	CHO	Fat	Protein	GUP	Iron	Calcium
Serving:	330	24g	22g	11.8g	7.1g	3.8mg	312mg

Yield: 6 servings

½ c bulghur wheat, soaked
2 cucumbers
10 radishes
2 green peppers
6 oz feta cheese
1 c Greek brined olives
½ c lemon juice
¼ c olive oil +
½ c chopped fresh mint
½ c chopped fresh parsley
romaine leaves
salt, pepper

Chop vegetables, drain bulghur. Toss everything but romaine together and taste for seasoning. Arrange romaine leaves in bowl and fill center with mixture. May be served with yoghurt for higher protein. If you don't use the feta, definitely use about 1 c yoghurt and toss with everything else.

Sprouts

Although many people think of sprouting as a recent innovative technique, the Chinese developed sprouting centuries ago. Sprouts are economical (in salads they are much crisper and cheaper than lettuce), low in calories, delicious, and nutritious. A handful of certain bean sprouts can supply close to one-third the RDA for thiamin and riboflavin, and almost all the RDA for vitamin C for an adult woman. Recent research has shown that the vitamin content of sprouted grains or beans may increase from 200% to 1,300% over the unsprouted form; that the natural phytate decreases; and that iron is more available.

Sprouts are also absurdly easy to germinate in a variety of ways, even for confirmed "black-thumb" gardeners. Equipment found in most kitchens can be used to grow them, and they give phenomenal returns in delicious, sweet crunch (and nutrition) for a minimal investment of time or money.

You can sprout alfalfa (great on sandwiches), mung beans (Chinese bean sprouts), rice, wheat (sweet-tasting and delicious in bread), lentils (my favorite in salads), soy (good stir-fried), sunflower, and sesame seeds—or almost anything that holds the germ of a new plant.* Although they require slightly different handling, most sprouts are made the same basic way: start with only 2 to 3 tablespoons of sprouts per quart jar—they expand enormously and overcrowding can lead to rotting.

SPROUTING INSTRUCTIONS

1. Soak (overnight is best)—pour seed soaking water on your house plants—they'll thank you for it—or save for soup.

2. Either put soaked seeds in a quart jar with a piece of netting or cheesecloth tied over the mouth (to allow air circulation); or place soaked seeds on a very moist but

---

*Don't use commercially packed seeds intended for planting, which have probably been covered with a poisonous fungicide.

164

not dripping wet paper or cloth towel on a tray. We have often used a plastic shoebox—50¢ in any variety store—which very nearly duplicated the expensive sprouting trays. *Or* make a sprouting tray by nailing small-mesh hardware screen onto a wooden frame. Spread the soaked seeds on the mesh and put a towel drainboard underneath.

3. Rinse the seeds at least once a day—twice if they seem dry: run water into the jar and then invert it for at least 15 minutes, netting still in place to drain thoroughly; *or* drench the sprouting tray (it will drain itself); *or* sprinkle water into the shoebox (if you have the lid, it will tend to hold the moisture in, as in a miniature hothouse). Don't keep the seeds *wet*, only damp—or they will rot.

4. Keep in a dark, warm place about 24 hours—until you see some shoots. (Alfalfa seeds sometimes take two days.) Then put the sprouts in the sun to develop chlorophyll. Don't "burn" them with too much direct sunlight or they will turn brown—but they'll still taste fine.

Alfalfa, mung, and lentil sprouts grow to about five times the length of the original seed, but mung and lentils take three to four days and alfalfa can take six. They will also develop delicious tender green leaves, if you can wait that long. Wheat and rice don't usually develop sprouts as quickly as they develop roots. In fact, after three or four days, the rapidly growing fine root hairs will start to mat together. Don't confuse that with the matting of decay—which smells rotten and is somewhat slimy. Sunflower seeds and sesame seeds should be eaten when the sprout is as long as the seeds —about two days—or they'll turn slightly bitter.

» Sautéed Sprouts

1 Tb butter	1 tsp tamari
1 clove garlic, pressed	large dash pepper
2 c sprouts	1 oz grated Parmesan cheese

Melt butter in a heavy skillet. Add garlic and sprouts and sauté about 2 minutes, just until sprouts are hot through. Stir in tamari, pepper, cheese, and additional salt to taste. May be served in hot pita.

» Sprout-Cheese Sandwich

Add sprouts to cheese in pita and heat in oven until cheese is melted. Or make regular skillet-grilled cheese sandwich with sprouts. Or soften tortilla on oiled griddle, stuff with cheese and sprouts and grill until cheese melts. If desired, chopped tomatoes, green peppers, cucumbers and/or piquant sauce may be added, too.

» Sprout Salad

2 c sprouts
1 chopped cucumber
1 chopped pepper

handful ripe olives
romaine leaves
dressing

Combine sprouts, other vegetables, olives and dressing. Serve on bed of romaine leaves.

Nutritional Yeast

As opposed to yoghurt, wheat germ, or molasses, which are all good for you and taste good too, brewer's yeast is good for you and tastes terrible. Always. You can get used to it enough to tolerate it, but I've never met anyone who honestly claimed to delight in the taste. But since it is an amazing food, it pays to develop a tolerance.

Food-yeast analysis reads like a trace mineral and vitamin treasury. For "pure" vegetarians, one tablespoon of fortified yeast provides the daily requirement for Vitamin B-12.

It is also an excellent source of biologically active chromium, a necessary trace mineral usually marginal in refined carbohydrate diets. Originally, nutritional yeast was a by-product of the beer industry—hence, the term "brewer's yeast." At least one company now produces "primary grown" yeast—meaning it's not a by-product: it's *the* product. They also produce yeasts with varying strengths of certain vitamins (perhaps by fortifying the growing medium). Precise figures are hard to get but it appears that the chromium content of *brewer's* yeast may be considerably higher than that of *primary grown* yeast. On the other hand, primary grown yeast has the least objectionable taste. Scylla and Charybdis—take your pick.

There are two ways of eating something that you know is going to be awful: you can either drown it in a lot of something else and then work your way through that until you've gotten it all down, or you can make it a small, bitter pill and get it down all at once. I opt for the second, but many people argue convincingly for the first. Here they both are anyway.

» Yeast I

Put ½ tsp of yeast in an 8 oz. glass of orange or tomato juice. You will not taste it (I hope). After 1 week, put 1 tsp in an 8 oz. glass. (Do I make myself clear?) Work up to 2 Tb a day. If you can stand doing it more than once, take the 2 Tb in divided doses—say 2 *tsp* three times a day. As with so-called one-a-day vitamins and the over-fortified children's cereals, larger doses of nutrients than your body can use at one time are partly wasted. If the repetition seems too horrible to contemplate, remember: the less you take at any one time, the less your taste buds will recoil. One lady said that after she'd been adding yeast to her orange juice for several months, she couldn't drink the orange juice without it. She said that the yeast took the edge off the acidity. That's her story, anyway. You can also put yeast in malts, milkshakes, or blended fruit drinks.

» Yeast II

4 oz juice   4 oz juice
2 Tb yeast

Put the yeast in the first 4 oz. of juice. Have the second 4 oz. ready. Without actually holding your nose (unless it's absolutely necessary), chug the first concoction down (no breathing) and immediately down the second. Do not breathe through your nasal passages until you're well into the second glass. You may want to work up to this method by using Yeast I first, just in case you breathe at the wrong time.

VIII
Meat Is Bean Replaced

Reprinted with permission of The McNaught Syndicate, Inc.

Meat consumption in this country is preposterously high, and cannot be justified on a nutritional basis . . . The overemphasis on protein . . . has resulted in all sorts of useless activities to increase the protein content of everything from soup to nuts and has led many people to believe that the sine qua non *of a good diet is meat.*
     —Dr. D. M. Hegsted, *Journal of the American Dietetic Association,* April, 1974

VEGETARIANISM is no longer a mode of life peculiar to saints, zealots, or faddists: these days, everybody knows *somebody* who is one. Although historically vegetarianism was often an expression of religious and ethical beliefs, modern vegetarians may have a wider range of objections to meat-eating.

Beans have long been rightly called "poor man's meat." But this has given them a negative social status. As soon as they are financially able, people replace the excellent and cheap nutrition which beans offer with the costly—and often less balanced—nutrition of meat. Except for a lower protein availablility, beans generally contain better nutrition than meat: high in the nutrients that American diets are likely to lack; low in excess sodium, fats and calories. Even their relatively low NPUs should not dissuade bean-eaters: supplementation increases their protein availability to a level comparable with or *surpassing* that of meat, and at a fraction of the cost. T-bone steak protein costs about ten times as much as the same amount of available protein from a grain-bean combination; and about 20 times as much as soybean protein.

FEDERAL MEAT INSPECTION

Upton Sinclair's famous exposé of the meat industry led directly to the Wholesome Meat Act of 1906. Today, all meat which is sold in interstate commerce must be Federally inspected, and laws passed recently have set a deadline for the states' inspection to meet Federal standards. The optimal standards are quite high: there is a long inspection procedure which according to law, must be performed on every four-footed animal and bird. (Actually, non-birds must be inspected twice: the first time when they are alive and in holding pens.) Unfortunately, the application of the law is not as thorough as it would seem on paper. According to Federally published figures, there are 8,800 inspectors and

169

veterinarians to cover 5,763 meat plants (plus less than 1,000 auxiliary personnel who do not make inspections). Each plant must have at least one veterinarian in charge of one or more inspectors.

In 1974, 3 billion birds and 124 million meat animals were slaughtered and inspected. It has already been established by several researchers that poultry inspectors (whose specialized training may have consisted of nothing more than three weeks of on-the-job instruction) have between three and six seconds to view each bird as it advances on conveyors.

Assuming an 8-hour day (the Federal Government does not pay overtime), and no time out for paperwork (which is actually a prime responsibility of the professionally-trained veterinarian), each of the 124 million inspections of meat animals averaged no more than 3 minutes.

Although the USDA claims that less than 1% of the meat that reaches packing plants is condemned, there is some suggestion that the defects in the inspection system, rather than the quality of meat, may account for the good showing.

DES

The practice of using hormones to induce greater weight gain in food animals has also come under fire. Hormone feeding is a kind of chemical neutering—and just as your cat or dog got lazier and plumper shortly after being "fixed," the food animal gains more weight, though it eats less. But the increased weight is primarily in water and fat, which is of no value to the consumer, though it represents increased profit to the feed lot operator.

For over twenty years, most food animals in this country were either fed or had implanted pellets of diethylstilbesterol (DES), a synthetic hormone. Did the low—a few parts per billion—levels of DES residue in meat represent a hazard to the consumer?

Even though they are produced within the body and are essential to life, hormones have great potential for causing harm. For example, the hormones naturally present in a woman's body can be an important contributing factor to the incidence of breast cancer.

The most startling results of DES usage are occurring twelve to twenty years after its prescription for miscarriage-

170

prone women: over 200 cases of extremely rare vaginal cancer have been discovered in the *daughters* of women who took DES while pregnant.[1,2] DES has also been linked to breast cancer in men taking hormone treatments for prostate cancer.

At Senate hearings on the proposed DES ban,[3] the following points were made by specialists in carcinogenesis: DES is many times more potent in its activity than the natural hormones each person produces (or the additional hormones which could be present in the tissues of a cow in heat); although hormone-like substances are also found in some plant sources, DES is *10,000 times more active* than the *most potent* plant sources; no determination has been made that a small amount of a carcinogen (DES is used in laboratory experiments as a cancer-producing agent because it is so *reliable*) is harmless—rather, current theory holds that smaller amounts will still produce cancer but in fewer numbers of people; that the absolute amount of DES may not be as relevant as the alteration in the delicate balance of the body's own hormone burden.

In 21 countries, the use of DES in animal feed is banned; in Sweden and Switzerland, the import of DES-residue tainted American beef is also banned.

The attitude of the FDA in the DES controversy has been ambivalent, at best. During the 1972 hearings, the then-Commissioner of the FDA testified that the carcinogenicity to man of such small doses was unproven.[3] However, in response to the demand of the Senate Committee, DES was banned; the ban was partial—it applied only to DES feeding and not to DES implants. But more importantly, the FDA Commissioner chose not to declare an "imminent health hazard" which would have given him the power to ban DES summarily; neither did he give the pro-DES forces the required hearing for a substance which was not an imminent hazard. As a result, the ban was successfully overturned in the courts. After that, there was no further attempt on the part of the FDA to reinstate the DES ban. The current ban on DES is the result of Congressional legislation in late 1975.[4]

Other hormones are now used in place of the banned DES; though they are not as potent, their use is open to essentially the same questions of safety.

ANTIBIOTICS

Antibiotics, too, are routinely given to farm animals. They help put weight on young animals and combat infections which can spread quickly in unsanitary chicken houses or over-crowded feed lots. One American in ten is known to have the potential of allergic reaction upon contact with antibiotics, and if the person is sensitive enough or the dose is strong enough, exposure can lead to fatal anaphylactic shock.[5] Further, even those who don't become allergically sensitized to small but continuous doses of antibiotics may develop drug resistance—the antibiotic loses its clinical effectiveness.

BEEF AND CANCER

Whether or not the meat contains harmful residues, some researchers are linking beef consumption with bowel cancer. Countries with the highest per capita beef consumption also have the highest incidence of this cancer. A high fat (beef) diet both alters normal intestinal flora and raises the level of bile acids in the intestine. This combination may be conducive to production of carcinogens. In addition, the prolonged intestinal transit time of high-meat, low-fiber diets allows carcinogens longer contact with intestinal tissue. (See Chapter VI.)

WORLD FAMINE

In the last ten years, still another reason for vegetarianism has become increasingly important. Meat-eating is not ecologically justifiable in a world where millions are starving. Global malnutrition is the name of the game. The term "world famine" is actually misleading; for at least the next ten years there will be enough food grown world-wide to feed the earth's population, even at its present rate of increase.[6] The problem is rather a famine of maldistribution: the people are where the food isn't.

Sporadic famine has been a chronic plague throughout man's history. The current problem is a culmination of political, agricultural, and atmospheric conditions. Several events followed one another in rapid succession, any of which might have been enough to upset the grain-cart, but which in combination precipitated the already developing food-population-distribution problems.

172

For many years, America's surpluses were given or sold at low prices to countries whose agricultural production did not meet the needs of their people. In some cases, rich native soils which could have produced abundant food supplies were (and still are) planted in non-nutritive cash crops such as coffee, tea and sugar to be sold to the United States and other countries. With the incredible agricultural advances of the post-war years, production increased dramatically while the market for cash crops expanded slowly, forcing prices down. At the same time, the grain silos of the United States were depleted by increasing cattle food demands and the unprecedented volume of grain sales to China and Russia. Meanwhile, the sub-Sahara lands were experiencing a long and severe drought; and for two years, the much-needed monsoon rains of India fell uselessly into the ocean while cyclones and floods ravaged high production areas. The last straw was the enormous rise in the price of petroleum, and concomitantly of its agriculturally linked by-products—fertilizers, and fuel for tractors and shipping.

Now, countries which need our grain can ill afford it, but our annual donations to the world's needy have steadily declined.

MEAT AND ECOLOGY

While at first glance it seems our resources have been so depleted that greater donations would raise the domestic price of grain unbearably, there is another factor which alters the picture—the ecological inefficiency of producing animal protein.

Grain-staple countries, like Japan, consume about 400 pounds of grain per person per year, yet Americans consume almost five times as much.[6] If you stop to add it all up, you'll realize that no matter how fond you are of pasta, grits, or rice, you couldn't possibly have eaten 5½ pounds of grain a day. You didn't: American per capita consumption of bread and other grain products actually amounts to only 5 or 6 ounces per day.[7] The other 5 lbs. were eaten by animals which, in return, provided less than one-half pound of meat.

American "corn-fed" meat-raising practices were supported because they turned many pounds of (then) cheap grain which were otherwise stored in silos (lest the laws of supply and demand depress the market too much) into fewer pounds of high-priced meat (not in such plentiful supply worldwide, and therefore a lucrative export to those countries which could afford it). Grain-fed meat was a product of the same kind of endlessly-expanding consumption mentality which produced in the auto industry huge tailfins and monstrous horsepower.

Meat, as we use it, is an extravagance—we eat it to the point of detriment to our own health and starvation for others. Turning grain protein into animal protein reduces the protein available for consumption by 90% (the ratio of grain to animal protein is an average 10 to 1).[8] Beef is the worst offender—the cow requires 16 pounds of grain protein to produce one pound of animal protein! *If it were a car, no one would buy it.*

LOST PROTEIN

It's a simple statistic: 60% of America's high-quality annual agricultural production is fed to livestock. An additional 14% is fed to other domesticated animals including our housepets. Consider this anomalous situation: in a world where "more than two-thirds of the 800 million children now growing up in developing countries . . . (will suffer the effects of malnutrition),"[9] Americans buy dog food which is "all meat, not a speck of cereal" and obese pets are put on special reducing diets.

Articles have recently been written which claim that meat animals are only "topped off" with grains that aren't useful in human nutrition, and we should therefore not curtail our meat-eating habits. The fact is that during the short topping off period, livestock consumed 86% of the corn crop, 84% of the oat crop, 100% of the sorghum crop, and 70% of the barley crop[10]—all edible *people-food* (grain sorghum is a staple in other countries). Topping off is a systematic, concentrated program used to put as much weight as possible on the animal before slaughter. The weight gain is primarily fat, and therefore, the much-heralded "increase in the food supply" is useless to the consumer. In any event, the acreage which produced the topping off grains might have been used to produce even higher-quality protein food for human consumption.

As a conservative estimate, the total amount of grain consumed by livestock in 1971, 179 million tons, could have provided the protein needs for 419 million people for one year—or more than enough to feed the actually starving, and to raise the nutritional status of the marginally nourished (author's calculation).[10]

PROTEIN

The ancient Greeks (who knew a lot) thought enough of protein to name it "that which comes first" *(is of prime importance)*. In fact, not counting water, protein is the most abundant element in the body—it's a component of every cell and all enzymes and hormones. Hundreds of millions of cells are destroyed and rebuilt in the never-ending process of metabolism. Protein is essential to this cell-building as the stuff which new cells are made of and as the regulators of the process.

Proteins are made up of smaller units—about 22 amino acids. The body synthesizes some of the amino acids, but the others must come from food. These last are called the essential amino acids or EAAs.

ESSENTIAL AMINO ACIDS AND
NET PROTEIN UTILIZATION

Like a recipe which requires a certain proportion of butter to flour, the body's protein recipe requires a certain proportion of essential amino acids. If an essential amino acid is totally missing from a food protein (as is the case with gelatin), the protein has no value in cell-building. And if the proportion of one or more of the EAA's is less than ideal, less of the total protein can be used. (If a recipe calls for one cup milk, but you have only ½ cup, you can make only ½ the recipe.)

An expression of a food's protein value after it has been adjusted for varying amounts of the essential amino acids (biological value-BV) and digestibility is NPU or Net Protein Utilization. Theoretically, at least, a protein could exist with an NPU of 100—meaning that the protein was totally utilizable by the body; in that case *total* protein and *available* protein would be the same. Actually, however, NPUs vary widely. With low NPU foods, less of the total protein is

175

available to the body for cell building. Almost all protein analysis charts are based on *total* protein, which can be confusing and give an exceedingly inaccurate picture of what the body can use.

Different foods contain varying proportions of essential amino acids, and have higher or lower digestibility, hence have different NPUs. Some foods are comparitively high in all the Essential Amino Acids—these foods are, primarily, animal protein, like eggs (closest to the body's ideal protein with an NPU of 94), milk (82), cheese (70) and meat (67 —makes no difference what cut it is). Related foods tend to be consistently high, or low, in certain amino acids: beans are generally low in the sulfur-containing amino acids and high in lysine; conversely, grains are low in lysine. Soybeans, (NPU 61) and brown rice (NPU 70—white rice is only 57 because some of the amino acids are milled away, reducing the biological value of the whole) are comparable to meat in their EAA sufficiency.

Biologically speaking, the source of an amino acid makes no difference—isoleucine from beans is chemically identical to isoleucine from meat or eggs. The concept of first or second class proteins is outdated—NPU has taken its place.[11, 12]

MUTUAL SUPPLEMENTATION

When foods of varying amino acid patterns are eaten at roughly the same time, the overall (combined) amino acid pattern may be closer to the body's ideal "recipe" than the pattern of either food if eaten alone. In fact, dozens of protein combinations exist which have a higher NPU than would have been predicted by averaging. An NPU of 61 (soy) and an NPU of 60 (wheat) can result in an NPU of 71 (wheat-soy) if the proportions are right.

Many combinations which reflect foods native to a geographical area have been empirically discovered, and are identified with certain ethnic groups: bean-rice and corn-bean (Latin); fish-rice and soy-rice (Oriental); bulghur-leben (which is wheat-milk) and sesame-chickpea (Middle Eastern). Additional combinations have been scientifically calculated from analysis of supplementary amino acid patterns.

One great practical benefit of this mutual supplementation is to reduce the cost of protein in your food budget.

SINGLE FOODS			MUTUALLY SUPPLEMENTED FOODS
Cost and Pound Amount for 100 grams protein		Price/lb.	Cost of 100 grams Protein

$5.90	(2½ lbs)	Porterhouse Steak	$2.40	
$2.20	(1¼ lbs)	Cheddar cheese	$1.75	
$1.73	(4½ c)	Creamed cottage cheese	$ .80	
$1.68	(4.3 lbs)	Brown Rice	$ .40	
$1.65	(1.8 lbs)	Hamburger	$ .90	
$1.61	(2.7 lbs)	Whole chicken	$ .60	
$1.54	(14 c)	Whole milk	$1.75 /gal.	
$1.49	(1 lb)	Tuna, water pack	$1.50	
$1.48	(1.9 lbs)	Peanut butter	$ .80	

$1.21 Brown rice (2 lbs) + milk powder (1¼ c)

$1.08 (16 lg.) Eggs $ .79 /doz.

$1.04 Brown rice (2¼ lbs) + beans (¾ lbs)
$1.03 Sunflower (2¼ c) + peanuts (1½ c)

$1.01 (2½ lbs) Beans, average $ .40

$ .98 Brown rice (2½ lbs) + soybeans (¾ c)

$ .94 (¾ lbs) Milk powder $1.25

$ .88 Milk powder (2¼ c) + potatoes (3¼ lbs)
$ .83 Milk powder (½ c) + peanuts (2½ c)
$ .80 Wheat flour (2½ lbs) + milk powder (1 c)

$ .75 (.8 lbs) Low-fat soy flour $ .90

$ .75 Beans (1 lb) + cheese (6 oz.)
$ .74 Beans (1 lb) + cornmeal (3½ lbs)

$ .69 (2¾ lbs) Wholewheat flour $ .25

$ .65 Wheat (1.8 lbs) + peanut ⅞ c
       + soy (3.5 Tb)
$ .61 Wheat (2¼ lbs) + beans (½ lb)
$ .44 Wheat (1.6 lbs) + soy (⅓ lb)

$ .43 (1.2 lbs) Wheatgerm, raw $ .35
$ .32 (1 lb) Soybeans $ .30

LEGEND

100 grams of *useable* protein represents the approximate daily protein requirement for a man, woman or child under ten.

Though some of the above mutually supplemented food combinations may look peculiar at first, try to think of them as foods rather than raw commodities. A combination of Wheat + peanut + soy makes sense as a peanut butter sandwich on Triple Rich bread. Where milk powder is used, cheese or other milk equivalent may make the combination sound more edible, but there will be some difference in cost. Wheat can represent bread, pasta, etc.

177

	T-bone	Ham-burger	Frank-furter	Av.\Meat\	Av. non-Meat	Beans Cheese	Milk, Soy, Sesame	Wheat & Soy
Quantity	1.21 lbs	.85 lbs	1.32 lbs	—	—	2⅓ c dry beans 6.4 oz. cheese	1 c powdered milk 1⅜ c sesame ½ c soy	4⅔ c flour ¾ c soy
Cost	$3.32	$1.24	$1.58	$2.05	$.42	$.55	$.50	$.22
Calories	1745	1121	1321	1396	1211	1174	1058	1402
Fiber gm.	0	0	0	0	11	11	10	11
Fat gm.	159	89	107	118	38	30	64	21
PUFA gm.	3.4*	1.9	3	3	16	2	33	12
Sodium mg.	299	194	5777	2090	334	615	373	14
Calcium mg.	43	41	32	39	1138	957	2140	316
Magnesium mg.	88*	88	88*	88	479	419	438	580
Iron mg.	11	11	6	9	17	16	17	17
Zinc mg.	18*	18	8	15	9	9	8*	10
Thiamin mcg.	322	323	853	499	2210	2040	1921	2668
Riboflavin mcg.	655	664	954	758	1001	894	1470	639
Niacin mg.	18	18	13	16	8.5	5	6.4	14
Pantothenic Acid mg.	2.8	1.9	2.3	2.3	4.4	2.1	6.1	4.9
Vitamin B-6 mg.	1.9	1.4	.75	1.4	1.4	1.4	1.1*	1.8
Folic Acid mcg.	21*	21	21*	21	334	433	300*	269*
Vitamin A IU.	310	148	0	153	845	1110	1369	65
Vitamin E IU.	2.6*	1.5	1.5*	1.9	16.4	2	34.1*	13*

*starred values are estimates

gm.=grams, mg.=milligrams, mcg.=micrograms, IU.=International Units

Mutually supplemented foods not only cost less for the same amount of useable protein (in this case, 50 grams) but they also provide a better range of those nutrients in which the American diet is probably marginal. The calorie "cost" is about the same, though fewer calories are derived from fats, especially saturated fats, in the mutually supplemented foods.

Relatively inexpensive (low NPU) foods can be combined, resulting in an overall lower cost per gram of *useable* protein. Combinations with moderately priced supplementary foods (see chart, page 177 for cost of individual protein foods) still result in overall savings.

How much protein is enough? It is virtually impossible to eat a low-junk, sufficient-calorie vegetarian diet and not get enough protein (unless you're eating a one-food diet).[13] In fact, the nutritional content of your diet will most likely improve. Plants are much better sources of magnesium, vitamin E, potassium, phosphorous, Vitamin B-6, folic acid and linoleic acid, all of which are found abundantly in the supplementary protein combinations. Although most people think of meat as low in calories, because of meat's high fat content (fat provides more than twice as many calories per gram as carbohydrate does) and because non-meat protein combinations generally have a better NPU than meat, the calorie "cost" of these combinations compares favorably to an amount of meat equal in available protein. (See chart on page 178.)

THE "COST" OF MEAT PROTEIN

A benefit which does not accrue (at least directly) to the consumer but rather to the globe as a whole can be expressed in terms of earth space. There is now (according to U.N. FAO population and arable land figures) less than one-half acre of cultivated land on the globe per person, or conversely, each acre has to provide sufficient calories, nutrients, and most importantly, protein for 2½ people. It can be done, but it isn't.

Well-documented studies have established that a diet based primarily on animal protein sources (meats and milk) requires 3½ acres per person; a diet based on wheat protein requires only one-quarter acre; and a diet based on the combination of rice and beans (which is very similar to Japan's diet) needs only one-sixth acre per person.[14]

Aside from what it is *not*—wasteful of earth's resources —the vegetarian diet is attractive for what it *is:* it is less expensive, higher in fiber,[15] and lower in both saturated and total fats.[16]

179

LINGERING MEAT MYTHS

Hard though it is to believe, some authorities still claim that meat is essential to a healthful diet,[17] despite the fact that extensive studies of American vegetarians (both lacto-ovo and pure) have shown no evidence of nutritional deficiency.[18-20] In fact, the overall health of one large group of American lacto-ovo-vegetarians (in this study, Seventh Day Adventists) is better than that of comparable meat-eaters.[21]

In various clinical studies, vegetarians have been shown to have: lower serum cholesterol,[16, 22-4] lower serum triglycerides,[24] lower incidence of many cancers,[21] lower incidence of osteoporosis,[25] and a capacity for greater physical endurance.[26, 27] They also have their first heart attack ten years after the national average.[21] And next time you hear someone say it's impossible to live without meat, gently remind him/her that over 2 billion people do.

SOYBEANS

After 6,000 years' use in the Orient as an excellent protein source, soybeans have been discovered by Americans to have other food uses besides being turned into edible oil (or fed to livestock). The food technologists have even discovered them, and one can now find ersatz (soy) hamburger and imitation meat products made mainly from texturized soy on the shelves of most supermarkets.

Since those of us who may have grown up on pork 'n beans (or kidney beans, or lima beans) have little experience of soy beans, they are often thought of as "funny tasting"— usually by people who have never tasted one. Actually, they have practically no taste. If anything, they are blander than most beans. In fact, soybeans have to be cooked with some exciting spices or sauces to have any recognizable taste at all; otherwise they tend to sit in the pot adamantly ignoring the other ingredients—little blobs of blandness in an otherwise interesting dish.

Yet they are worth getting to know and love because of the quantity and high quality of their protein. With an NPU of 61, soybeans are almost exactly comparable to meat (NPU 67) in their protein availability. And they have a favorable nutrient balance: cooked soybeans have 7 times as much calcium as hamburger; 3 times as much thiamin, 2½ times as much potassium, and the same amount of iron. But soybeans have only half the calories and one-quarter the amount of fat—most of it unsaturated. They are also almost sodium-free. Defatted soy powder, which you should toss into everything that will stand still long enough, has more protein on a dry-weight basis than any other food.

Whatever else you choose to do (or not do) about protein complementarity, *always* follow the soybean rule: to *every* grain you cook, however you cook it, add two tablespoons of soy grits (or granules) per cup of grain. And to *every* cup of wheat flour, whether for cakes, cookies, thickening or whatever, add 1 tablespoon of soy powder (full fat has more essential fatty acids but low- or de-fatted has more protein)— unless you use the Triple Rich Formula everywhere—in which case you're going one better. And learn to substitute soybeans for other kinds of beans in whatever favorite bean dishes you ordinarily make.

» Soybeans (Pressure Cooked)

Analysis	Calories	CHO	Fat	Protein	GUP	Iron	Calcium
One Cup	260	22g	11g	22g	13.4g	5.4mg	146mg

Yield: 6 cups cooked soybeans

3 c soybeans
1 tsp basil (or other herb, opt)

5 c water
1 tsp-1 Tb oil

Do *not* soak soybeans you're going to pressure cook: The few minutes extra cooking time will be amply repaid in lessened flatulence. That's also what the basil is there for— it may not work (I've never seen a controlled study on the subject, but just in case it does . . .). Use *no* salt because it toughens the soybeans and the last thing you need is a tougher soybean. They are the toughest bean to cook, requiring 45 minutes to the baked-bean (i.e. holds its shape) stage, and 1 hour to the ready-for-mashing stage. The oil is extremely important since it helps prevent the soy skins from clogging the steam vent. Cook at 15 pounds pressure.

» Soybeans (Not Pressure Cooked)

Start 4 days in advance. On the first day, soak the soybeans for 12 hours in enough water to keep them covered —or about twice as much as there are beans. They swell a lot, so put them in a big enough container. The second day, freeze them in their soaking water (this helps tenderize them—a decided benefit). Then cook them with whatever spices the recipe calls for (at an active simmer for the next two days)—but you'll never be able to mash them. See what I mean about the pressure cooker?

» Baked Beans

Analysis	Calories	CHO	Fat	Protein	GUP	Iron	Calcium
Serving	380	41g	14g	28g	17g	9.3mg	284mg

Yield: 5 servings

cooked soybeans (2 c raw)
1 lg onion, coarse dice
2 Tb dry mustard
3 Tb Worcestershire sauce
¼ tsp ground cumin
¼ tsp ground coriander

3-4 Tb blackstrap molasses
¼ tsp cayenne
2 tsp vinegar
3 cloves garlic, chopped
2 dashes ground ginger
3 oz. tomato paste or ketchup

Combine all ingredients (boil down excess soybean liquid until it is reduced to a syrup). Bake as long as possible to mingle flavors. A 250° oven for about an hour is fine. Check to see if it needs a few tablespoons added liquid.

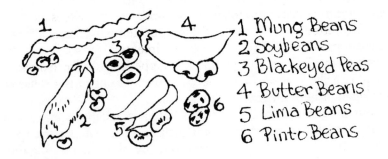

1 Mung Beans
2 Soybeans
3 Blackeyed Peas
4 Butter Beans
5 Lima Beans
6 Pinto Beans

» Soy Cheese (Tofu)

Analysis	Calories	CHO	Fat	Protein	GUP	Iron	Calcium
3½ oz:	72	2.4g	4.2g	7.8g	5.1g	1.9mg	128mg

(Analysis for commercial tofu)

Soak soybeans overnight (proportions don't matter much). Next day, blend soybeans with about 3 times as much water in a blender for at least one full minute blending time per cup of beans. Repeat, filling and emptying blender jar as often as necessary to accommodate beans. Drain (through a cheesecloth, unbleached muslin or clean old diaper) the soy milk from the mash. This will take some time and a strong wrist. Boil the soy milk for ten minutes. Watch carefully since it loves to boil over unexpectedly. Off heat, stir in epsom salts dissolved in a little cold water (about ¾ tsp salts per cup of beans). Let this stand several minutes; at least 15, or until you can see the whey separating. (Longer doesn't hurt —you can go away and forget it until it cools, if you like.) Then drain again. What's left in the drain-cloth this time is very high protein soy cheese. It can be sautéed, used in Chinese stir-fry recipes, or eaten plain, as in a salad. In a dish like Lasagna, it could be substituted for part of the cottage cheese. Chuck the whey—it has most of the epsom salts.

» Soybean Curry

Analysis	Calories	CHO	Fat	Protein	GUP	Iron	Calcium
Serving:	274	24g	13g	18g	12g	3.6mg	248mg

Yield: Serves 8 as a soup; more as a sauce.

1½ c raw soybeans, cooked
2-3 Tb butter
2 medium onions
1 tsp turmeric
1 tsp paprika
1 tsp ground coriander
¼ tsp ginger
¼ tsp cayenne
1 tsp salt
1 quart yoghurt

1 28-oz. can tomatoes
wine or lemon juice
Condiments:
  chopped apple or banana
  raisins or currants or dates
  coconut
  chopped nuts
  chopped green pepper or
  onion

Melt butter, sauté onion (maybe some garlic?). Add spices, sauté briefly. Add yoghurt, making a medium-thick sauce. Add tomatoes, soybeans; add seasoning as desired. Let simmer as long as possible for flavors to blend. Serve, either as a soup or over a bed of cooked grain, with as many condiments as possible.

» Mexican Beans (Frijoles Refritos)

Yield: Makes filling for about 2 dozen tostadas.

cooked soybeans (2 cups raw)
2 Tb oil (or lard)
1 lg onion, coarse dice
4 cloves garlic, chopped
2 canned peeled chilis (or fresh)
3-4 oz. tomato paste
1-2 Tb chili powder

1 Tb salt (or more)
½ tsp cayenne
2 Tb butter (or lard)
1½ tsp cumin
cheese (approx. 1 c cheddar or jack)
bean liquid as necessary

Sauté onion and garlic in oil (lard is traditional) about 3 minutes, then add chili (this amount is *not* hot, only tasty —add more if you like). Slightly mash the cooked drained (reserve liquid) soybeans into the oil and onion a cup at a time. Add a little bean liquid as necessary to keep the beans moist but not soupy. Continue adding and mashing beans until all are used. The point is to have a thick, fairly smooth consistency. If you prefer, use the blender to purée beans. Add the tomato paste, salt, cumin, cayenne (or red pepper), and cook until thick but not dry (add liquid if necessary). When ready to serve, stir in cheese, cubed or grated, and butter or lard. You can stir in half the cheese and sprinkle with other half, if desired.

» Tostadas (Using Mexican Beans)

1 dozen tortillas
chopped lettuce (approx. 2 cups)
chopped tomatoes (approx. 1 cup)
chopped onion

'taco sauce' bottled, made with tomatoes and chilis, hot or mild
oil
1 c Guacamole (opt)
½ recipe Frijoles (see above)
additional grated cheese

184

Fry the tortillas in an inch of oil about 2 minutes on each side, or until slightly brown and crisp. Keep in a warming oven (200°) on paper towels until all are done. Put the lettuce, tomatoes, onion, taco sauce, (olives if you like them) in individual serving dishes on the table. Heat the refried beans and put them out too. Serve the warm tortillas and let each person make his own tostada: a layer of beans on a crisp tortilla topped with choice of salad, then cheese and optional guacamole. If desired, add a spoon of "taco sauce."

» Soybean Chili

Analysis	Calories	CHO	Fat	Protein	GUP	Iron	Calcium
Serving:	400	41g	16g	25g	13.4g	7.4mg	169mg

Yield: 10 servings

2 c soybean, raw (4 c cooked)
½ c bulghur wheat
½ c unflavored vegetarian "burger"
4 Tb olive oil
5 cloves garlic
2 large onions
2 28-oz. cans tomatoes with liquid
6 oz. tomato paste
pinch cayenne

1 bay leaf
2 Tb + chili powder
2 tsp salt +
1 Tb paprika
1 tsp ground cumin
1 tsp rosemary
1 tsp oregano
¼ tsp cloves
½ tsp pepper
cheese (2 Tb grated per person)

If vege "burger" is unavailable, use double the amount of bulghur wheat. Soak wheat and/or "burger" in about 1½ cups water while assembling rest of ingredients. Sauté onions and garlic in olive oil. Add rest of ingredients. Simmer 10 minutes to 1 hour.

» Felafel

To call this crisp, lemony-spicy dish a Middle Eastern bean ball is to do it no justice at all. It is consumed in the Middle East like the hot dog once was on the streets of New York: venders offer Felafel stuffed into fresh Pita, an optional handful of greenery and a splash of sesame-seed dressing. Not even much-treasured childhood memories of the smell of hot sauerkraut wafting from the pushcart under the yellow and blue umbrella can compare.

Analysis	Calo-ries	CHO	Fat	Pro-tein	CUP	Iron	Cal-cium
Serving:	39	6.4g	.7g	2g	1.4g	.72mg	15mg

Yield: 40 felafels

1 20-oz. can garbanzo beans or 1 c dry beans pressure cooked for 30 mins.
½ c bulghur
8 large cloves garlic
2 tsp ground cumin
⅓-½ c lemon juice
½ c wheat germ

at least ½ c chopped fresh parsley
2 tsp salt or more
¼ tsp cayenne
2 eggs
1 tsp paprika
2-4 Tb wholewheat flour
1 tsp baking powder (opt)

Drain cooked or canned garbanzos; put in blender. Add eggs and a few Tb lemon juice and blend; it is not necessary or even desireable to have a completely smooth purée—just get the big lumps out. Meanwhile, soak the bulghur in the rest of the lemon juice—add a spoon or so of water if necessary to barely cover. Blend in the garlic, parsely and spices. Stir everything else together. Start with the smaller amount of flour; add more only if your first felafel tends to fall apart in the oil. The baking powder is optional but makes a lighter, less doughy felafel. Deep fry for 3-4 minutes at 375°. They may be kept in a warming oven until all are done, but best served sizzling hot. If you prefer not to deep-fry, oil a skillet and make thin patties. Traditionally served in a hot, split pita with cucumbers, tomatoes, lettuce or what-have-you and topped with either hot sauce or sesame dressing. (See recipe index for Sesame Dressing.)

» Moors (Black Beans) & Christians (Rice)

Analysis	Calo-ries	CHO	Fat	Pro-tein	GUP	Iron	Cal-cium
Serving:	213	31g	7g	7.6g	4.3g	2.5mg	59mg

Yield: 8 servings

2 c black beans
2 quarts water
2 bay leaves
4 ribs celery
2 onions, chopped
2-3 cloves garlic
large dash clove
1 tsp American saffron (or
few threads real)

10 red pepper seeds
½ tsp Dijon mustard
1 tsp salt +
2 Tb butter worked with 3
Tb whole wheat flour until
smooth
2 Tb oil

If you have no pressure cooker, soak beans in water overnight, then simmer with spices until tender—about 2 hours. Otherwise, combine beans, water, spices, and pressure cook at maximum pressure about 25 minutes. Meanwhile, sauté onions, garlic and celery in oil. When beans are tender, add to vegetables. Blend flour and butter with a little bean liquid and whisk this into beans. Simmer to thicken. Serve over steamed rice.

VARIATIONS:

1. Use 3 quarts water, serve as soup.
2. Garnish with chopped onion and chopped parsley.
3. Serve with chopped hardboiled egg or cottage cheese—improves protein considerably (if this is to be main dish).

» Bean and/or Grain Patties (in General)

Almost any bean and/or grain can be turned into delectable patties. This is especially useful when you have some of each left over, but not enough of either to be a meal by itself. As long as the beans are fairly dry, they can be mashed and will act as binder to hold the grain together. Lentils are especially good, since they tend to stick together anyway. By adding various sautéed vegetables, nuts or seeds, herbs and spices, you can create your own *specialité de la maison*. The chances are that without even thinking about it, you'll have complemented the protein enough to make the dish comparable to hamburger. And you'll have used up leftovers to boot!

If your first few patties won't hold together, try adding egg as binder. If all else fails, turn the whole thing into an oiled pan and bake as a loaf. Be sure to serve loaves with some kind of sauce, however, since they otherwise tend to be fairly dry. Each cup of grain/bean combo will make 4-6 patties.

» Cheese Surprise Patties

Analysis	Calories	CHO	Fat	Protein	GUP	Iron	Calcium
1 patty:	199	19g	8g	11.4g	7.7g	2.1mg	182mg

Yield: 12 patties

12 oz. pkg. kidney beans
4½ c water
1 bay leaf
1 4-oz. can chilis, chopped
3 cloves garlic, pressed
1 tsp salt +

2 Tb minced onion
1 tsp chili powder
1 tsp cumin, ground
½ lb cheese
2 Tb oil

Pressure cook beans in water with bay leaf for 30 mins. Reduce pressure. Water should be almost completely absorbed; if not, drain beans, then mash. Divide cheese in half: grate one part, cut the other into 12 cubes. Reserve cubes, add remaining ingredients to mashed beans. Pick up about 1 Tb bean mixture, press a cheese cube into it, then cover with another Tb or so bean mixture. Roll in moistened hands to completely cover cheese cube. There should be about 12 bean balls (2½" in diameter). Heat 1 Tb oil in a large skillet. Put half the bean balls in, pressing down lightly into a patty shape. Fry until browned, turn and do other side. Repeat with remaining oil and patties. Patties may be kept warm in oven. May be served as is, or with tomato sauce, or even ketchup. Each patty has a melted cheese "surprise" in its center. If desired, patties may be rolled in sesame seeds just before frying; or they may be baked on a lightly oiled cookie sheet.

IX

Saucery and Other Magic

Beetle Bailey

ONCE YOU CAN make white sauce, a simple thing in itself, you can also make cheese sauces, soufflés, croquettes, gratinées and all the wonderful dishes which are essentially just variations on a theme.

Standard white sauce recipes caution that careful cooking is necessary to dispel a gluey, uncooked flour taste. What they neglect to mention is that only white flour produces an unpleasantly raw taste. Wholewheat "white" sauce is therefore even simpler to make, and tastes much better—it actually has flavor and is not merely a bland thick background with no character of its own.

Classical white sauce recipes are expressed in proportions of fat and flour to milk (or other liquid, occasionally). Increasing the proportion of flour (and of necessity the fat to cook it in) makes a thicker sauce. A little more wholewheat flour (than white flour) is necessary to achieve the various thicknesses. That's because white flour is almost pure starch, hence has more thickening power. To convert a white flour sauce recipe to wholewheat, increase the amount of flour called for by about one-half. You will have to increase the fat somewhat as well. (See Appendix for general substitution rules.)

White sauce recipes call for cooking the fat and flour (*roux*) together without browning—impossible with the whole flour which starts with a lovely tan. Just cook about two minutes, or until the *roux* smells nut-like.

As with all flour-thickened sauces, the problem is to avoid lumps. Here are some suggestions to choose from: heat the milk or other liquid before it is added to the *roux*. (Since I am lazy and hate to wash out an extra milky pan, I rarely do this.) Remove the pan (with *roux)* from the heat before the milk is added. Use a wire whip and stir like a madman

190

all over the pan, especially at the beginning, while slowly adding the liquid. If all else fails and it looks like oatmeal, throw the whole thing into the blender, zap it for a few seconds, then return it to the pan and pretend nothing happened. It'll be as smooth as silk (and no one will ever know).

Another major problem (with a simple solution) is trying to prevent cheese from curdling when it it is added to sauce. Simply add cheese last, then turn off the heat immediately letting the retained heat of the sauce melt the cheese. Reheat cheese sauces at your own risk. Cheese curdles quickly at temperatures well below simmering.

Sauces

» Basic White (Tan) Sauce

Analysis	Calo-ries	CHO	Fat	Pro-tein	GUP	Iron	Cal-cium
1¼ cups:	344	25g	23g	11.2g	8.7g	.6mg	311mg

Yield: about 1¼ cups sauce

2 Tb butter   1 c milk
2-3 Tb wholewheat flour   salt and pepper

Melt butter; when bubbling add flour. Cook over medium heat for 2-3 minutes until flour is lightly browned and smells slightly nut-like. This is called a *roux. Either* scald milk and add to *roux* all at once, stirring; *or* add cold milk slowly, stirring constantly (preferably with a wire whip). Add salt and pepper, and nutmeg if you like.

» Cheese Sauce

Cheese sauce, with or without the wine, is the basis of most non-sweet soufflés. Either one is delicious served over barely steamed vegetables like zucchini, broccoli, cauliflower. A cheese sauce plus some sautéed mushrooms and whatever leftover vegetables you find lurking make a fine filling for entrée crêpes. It can also be the base for macaroni and cheese or scalloped potatoes.

Analysis	Calo-ries	CHO	Fat	Pro-tein	GUP	Iron	Cal-cium
1½ cups:	568	26g	41g	25.2g	18.5g	1.2mg	733mg

Yield: Approx. 1½ cups

To Basic White Sauce, add:

½ c grated cheese   ¼ tsp dry mustard
¼ tsp paprika

   Remove from heat. If cheese sauce is overheated, it will curdle; heat of sauce is usually enough to melt cheese. If necessary, heat *very* carefully stirring until cheese melts.

VARIATION:

To Cheese Sauce add:

¼ c dry white wine (sherry or vermouth)

   If you plan to make this wine sauce, it may insure a sufficiently thick end product if you either increase the flour in the original white sauce by 1 Tb or reduce the milk by ¼ cup.

» Italian Tomato Sauce

Analysis	Calo-ries	CHO	Fat	Pro-tein	GUP	Iron	Cal-cium
Serving:	90	13g	3.7g	2.5g	1.3g	1.8mg	25mg

Yield: 10 cups Sauce

3 Tb butter or olive oil
2-3 stalks celery
2-3 carrots
1 lg onion
3-4 cloves garlic
½ c water or wine
2 28-oz. cans tomatoes

2-3 6-oz. cans tomato paste
at least 1 Tb mixed herbs:
   marjoram, oregano, basil,
   parsley, bay
salt, pepper, yeast extract
other vegetables (not ana-
   lysed for)

   Sauté chopped celery, carrots, onions and garlic in oil or butter. Butter is usually for milk-based soups; olive oil is usually for tomato-based soups or sauces—but you may do as you prefer. When everything smells incredible and the sautéeing vegetables are beginning to stick to the pan and brown slightly—not burn— deglaze with water or wine: add the liquid and scrape the pan to add any stuck-in bits into the vegetables. Add the tomatoes and part of the paste. Add the seasonings. Let simmer at least 15 minutes, then taste and adjust seasonings. Add more tomato paste, as necessary, to give the desired thickness. Other vegetables which may be added include: okra—makes fantastic gumbo base; zucchini or other summer squash; green beans; eggplant—great on pizza; parsnip. Large families should double this recipe and store the extra.

» Mexican Tomato Sauce

Yield: 5 cups Sauce

2 Tb olive oil	1 tsp salt
2 c onions, chopped	1 tsp cumin
6 cloves garlic	1 tsp oregano
1 c celery—2 stalks, chopped	½ tsp ground coriander
1 c carrots—2 small, chopped	1 or more canned green chilis
1 28-oz. can tomatoes	(opt)
2 Tb chili powder	

Sauté vegetables in oil. Add everything else. If hotter sauce is desired, one or more canned green chilis can be added to sautéeing vegetables.

» Enchilada Sauce

Yield: about 5 cups Sauce

Ingredients above plus: ½ c wine
6 Tb wholewheat flour

When Mexican Tomato Sauce is done, add flour and whizz in blender for a few seconds: you don't want a complete purée, but you do want to get rid of the biggest lumps of vegetable. Return to pot, add wine and cook. At that point, stir in the other enchilada filling ingredients (see index for Enchilada recipe).

» Handmade Mayonnaise

Analysis	Calo-ries	CHO	Fat	Pro-tein	GUP	Iron	Cal-cium
Yield:	1894	2.6g	210g	5.8g.	5.4g	1.8mg	50mg

2 egg yolks
½ tsp salt
dash cayenne
½ tsp dry (or Dijon) mustard

2 Tb lemon juice (or vinegar)
1 c oil
½ tsp sugar (opt)

Egg yolks should be at room temperature. If not, warm bowl by running under hot water for a few minutes, then dry thoroughly. Beat egg yolks for about a minute with a wire whip (or hand beater) until thick and lemony. Add dry ingredients and about 1 Tb of lemon juice. Now, *beating constantly* (you don't have to beat very quickly, but you mustn't stop), add about ¼ c of oil, in dribblets. When the emulsion has thickened, you can stop beating and rest for a moment. It may take a little more or less than ¼ c to reach that point, but keep going until you do. Then beat in rest of the oil in dollops. Put in jar and refrigerate.

Dressings and Dips

» Basic Mayonnaise Dressing

Analysis	Calo-ries	CHO	Fat	Pro-tein	GUP	Iron	Cal-cium
Per Tb:	28	1.5g	2.3g	.5g	.4g	—	17mg

1 c yoghurt
⅔ c mayonnaise

juice of 1 lemon
salt

Shake well.

» Coleslaw Dressing

Mayonnaise dressing plus:

½ tsp celery salt
1 tsp Worcestershire sauce
1 tsp bottled taco sauce (opt)

1 tsp dry or Dijon-type
   mustard

   Combine.

» Louis Dressing

Mayonnaise Dressing plus:

1 tsp Worcestershire sauce
1 sm onion, minced
additional lemon juice
few drops hot sauce

1 clove garlic—minced or
   pressed
1 sm tomato (opt)
¼ c chopped green pepper

   If tomato is used, whizz briefly in blender. Otherwise shake well to combine.

» Roquefort Dressing

Mayonnaise Dressing or Coleslaw Dressing plus:

2-3 oz crumbled Roquefort
   or Bleu cheese

   Shake well—do not blend.

VARIATION:

To any of the above, increase the yoghurt, decrease the mayonnaise proportionately; or use some or all cottage cheese, blended until smooth, in place of as much yoghurt.

» Lemonette Dressing

Juice of 1½ lemons—about
2½ Tb
Twice as much olive—or
other—oil, about 5 Tb
½ tsp dry or Dijon-type
mustard

salt, pepper
few grains cayenne (opt)
1-2 cloves garlic, pressed (opt)
1-2 Tb fresh grated Parmesan
cheese (opt)
½ tsp anchovy paste (opt)

Yield: about ½ cup; enough for 4-6 cups salad greens.

Combine everything just before you're ready to use. Shake in a jar for about 10 seconds. Increase the oil or lemon juice to taste. A teaspoon of fresh or a pinch of dried herbs may be added, too. Do not let this dressing sit with dried herbs, however—they get strong and bitter.

» Eggplant Guacamole

Analysis	Calo-ries	CHO	Fat	Pro-tein	GUP	Iron	Cal-cium
Yield:	398	26g	33g	6.2g	3.1g	3mg	65mg

about 2 c eggplant pulp
3 Tb minced onion
2 Tb olive oil
3-4 cloves garlic, pressed
½ tsp each salt and pepper
1 tsp chopped green chili
1 tsp + "taco" sauce

juice of ½ lemon
1 tsp mayonnaise
½ tsp + ground cumin
2 Tb toasted sesame seeds
(opt)
fried tortilla chips (opt)

For eggplant pulp, bake whole eggplants—about 1 large or 2 medium—in 350° oven for one hour, or until quite soft and skin crackles to the touch. Remove pulp with spoon and discard skins. Sauté minced onion in olive oil; add to eggplant. Press garlic right into eggplant. Add everything but seeds and chips; adjust seasoning. May be served in place of Avocado Guacamole; this recipe has fewer calories. May be sprinkled with toasted sesame seeds, or served with tortilla chips or garlic toast.

» Hummos or Chummus
(Garbanzo bean dip)

This Middle Eastern dish is enjoyed by both Arabs and Israelis: on *some* things, they agree.

Yield: 3 cups

1 20-oz can garbanzos or
2 c cooked garbanzos
3-4 lemons
1-2 Tb olive oil
1 sm *head* garlic
½ tsp + salt
1 tsp cumin (opt)

1 tsp paprika (opt)
⅛ tsp cayenne (opt)
¼ c tahini or sesame butter
additional olive oil and lemon
juice
raw vegetables, sliced

Drain garbanzos, reserve juice. Blend garbanzos using as little reserved bean liquid as possible. Home cooked garbanzos do not blend as easily as canned, but they blend best when still slightly warm. To avoid an "over-beany" taste, use some of the lemon juice for blending in place of some of the bean liquid. When the beans are fairly smooth blend in the garlic, lemon juice, oil and spices. This makes a fairly spicy dip—decrease or omit the spices as desired. The garlic flavor will increase on standing—you may wish to use less and allow to "ripen" before using the whole amount. To serve: drizzle with a small additional amount of olive oil and lemon juice. Serve with vegetable "dippers."

» Bagdoncia

You have to love garlic to like this one. Arabs eat it for breakfast. The rest of us might be more comfortable with it as an appetizer. A tablespoon or so may be added to any ordinary salad dressing; even people who don't think they like parsley will love it.

Analysis	Calo-ries	CHO	Fat	Pro-tein	CUP	Iron	Cal-cium
Yield:	635	63g	39.4g	28.1g	14.5g	29.4mg	1539mg

Yield: 2-3 cups

2 c very tightly packed parsley clusters—about 40
stems
1 c fresh lemon juice

½ c sesame butter or tahini
1 tsp salt
8 cloves garlic

To get clusters of parsley, break off the main stem where it divides—this part is very pithy and if left on will make stringy Bagdoncia. Put the lemon juice, salt, garlic and half the sesame butter in the blender; blend until smooth. Add the parsley, a handful at a time. You may have to turn the blender on and off and push the parsley back into the blade action. When all the parsley has been added, add the rest of the sesame butter.

» Sesame Seed Dressing
("Sesammaise")

4 Tb tahini or sesame butter
½ c liquid, approx. half
water, half lemon juice,
adjust to taste

¼ c freshly chopped parsley
optional: pressed garlic, dash
cayenne, paprika, ground
cumin

Stir liquid into sesame butter or tahini; it will form a smooth, thick paste. Stir in parsley and any or all optional ingredients. You may need salt if unsalted tahini is used. Use over felafel, on broiled eggplant, or as a substitute for mayonnaise on sandwiches. May also be used as salad dressing.

Beverages

» Fruit "Soda"

⅔ c grape juice (the best you ⅓ c carbonated water
  can afford)

    Mix—tastes a lot like grape soda.

Or:
1 can orange juice concentrate
3 times as much carbonated
  water or part water and
  part carbonated.

    Mix. This only works well if there's enough call for orange soda to use it up almost at once; otherwise it goes 'flat.' For smaller amounts, reconstitute frozen juice with ⅔ to ½ the water called for. When "soda" is desired, add carbonated water to proper dilution.

» Thick Shake

Analysis	Calories	CHO	Fat	Protein	GUP	Iron	Calcium
½ recipe:	158	23g	.3g	15.4g	12.5g	1.7mg	523mg

Yield: 2 lg glasses

1½ c milk   1 tsp vanilla
½ c milk powder   6-10 ice cubes
3 Tb malted milk powder—   2 Tb honey (opt)
  unflavored   flavoring or fruit

    Combine ingredients in a blender until fairly smooth. Adjust sweetening and malt to taste. More ice cubes make a thicker shake, but if you let it melt, it gets very watery. For flavoring you may use de-caffinated instant coffee, plain Ovaltine, a *small* amount of chocolate syrup, additional vanilla, carob powder, etc. If you can, get real fruit syrups at the health food store and add fresh fruit too. Some people claim success with a date-coconut shake! On special occasions, you can even put in a little ice cream.

X
The Waistland

It is wrong to imagine that the ill effects of a large intake of sugar lie solely in the fact that it contributes nothing but calories to the diet, and thus would become a wholesome food if it were simply "fortified" with nutrients such as vitamins and mineral elements. This assumption entirely ignores the deleterious effects of sucrose itself on the organism.
—John Yudkin, *Senate Hearings on the Role of Sugar in Diet, Diabetes and Heart Disease,* April, 1973

You've probably heard all about that white powdery stuff that causes addiction: it's called sugar. The fact that sugar is empty calories is only the frosting on the cake (more about cakes and frosting later). New research is disclosing that today's relentless sugar consumption—120 pounds per year for every American man, woman, and child, according to government figures—is implicated in the rising incidence of several diseases plaguing modern Western civilization. Sugar is linked with everything from elevated blood lipid levels and heart disease to diabetes and obesity; to say nothing of tooth decay which costs Americans more than $4 billion annually —a sum equal to that spent on carbonated beverages during the same period.

Dr. Thomas J. Cleave has written a comprehensive overview of the problems caused by sugar (and the other major refined carbohydrate, white flour). During Senate hearings on *The Role of Sugar in Diet, Diabetes, and Heart Disease,* Dr. Cleave outlined his theory of the "Saccharine Disease."*

THE SACCHARINE DISEASE

The refining of carbohydrates affects the body in three ways. First, through concentration: refining removes a large part of the original foodstuff, leaving behind only sucrose, in the case of beet or sugar cane, or starch, in the case of wheat. This concentration or "packing" leads to overconsumption, causing diabetes, obesity and, indirectly, coronary thrombosis. Second, the refining of carbohydrates removes fiber, causing tooth decay and gum disease as well as diverticulitis, etc. (see Chapter VI). And third, refining removes

---

*Saccharine, derived from the Greek word for sugar, is pronounced to rhyme with the River Rhine, to distinguish it from the artificial sweetener.

201

protein, causing peptic ulcers.[1] Recent research by other scientists has vindicated much of Dr. Cleave's startling claims.[2-8]

CONCENTRATION

When whole grains are refined, most of the calories are retained (few of the nutrients, however) but 30% of the volume is lost: white flour contains only 70% of the original wheat. Sugar is even more "packed". It is eight times more concentrated than white flour. The average daily intake of sugar (5 oz.) is refined from a sugar beet the size of your head—about 2½ pounds. Severely reducing bulk through refining encourages overconsumption. Who could eat over two pounds of beets per day—or having eaten that, eat anything else? The feeling of fullness—which is necessary for the body to know it has had enough—is missing, even though more than enough calories are being supplied.

Taste bud titillation is essential for satisfaction, too. The nature of sugar and white flour products—light, airy, melt-in-your-mouth—makes them easier to eat quickly or to merely swallow, and the calories are already on their way to digestion before the taste buds have been gratified. Chewing an unrefined food allows "mouth hunger" to be satisfied before a disproportionate number of calories have been consumed.

REMOVAL OF FIBER

The concentration of refined carbohydrates is achieved by removing fiber, water, and nutrients. Overconsumption is only one result of this removal. Without fiber, the need to chew is drastically reduced. (Before the Industrial Revolution, it was a lot harder to "eat and run".) Without the gum exercise of chewing, periodontal disease develops. In addition, refining removes the tooth enamel-sparing phosphates present in the whole grain.[8] While the gums work less, the intestine works more. Without the bulk of indigestible water-retaining fiber, the muscles of the intestine strain and herniate; the prolonged intestinal transit time of compacted fecal matter may allow cancer-causing substances additional time to act.[4, 6]

CARBOHYDRATES AND HISTORY

Though at first it seems hardly credible that foods so

widely eaten and enjoyed can be so detrimental to health, one must realize that only in the last hundred years or so have they accounted for a significant part of the human diet.

Unrefined carbohydrates have been around since the dawn of time in the form of wild fruits and grasses. When agriculture began, production and consumption of unrefined carbohydrates increased until they became staples of most diets. Only since the mid-1800's, however, has it become possible to remove and refine out the fiber and nutritional "impurities" of these formerly natural foods. The body's systems for energy metabolism (including the pancreas) are designed to handle slowly absorbed carbohydrates, limited by their bulk to small quantities at any one time.

Rapidly absorbed carbohydrates—sugar and white flour —enter the system in massive amounts, molecularly speaking, putting strain on the pancreas (see Chapter III). Researchers have suggested that it is the consistent consumption of sugars in this unnatural form that may be responsible for the "initial lesion" of diabetes.[9]

REMOVAL OF NUTRIENTS

The emptiness of refined carbohydrate calories is not *just* the loss of a few nutrients. Some of them are not so easily replaced. When sugar is processed from beet or cane, chromium and other important micronutrients are removed. But chromium is essential for carbohydrate metabolism; the removal of chromium from carbohydrate foods eventually leads to a negative balance or deficiency. This has been verified by comparing populations with differing amounts of refined carbohydrate intake. In the tissues of most non-Americans, the body burden of chromium remains constant throughout life; in Americans, it falls almost continuously after birth. In twice as many American as foreign tissues, there was no detectable chromium at all. Animal studies have shown that chromium can lower serum cholesterol;[7] human studies have indicated that chromium insufficiency may play an as yet unidentified role in the hows and whys of diabetes and atherosclerosis.[2, 3]

IS DIABETES GENETIC?

One of Dr. Cleave's more startling conclusions is that diabetes is not, strictly speaking, caused by a genetic defect. He offers this analogy: taller men were more likely to be killed in WWI because they made bigger targets. If a tall man's son was subsequently killed in WWII, it would make no sense to say that his inherited tallness had killed him; rather, a bullet killed him. In the same way, although an individual's pancreas may be susceptible to the diabetic manifestation of the Saccharine Disease, it would be equally wrong to say that his inherited pancreatic weakness *caused* diabetes; sugar caused it.

To support this thesis, Dr. Cleave points to societies that have had practically zero incidence of diabetes: Zulu, Bantu, Eskimo, and Yemenite. Yet, within twenty years of changing to a refined carbohydrate diet, their incidence of diabetes closely parallels (or even surpasses) that in most Western countries. A disease caused by a genetic defect would not make this quantum jump.

Another important researcher on diabetes, Dr. Aharon Cohen, does not rule out heredity; but he too considers diet to be the precipitating factor. His work with immigrant and settled Yemenite Jews underscores the role of sugar in causing diabetes. Dr. Cohen's study compared 5,000 immigrant Yemenite Jews who had no appreciable incidence of diabetes (three cases) with settled Yemenites of the same racial and genetic stock who had been living in Israel for 25 years. The settled Yemenites' incidence of diabetes was equivalent to 150 cases out of 5,000. An analysis of the difference in diet between the immigrant and the settled Yemenites showed that the greatest change had occurred in the carbohydrate source—there were only slight changes in protein and fats: immigrant Yemenites ate lightly ground whole grains, settled Yemenites ate more refined flour and ten times as much sugar.[10, 11]

To test the diabetes-sugar connection, Dr. Cohen used two groups of genetically selected rats. One group was predisposed to diabetes, the other group was decidedly normal. By altering the carbohydrate component (72% of the diet) Dr. Cohen could either produce (with all sugar) or inhibit (with all starch) the onset of diabetes. While no normal

204

human diet would contain 72% sugar, Dr. Cohen also induced diabetes in genetically pre-disposed rats with a diet containing only 25% sugar—which is comparable to the average American sugar consumption. In Senate testimony on the role of sugar in diabetes and other diseases, Dr. Cohen suggested limiting consumption of refined sugar to 5% of the carbohydrates—or about 1 Tb per day.

SUGAR

It's not enough to just limit digging in the sugar bowl. Three-quarters of the sugar consumed in America is in processed foods—some obviously sweet (candy, carbonated beverages, and cakes), some quite subtle (soups, bread, pickles). One half-cup serving of most canned fruits or one ounce of most children's breakfast cereals (the "recommended" serving) has the entire day's suggested limit of one Tb of sugar. Other prime offenders are cola with 1 Tb in 4 ounces, and Jello with almost 2 Tb in ½ cup.[12] Your best defense then is to read product labels and avoid foods containing sugar or any of its disguises: glucose, dextrose, corn syrup, sugar.

KIDS AND KANDY

You'll find that the greatest number of products that contain sugar as a primary ingredient (in first or second place on the ingredient panel) are aimed at children. Even if you've been aware of the potentially harmful effects of too much junk food, especially on children, it seems that everything conspires to ruin your healthful eating patterns. The kids next·door all seem to live on sugar; grandma looks lovingly at baby and assures you "it's just a little piece;" and holidays and birthdays fall with insidious regularity, just after you've almost convinced everyone they can live without Gooey Bars and Nause-Ade. Most Home Economics classes still center their cooking experiences around cakes; and the Type A school lunch wouldn't be complete without its chocolate brownie or peach slices in heavy syrup.

There is an answer—several answers, actually—but it takes a certain amount of conviction, willingness to cooperate, and change in your own patterns. If there's junk food in the house, it's going to become an issue.

It's much simpler *not to have it around*. Then there's

no issue: you can't be asked for what you don't have. Surprisingly enough, kids, particularly young kids, won't ask you to buy junk either, unless you take them shopping, which can be a big mistake. They seem to think that if it doesn't appear in their very own kitchen cupboard, it's because it doesn't grow there, and that's that.

Which is not to say that children never get treats. But "treat" is a state of mind—if you offer a child a carrot stick with a wavering eye and a fearful demeanor because you *know* he's going to prefer something you're not willing to give him, he will "read" you and feel *insulted*. Whatever you do, though, it helps to start them young. Our own children really believe that fruit is the best thing since Sunday, despite the fact they've been exposed to their share of junk by now.

Holidays seem to present special problems. For Halloween, the paradigm "crud" festival, our entire family conferred about each person's desires and needs, and in the end hit on a unique solution. The children went out trick-or-treating (and got to dress up and go door-to-door, which is the fun part, anyway) but agreed that when they got home they would throw out most of their candy, especially the nothing-but-sugar-additives-and-dyes confections. They kept a few small pieces and everyone was satisfied. Easter Egg hunters can hunt for real eggs instead of jelly beans—or even nuts and raisins if you say it with a straight face. Children's prejudices are usually set by their parents; if *you* feel you are depriving them, *they* will feel deprived.

GRANDPARENTS

Unless you grew up in a home where candy was anathema, chances are the grandparents act as though they're your child's only link with "normal" nutrition. Since you can't expect that they'll never feed your kids junk, we have found that it helps to suggest somewhat more acceptable treats: I'd rather have my kids eat "all-natural" ice cream than an all-day sucker; better a granola cookie than a chocolate-marshmallow pie; better a natural food store's (additiveless) high-protein candy bar than a box of jelly beans.

OLDER KIDS AND TEENS

If your kids have grown up from the cradle thinking that a green pepper was a snack and a handful of nuts was nirvana, you'll have fewer problems than if you suddenly decide you've been doing it all wrong and everyone is going to have to chew the party line. There's much less friction and a much greater chance of success if everyone discusses and enters into an agreement on the "new" diet and what each person's commitment is: you will have greater cooperation if you explain what you're trying to do—children are perfectly capable of understanding mounting dental bills as well as rudimentary nutrition.

The 12-18 year old male has the greatest caloric need of any group in the population. It is all too often satisfied by a succession of fast-food meals, empty calorie snacks, and carbonated beverages. This may be the hardest group of all to tackle, since the frequent adolescent-parent frictions may be exacerbated by a high-level decision about diet, as it has been in the past about hair and other things. All you can do is start buying and preparing more nutritious foods and hope that some of their friends are health food faddists.

DESSERT REALITIES

After having made as strong a case as possible—to try to counteract what is, for most people, a lifetime of exposure to junk food advertising—we will soften our stand somewhat to reflect the realities. Of course you're going to want dessert occasionally, but you will have to rethink your dessert and sweet eating patterns. You can start by kissing white sugar good-bye (and most of the myriad products made with it). If it is true that chromium deficiency is one of the contributing causes of the many diseases that can be traced to refined carbohydrate consumption, then there are possible substitutes for white sugar: dark brown sugar, honey, and molasses.[3, 7] Of these, molasses (third extraction or blackstrap) has the highest chromium concentration. It is also extremely high in iron and other vitamins and minerals. Molasses is the by-product of sugar-making and contains all the nutrients that were stripped from the sugar. Honey also contains chromium and some minerals and enzymes. The chances are that raw, un-filtered honey contains a better nutrient profile than the pasteurized stuff the supermarket sells. Dark brown sugar is the least desireable of these, but where the crystalline structure of the sugar is important to the final result (in creaming with butter for lightness), it has an advantage. On the other hand, in many cakes, honey and/or molasses can be successfully substituted by changing the proportions slightly.

None of this is meant to suggest that you can go on eating several desserts a week by changing the ingredients somewhat. Sugar—white, brown, honey, or molasses—still has no fiber, still provides too many relatively empty calories, and still figures prominently in obesity and tooth decay.

OVERWEIGHT

Vegetarians tend to weigh about 10 pounds less than carnivores of the same age; and pure vegetarians weigh about 10 pounds less than their egg-and-dairy-eating counterparts. But vegetarians come in all shapes and sizes; we're not all lean and ascetic-looking. We, Kathy and D'Ann, are most certainly not. (Who do you think tests all these recipes?) Yet, each of us weighs less now than we did when we ate the typical Western diet, despite the fact that we haven't counted calories in years. Which is not to say that vegetarians can never be fat; one long-time vegetarian friend's inordinate fondness for butter and sour cream more than made up for whatever calories he saved by not eating meat.

The principles upon which our diet is based, however, mesh neatly with Dr. Humphrey Sassoon's recommendations for an anti-obesity diet. "An optimal diet for man would supply restricted amounts of protein, and energy coming mainly from fats and slowly available starches."[13]

It's not just what you eat, it's what you do—or don't do. In one study of adolescents, obese girls ate fewer calories than girls of normal weight, but they were so much less active, they stayed fat.

TOOTH DECAY

Despite the fact that everyone seems to know sugar consumption leads to tooth decay, banks, doctors, and even some dentists routinely give out candy—lollipops to be exact, the favorite food of germs that cause tooth decay. And the notion that natural sweets are just as bad has finally been

208

put to rest: in one experiment, subjects fed sugar had significantly greater incidence of caries and more growth of caries-causing bacteria than subjects fed raisins, dried figs, dates, maple syrup, or honey. In fact, unrefined cereals contain enamel-sparing factors, and the exercise of chewing natural foods may itself produce some protective benefit.[14]

Dr Abraham E. Nizel, testifying before the Senate Select Committee on Nutrition and Human Needs, said:

> Every package of sugar-sweetened cough drops, breath mints, candies, chewing gum and soft drinks should be labeled with a statement that . . . these products can produce significant amounts of dental plaque and dental decay.

Dr. Howard Ausherman has neatly summed up the connection between excess sugar consumption and health: "Don't dig your grave with your [carious] teeth."[15]

"WHAT'S FOR DESSERT?"

The recipes that follow fall into two classes. Most are nutritious enough to be considered part of the meal—they're not just stuck on at the end. There are a few exceptions—for birthdays, for company, and sometimes for the fun of it.

Fruit desserts, provided they are not excessively sweetened, are the kind of desserts we most recommend. The simplest of all is to pass a bowl of fresh whole fruit at the table; few turn it down. If you're feeling more sophisticated, you can pass a bowl of nuts, or a platter of cheese, in the other direction.

After a light supper such as soup and salad, the nutrition of a slightly more elaborate fruit dessert might be welcome; you can get a surprising amount of protein from fruit with yoghurt or fruit with a complementary grain topping. Custard and its variations are high-protein desserts too, and children are especially fond of them. Cakes, even those with highly nutritious variations, should be made less often; they contain a lot of calories, fat, and carbohydrates.

For those dozen-or-so times a year (birthdays, holidays) when you don't particularly care how nutritious a dessert is as long as it's absolutely irresistible, we've included a few totally sinful recipes.

» Melon Basket

For a spectacular, non-junk dessert, go out and buy a melon-baller—less than $1—and make a watermelon basket. Begin by lightly scoring the pattern in the rind until you get the look you're after. If you think you can manage it, make a handle out of the rind, too. You can make pointy or scalloped edges if you're really in the mood. Make the depth of the basket roughly ⅔ of the whole melon—as it is, you'll have more melon balls than you can fit back into the melon basket. You can just scrape out and discard the parts that are wall-to-wall pits. But if you take the trouble to remove the pits you can make Watermelon Popsicles. Add any extra liquid to the popsicles, too.

If you also use honeydew or cantaloupe, the variegated balls make a gorgeous display. If you don't feel like bothering with the basket, you can get much the same effect with various colored balls in glass dessert dishes.

Only one "trick"—before you start planning the look of the basket, roll it around until you find its natural base; or cut a sliver to make the least attractive part of the melon flat enough to stand on. Otherwise your work of art may tilt annoyingly.

» Ambrosia

Analysis	Calories	CHO	Fat	Protein	GUP	Iron	Calcium
Serving:	185	41g	3g	3g	1.5g	2.7mg	61mg

Yield: 6 servings

3 medium bananas
2 pints strawberries
1½ c fresh orange sections
4 Tb dessicated coconut (opt)
1 Tb honey (opt)

1 cup blueberries, if available
large dash cinnamon
¼ tsp of fresh grated ginger (opt)

Combine. Alter the proportions at will. Tastes best when allowed to sit for about ½ hour before serving. May be served with yoghurt (or cream—shhh!), on whole wheat shortcake, on waffles, or plain. Delicious, in any case. During the winter, canned fruits (without heavy syrup) may be used; also one cup chopped dates is a nice addition.

» Strawberry Delight

Yield: 4 servings

1 pint strawberries	2-4 Tb liqueur (opt)
1 Tb sweetening	1 tsp vanilla ext.

Slice rinsed and drained strawberries. Add other ingredients and stir to bruise lightly. Let sit about 10 minutes.

Meanwhile combine:

1 pint yoghurt	1 tsp vanilla ext.
½ tsp almond ext.	1 Tb sweetener

In parfait glasses, layer first yoghurt, then strawberries, continuing in stripes. Garnish with a reserved berry and mint leaves, if available.

VARIATION:

If you don't have fancy parfait glasses, it tastes just as good all mixed together. You can leave the liqueur out, if you prefer, for the small fry.

» Fruit Compote

Dried Fruits:

prunes 4 c	Water to cover double
apricots 1 c	1 lemon
apples ½ c	cinnamon, a dash
pears ½ c	honey (opt)

Cover as much fruit as you can afford with water. (The fruits are listed in order of my favorites—yours may vary.) Simmer about ½ hour or until prunes are "done." Turn heat off, squeeze in juice of 1 lemon, throw the whole peel into the pot, add a dash of cinnamon and no more than 1 tsp of honey and let cool. Fish out the lemon and refrigerate the rest.

VARIATION:

Add about 1 Tb cognac to each serving of fruit compote. If you want an ecstatic experience, also add a Tb of half & half.

» Dessert Crêpes

Yield: about 18 crepes

4 eggs
1 c milk
1 c water
2 c wholewheat flour
⅓ stick melted butter or 3
  Tb oil

1 tsp vanilla ext.
2 Tb sesame seeds
1 tsp sweetening

Whizz in blender; let rest, refrigerated, at least one hour. Whizz again before using to redistribute heavy particles. Follow baking directions on page 99.

Fill with:

1. Ambrosia or winter ambrosia
2. yoghurt banana split
3. macerated strawberries
4. Combine 2 c yoghurt; ½ pint heavy cream, whipped; about 8 cups of assorted sliced fruits such as banana, berries, dates, peaches, pineapple; 2 tsp vanilla ext; 2 Tb sweetening— you will need to double Dessert Crêpes for this amount of filling.

» Custard

Analysis	Calo-ries	CHO	Fat	Pro-tein	GUP	Iron	Cal-cium
Serving	153	20g	4.2g	9g	8g	1.2mg	179mg

Yield: 8 servings

4-6 eggs (six for unmolded
  custards)
1 qt. milk*

½ c brown sugar or ¼ cup
  honey
1 tsp vanilla ext.
½ tsp salt

*(2 c milk plus 13 oz can of evaporated milk and enough water to make 4 c total liquid can be substituted)

Heat milk (or milk and water) until little bubbles show around the edge of the pan—until it is scalded. Meanwhile, beat the eggs, sweetening, and flavoring together. Beating constantly, add the hot milk in driblets until about half of it is added, then the rest may be added more quickly. If you have added the hot liquid too quickly, you can strain the custard to remove any scrambled egg particles. Pour (or strain) the milk and egg mixture into a mold or individual custard cups. Put the mold(s) in a pan of boiling water in a 350° oven—water should come about halfway up the sides of the custard dish. Cooking time will vary with the size of the mold—a tube pan cooks faster than a soufflé dish; individual cups cook very quickly. The range is 25-45 minutes; when a knife inserted in the center of the custard comes out clean, the custard is done.

VARIATIONS:

Caramel Custard: "Flan"

Heat ½ cup of brown sugar and 1 tablespoon of water in a cast iron skillet until the sugar melts: watch carefully, it burns easily. Stir with a wooden spoon until no granules remain. Rinse the mold in hot water; pour in caramel and quickly tip mold to spread as evenly as possible. Pour in custard mixture and bake as usual. When custard is done, it may be unmolded: cover cooled custard with a large platter and quickly invert both.

» *Peanut Butter Grahams*

Analysis	Calories	CHO	Fat	Protein	GUP	Iron	Calcium
Serving:	94	12g	4g	3g	2.3g	.6mg	19mg

Yield: 60 2" squares

1 stick butter
1¼ c honey
1 c peanut butter
4 eggs
1 tsp vanilla
1½ c Triple Rich Mix (see Recipe Index)

1½ c wholewheat flour
½ c maple syrup (opt. or ¼ c more honey)
½ tsp baking soda
1 cup oats +

Combine all ingredients. For grahams: roll as thinly as possible directly on buttered cookie sheet. Prick all over. Bake at 350° for about 10 minutes. Watch that edges don't burn; honey tends to burn easily. Cut into squares; let cool on sheet for 5 minutes. Remove squares to rack and let cool thoroughly. Also may be made into regular drop cookies.

» Halvah

Yield: 24 pieces

2 c sesame seeds
4 Tb honey
4 Tb butter or sesame tahini
1 c Triple Rich Mix
1 tsp vanilla extract

½ tsp salt
optional: cinnamon, almonds
  or other nuts, almond extract, coconut

For fuller flavor, toast all or part of seeds in a dry pan in a 250° oven for about ½ hour, stirring occasionally. Grind raw and cooled toasted seeds in either a flour mill, a nut- or coffee-type grinder, or a mortar and pestle. Force seeds to exude as much oil as possible. Add rest of ingredients and mix well. Press halvah into a container that has been rinsed out with cold water, chill for ½ hour or so. Turn out into a serving dish and cut in small slices or chunks to serve. Or roll into balls which can be coated with coconut or ground nuts.

» Nettie's Date-Nut Cake

This cake is unusual in that it contains no fat at all, and not much sugar either. In fact, it's mostly wall-to-wall dates and nuts, and keeps exceedingly well. It can be frozen for months, then sliced thinly and served with butter, cream cheese, or plain.

Yield: about 24 slices

4 eggs
1 c sugar, brown
1¼ c wholewheat flour
2 tsp baking powder
4 cups pecans

1½ pounds pitted dates,
  sliced once
1 tsp vanilla ext.
a few Tb liqueur, (opt)

Beat eggs and sugar with vanilla until light. Meanwhile,

214

dredge nuts and dates in flour to which baking powder has been added. Combine everything. Press into 2 well-buttered bread pans. Bake at 325° for about 1½ hours, until golden and thoroughly done. Cool and store.

» Christmas Fruitcake

Analysis	Calories	CHO	Fat	Protein	GUP	Iron	Calcium
Serving:	324	49g	12g	4.3g	3g	2.2mg	51mg

1¼ c dates
¾ c dried pineapple
½ c dried apricots
½ c thick fruit preserves
¾ c currants or raisins
¾ c dried figs (or pears)
1 tsp vanilla extract
¾ c cognac (or rum or whiskey)

½ c walnuts
½ c pecans
3 eggs
½ c brown sugar
½ c butter
1 c whole wheat flour

Combine all chopped fruits with liquor and vanilla extract. Let soak overnight. Next morning stir in nuts and fruit preserves. Butter and flour an 8″ square pan. Cream butter and sugar together. Beat in eggs; beat in flour. Pour batter over fruits and nuts. Combine thoroughly. Fill pan, pat batter down flat. Cover with a sheet of aluminum foil, sealing the pan. Bake in preheated 300° oven for 2 hours; remove aluminum foil and bake 40 minutes more, or until top of cake is nicely browned. When cool, turn out of pan. It may be eaten immediately or allowed to ripen as follows: wrap in liquor-soaked cloth, then in plastic. Check every day or two and re-soak cloth as necesary. A two-week soaking period is enough. The fruit and amounts suggested above may be changed according to your preference. Just keep the total of 4 cups constant.

XI

Times of Your Life

Hi and Lois

*A food additive that had no immediately toxic effects,
but that causes birth defects, cancer or mutations, might escape
detection indefinitely, because there is no simple way of as-
sociating the ingestion of the chemical in 1971 with the birth
of a deformed child in 1972, the occurrence of liver cancer in
1992 or a case of hemophilia in 2002.*
   —Michael Jacobson, Director, Center for Science in
   the Public Interest

LABORATORY animals used for research are healthy, sleek adults (or at least, they're healthy to begin with). They are kept in unstressful air-conditioned surroundings, and offered a full range of the nutrients they're known to need every day. This is a far cry from Americans as a whole, who may be old, young, fat, thin, sick, well, taking drugs, or living in polluted surroundings. It is these subpopulations that may be most sensitive to additives, and, for various reasons, it may be these people who receive proportionately more than their share.

Children are a case in point: in most foods geared primarily for the "youth" market—which goes up to teen-agers —sugar, artificial flavors, and artificial colors predominate. Pregnant women (who until recently were usually advised to limit their weight gain) could be found high on the list of consumers of various "dietetic" additives. And older folk, many of whom find cooking for one or two an onerous job, receive more than an average share of the additives that make instant meals possible.

Yet, you may say, all this is academic: the additives have been tested and declared safe by the awesome Food and Drug Administration (FDA). Have they?

SAFETY TESTING?

Obvious as it seems that the safety of an additive should have to be proven before it is used in our food, it was not until 1958 that such a law was passed. Until then the burden of proof went the other way—if the government could prove an additive caused harm or could show a reasonable doubt about its safety, they could petition to have it *removed*. While the legal machinery ground on, the additive stayed right where it was.

In 1958, Congress passed the Food Additive Amendment, which required safety testing of additives. But an exception

217

to the law was built in from the beginning: to avoid having to remove all the additives already being used in food—pending the outcome of saftety tests as the Act would have required—a list of "innocuous" substances was devised. These were substances that had shown "long and uneventful" usage and so could be assumed safe without laboratory evaluation.

GENERALLY REGARDED AS SAFE (GRAS)

These came to be called the GRAS list. At its inception there were perhaps 200 substances on it ranging from milk powder (an "additive" to frankfurters, though not to pudding) to MSG and cyclamates—which we were to hear more of later. Recent Senate testimony has divulged that there was no officially prescribed method for getting a substance declared GRAS; in fact, if a manufacturer decided a given additive was generally recognized as safe, he could consider it GRAS and proceed to use it in his food product—without even notifying the FDA. GRAS items—which finally unofficially numbered over 700—could be added *to any food in any amount.*

When some GRAS items were subsequently dropped (with enough "scare" headlines to make mothers gray), the concept of "long and uneventful" usage came under fire: is ten, twenty or even thirty years long enough to determine the safety of an additive used in foods for a population whose average life span is seventy-odd years? To understand that concept, one must understand how lab tests are conducted. There are at present four major areas of concern about the safety of a chemical: toxicity, carcinogenicity, teratogenicity, and mutagenicity.

TOXICITY

Toxicity means poisoning capability—will it harm or kill you if you eat enough of it? All new chemicals have been tested for simple toxicity since 1958. An additive is fed in varying doses to one or more species of laboratory animals and a count is made of how many die (compared with a control group who are treated identically except that the additive is left out). Many familiar substances are toxic; odd as it seems, some of them are also necessary nutrients. You can kill yourself with enormous doses of Vitamin A,

218

salt, or potassium. Toxicity is a matter of degree. A little aspirin can be a good thing, a lot can do you in.

CARCINOGENICITY

Testing for carcinogenicity, the ability to cause cancer, is less straightforward. Whereas with simple toxicity a "no-effect" level can be extrapolated from the results, much scientific controversy centers on the question of whether a "no-effect level" for cancer exists. Prominent cancer specialists testifying before the Senate agreed that, at present, no safe tolerance can be said to exist for carcinogens. No evidence exists to indicate that "just a little" is harmless. In fact, frequent small doses of carcinogens are more likely to cause cancer than one large dose.

One of the strongest features of the 1958 Act (which has come under subsequent and almost unremitting fire from manufacturers and even from the FDA itself) is the Delaney Clause. The Delaney Clause states that no substance found to cause cancer in man or animal when ingested may be added to food. (It specifically does not cover "incidental" additives or contaminents; nor does it cover any chemicals that have caused cancer as a result of injection, implantation, or other exposure.) Eminent cancer researchers have called the Delaney Clause an essential safeguard. They have stated that with a latency period of thirty or more years, the devastating effects of a few weak carcinogens added to our food today would go unrecognized until they wreaked havoc on tens of thousands of people half a generation from now. One researcher suggested that we could now be sowing the seeds for a cancer epidemic in the 1980's and 1990's (see Epilogue).

TERATOGENICITY AND THALIDOMIDE

Until the thalidomide tragedy, testing on pregnant animals was the exception rather than the rule; tests were usually run on healthy young males, in fact. Even now, although *new* food additives must pass tests for teratogenicity—capacity to damage the fetus—the hundreds of GRAS addititives have still not been tested. Since the FDA was mandated to begin its examination of GRAS items following the disqualification of MSG and cyclamates, fewer than twenty items have been unconditionally cleared. There is no way of knowing whether some additive currently in wide use will some-day be found to be weakly teratogenic.

Thalidomide was used by thousands of women. Although its effects were dramatic and the time lapse between taking the drug and producing a deformed child was less than nine months, it took scientists five years of sifting epidemiological evidence to work back to the cause. FDA employee Dr. Jacqueline Verrett has said, "It's likely that if thalidomide caused mental retardation instead of the gross skeletal deformities it did, we would still be using it today."[*1]

MUTAGENICITY

At present, mutagenicity—the ability to cause genetic changes—is the stepchild of safety testing. It is the least understood, and potentially the most terrible of the safety hazards. A toxic substance may kill you quickly. Cancer will kill you eventually. A teratogen may kill or harm your unborn children. But a mutagen may alter the human race for eternity. Now, additives are not screened for mutagenicity because scientists have not agreed on the standards for adequate tests.

TO WHAT END?

While some additives, used cautiously, may add to or enhance the food supply and benefit the consumer, the vast array of preservatives, humectants, sequestrants, flavorings, colorings, stabilizers, and conditioners are there to suit the manufacturer. Although the FDA's legislative guidelines declare that nothing may be added to food that would fool the consumer into believing it is something it is not, most textural, coloring, and flavoring changes are primarily cosmetic —they make the food appear better than it is.

Many additives are "necessary" because without them, fabricated, ersatz "foods" could not exist at all. Additives can turn inexpensive chemicals into what appears to be food. Even if they are not chemically harmful, the "foods" they make possible lower the nutritional value of your diet. Such

---

*For a chilling account of how close the FDA came to permitting the sale of thalidomide in the U.S., read *The Chemical Feast*.

additives are "essential"—to the manufacturer. While dairy-less cream and fruit-less blueberry muffins may have some curiosity value, they are in no sense valuable ingredients in the diet.

The picture is not unremittingly bleak. In a few cases, certain manufacturers of common products have chosen to use no preservatives or other additives; the consumer can choose. Recently, in response to consumer demand, some foods have been manufactured that claim to be "all natural"--apparently some "essential" additives *can* be avoided.

At present, it is fair to say that the safety of most chemical food additives has not been proven. More important, they haven't even been adequately tested. One wonders why some "authorities" insist that our food supply is the safest in the world and that no one has ever been able to prove that a food additive caused harm to a consumer.

Which leads us back to the whole question of who should assume the burden of proof. Should we assume safety unless we have irrefutable evidence that an additive has caused damage? Would that ever be possible without resorting to human testing that—even if it were morally acceptable—would take years?

We seem at present to be reduced to merely waiting for epidemiological evidence of an environmental hazard (a jump in cancer rates, an unexpected surge in certain diseases) that may then be traced back to its cause. But in a population of millions consuming thousands of additives, how could the effects of one be isolated from the effects of others? Suppose for a moment that someone added continuous small amounts of a poison to the water supply of a large city—just a simple poison, not one whose effects could very well take twenty years or lifetimes to notice. Depending on the particular poison and the amounts of water various people drank, some people would sicken and die, while some would show intermittent symptoms like nausea, headaches, weight loss, irritability, sleeplessness, or drowsiness. Most vulnerable would be the malnourished, the already sick and debilitated, the very young, and the very old. Unless the poison caused many sudden deaths, it is likely that these effects would pass unnoticed in a large population for quite some time and that the cause might never be clearly determined.

Few of the hundreds of chemical additives now used

are really necessary to insure a safe, nutritious food supply. Flavor enhancers are not necessary when high-quality ingredients are used. Thickeners, emulsifiers, and stabilizers are needed only when time-honored recipes are altered in favor of cheaper ingredients or short-cut methods. Antioxidants and preservatives can be largely avoided with more careful distribution procedures. And the most flagrant offenders, artificial flavors and colors, are in fact already proscribed under the rule that consumer deception is unlawful (though the FDA does not interpret it that way).

Unless it can be demonstrated that the *consumer's* best interest is served by the inclusion of a food additive (a case can be made for vitamins and fungicides, for example), concern for safety should far outweigh potential profit. Currently, safety testing is far from perfect and the potential vulnerability of certain subpopulations (pregnant women, children, the elderly) is unmeasurable.

PREGNANCY

For years it was assumed the placenta acted as a barrier that protected the infant from any harmful chemicals in the mother's system. We now understand that almost everything passes through the placenta in some form; chemicals that have no effect on the mother can have disasterous effects on the forming child.

As the food supply now exists, a pregnant woman, or someone who is planning to become pregnant, should avoid food additives. Most of the substances on the GRAS list have not been tested for their potential to cause fetal abnormalities or chromosome breaks. Cyclamates, now available by prescription only, but once widely used by weight-conscious mothers-to-be—as well as everyone else—have given indications of teratogenic potential in tests on chick embryos; they produced thalidomide-like deformities. Red-2, currently the most widely used food color,* has caused fetal resorptions in

---

*The partial ban on Red-2 (existing supplies were allowed to be used up) is a half-measure at best: the dyes which will replace it are open to the same questions of safety and inadequate testing.

rats—the equivalent of a miscarriage—at doses that would equal the amount consumed by a woman drinking two bottles of red-colored soda. It is not enough to avoid red-colored foods; Red-2 is in everything from *vanilla* frosting to *chocolate* cake.[1-4]

EATING FOR TWO

Nutritionally speaking, if you've ever felt the need for supplements, pregnancy is the time to take them, but only in addition to a fully nutritious diet. Pregnant women are known to need more iron, B-6, B-12, calcium (and therefore magnesium), folic acid, riboflavin, vitamin C, and fiber.[5, 6]

A lot of folklore exists about the diet for pregnancy: "eating for two," "strawberries cause rashes," "you lose a tooth for every baby." While most of the old wives' tales don't hold up under scrutiny, there's no better time to start eating properly. What you eat will have an effect on toxemia and other maternal complications, length of labor, newborn weight and size of baby, intelligence, and incidence of congenital malformations, as well as possible prematurity, abortion, stillbirth, and sterility.[6, 7]

The United States doesn't have the lowest infant mortality rate—it isn't even in the top ten. Even if you have heretofore thrived (?) on the meat-dairy-sugar-white flour diet (with its almost inevitable complement of synthetic foods and additives), eat right at least until you stop nursing. It might even become habit-forming.

It is not the case that a vegetarian mother-to-be has to start eating meat. With just a little attention, it is not at all difficult to get enough protein, calcium, and even iron on the vegetarian diet. A pregnant vegetarian should be sure to consume food yeast, leafy green vegetables, nuts and seeds, soy, dried fruit, whole grains, legumes, and occasionally molasses—in other words, the diet described throughout this book. For zinc you will have to eat small amounts of zinc-rich foods like pecans, oysters, Brazil nuts, and crab, in addition to the foods mentioned above, or use supplements.

FORMULA VS. BREAST-FEEDING

At a time when maternal childbirth mortality was higher, when societal changes had largely eliminated the practice

223

of wet-nursing, and when many marginally-nourished mothers may have had insufficient milk, infant feeding formulations probably saved many young lives. There are still cases in which formula is necessary or better; a baby with allergy to mother's milk, lactase deficiency, or certain metabolic defects cannot survive on his/her mother's milk.

But these cases form perhaps 1% of all babies. The 90%-plus of babies who are currently fed formulas in this country are receiving them for far less pertinent reasons: (1) it's more convenient to bottle feed, or (2) even if breast-feeding is considered, the mother-to-be may believe she "can't" and besides, (3) formulas are just as good as breast milk.

In fact (1) the breast is far more convenient than the bottle: there's nothing to sterilize, heat, cool, forget, run out of, or break. Formula advertisements that stress "convenience" somehow manage to avoid the obvious. It would be more accurate to say that breast-feeding is rarely thought of except in passing, and even more rarely encouraged. There's no profit in it. Advertising both for mothers and health professionals centers on *which* formula and *which* bottle. The factor of cost seems somehow never to enter into consideration, despite the enormous potential savings. In fact it is upper-class women in America who are more likely to breast-feed than women who can less easily afford formula.

One aspect of convenience is related to the woman's perceptions of societal pressures. Many women think they would feel embarrassed breast-feeding, even in front of friends. On the other hand, it is a simple thing to carry a light shawl for subtle drapery as the La Leche League suggests.[8] No one but a careful observer would notice that the baby was doing something other than being held closely. It is probably also the case that, as more women breast-feed openly, their singularity would decrease. Since today's new mother is herself likely to have been bottle-fed, she is breaking no new ground in continuing the practice.

As for (2), certain breast-feeding myths have been perpetuated. The most common are that many (or even most) women won't have enough milk; that their nipples aren't well-formed; or that they're too "nervous;" or that their mothers couldn't, therefore they can't. Unfortunately, many health professionals seem unable to counteract this misinformation. There is three times as much space devoted to formula as to breast-feeding in a widely used nutrition text for nurses and dietitians.[6]

Contrary to (3), even the most scientifically prepared formula based on up-to-the-minute nutrition cannot claim to be as good as mother's milk. As recently as 1968, essential nutrients were discovered lacking in commercial formulas. Sometimes the results have been tragic: Vitamin E deficiency led to hemolytic anemia for premature infants;[9] vitamin B-6 deficiency led to convulsive seizures.[10] No reputable scientist claims that all essential nutrients have been discovered. It is more likely that, a few years from now, errors in today's most up-to-date formulations will be discovered. Even if these are minor, no formula can hope to give the infant its mother's all-important immunologic protection against infection. Breast-fed infants are less likely to develop respiratory and gastro-intestinal infections and allergic reactions.[11] In fact the extraordinarily high incidence of allergic disease in the United States has been linked with this country's abstention from breast-feeding. In one study, adult ulcerative colitis occurred twice as often in subjects who had been bottle-fed rather than breast-fed as infants.[12]

One more caution about formula: breast milk is very low in sodium—cow's milk contains four times as much. The infant on a cow's milk-based formula is likely to receive much more sodium per day at a time when his kidneys are least able to handle the excess. This greater load may be linked to the later development of hypertension in sensitive individuals.[13]

In addition, high concentration of solutes (minerals in solution) in milk formula requires more water for excretion: the child is always thirsty and tends to drink more milk. This can lead to a vicious dehydration-thirst cycle.[14]

You can't know if it will work for you until you try it. Although six to eight months of exclusive breast-feeding has shown the greatest benefits, something is better than nothing. Be sure to get the La Leche Handbook; unless your doctor has herself breast-fed, there's a good chance that *he* won't know the right answers to your questions.

Just as in pregnancy, the mother's diet for breast-feeding is all-important, and it is certainly possible to maintain adequate milk on the vegetarian diet. If the mother's diet is deficient, the baby will be a parasite on the mother's system for a time, but eventually the volume of milk will be reduced and both will suffer. Lactating mothers should not take drugs, nor should they smoke anything. They should also read ingredient labels and avoid excessively "chemical" foods. They should eat a lot—the additional daily requirement of a mother fully breast-feeding a healthy 1-6 month old baby jumps about 1,000 calories (about 3,000 total) with commensurate increases in other nutrients. These calories must be wall-to-wall nutrition—there's no room for "empty" calories when the physiological needs of two people are dependent on the intake of one person.

And you don't have to pay any attention to the nonsense that says you're supposed to start eating with all the self-abnegation of a Trappist monk. Do you seriously think that an Indian, Mexican, or Italian mother stops eating garlic and spices because she's nursing? If you think you notice a relationship between your spicy indulgences and baby's petulance, that's another matter.

Although some substances in certain foods circulate in the bloodstream, and hence reach the milk, your child cannot become allergic to chocolate if *you* eat chocolate. In fact, the reverse may be true. Some measure of resistance to potential allergens may be conferred (as well as the obvious advantage to a completely nursed baby of delaying the moment when he will be exposed to the foods that can sensitize him).[13] It is true that breast milk is not entirely free of environmental contaminants such as pesticide residues, but then neither is cow's milk.

EARLY INFANT FEEDING

Despite the trend toward earlier and earlier feeding of solid foods to infants, no benefit for this practice has been proven and many potential difficulties exist. The early introduction of solid foods can contribute to overeating and an excess of fat cells that some researchers link to early obesity. Allergists claim that early solid feeding can bring about allergic reactions in some children. And remember that commercially prepared baby foods are salted and sweetened to please the palate, not of the infant, but of the mother. Most recent research indicates that "for the first four months of life, the average healthy baby needs only milk (about 2½ oz. per pound per day.)"[15]

Although some doctors have recommended skim milk for infants and children, the latest evidence indicates that this is not wise, especially before two years of age, and probably until school age. Infants tend to drink until their caloric needs are met. To get enough calories from skim milk, an infant must drink more, which enlarges his or her stomach and may be the beginning of a lifelong tendency to overeat. Pre-school children need the calories provided by whole rather than skim milk.[17]

BABY FOOD

Many modern mothers who are convinced that baby food isn't all they want it to be lack confidence in their own ability to provide nutrition. They're afraid that they can't design a nourishing diet for baby, and they fear bacterial contamination from improperly prepared foods.

While it is true that babies have high nutritional requirements, it is also true that these can be amply met by a diet chosen from a wide variety of whole foods. By definition, that will cut out the mountains of junk, questionable additives, empty calories, refined carbohydrates, and other foods of limited nutritional value so prevalent in the American diet.

And with the simplest of precautions, homemade baby food is safe as well. It is not too surprising to learn that commercial manufacturers are a major source of dire warnings about the dangers of home-prepared baby foods. One company sent out 760,000 "public service" leaflets—which also contained discount coupons for their product—warning of the "significant risk of bacterial contamination" in home-prepared baby foods. Yet a Consumer's Union analysis of commercial baby food found "insects, rodent hairs, and enamel paint chips in many of the samples." C.U. also found that in every case baby foods prepared at home from locally available ingredients were more nutritious than the commercial variety.[18]

Baby food grinders are available that can handle small amounts for instant, at-the-table preparation. Blenders work well for preparing in greater quantity—the extra can be frozen in an ice cube tray and the individual cubes warmed as needed. If baby objects to the slight grittiness of blended, cooked whole grains, push the blended grains through a tea strainer before freezing.

We reiterate that specialists in the field of infant nutrition recommend feeding nothing but mother's milk for the first four months; but then, what to feed baby? First, fruit. Introduce new foods one at a time, allowing a few days of exposure. Obviously, if baby develops odd blotches that can't be attributed to anything else, hold off on that food for a while. If you are an allergic family, hold off on berries and citrus—and anything you are allergic to. Most babies adore a banana: it should be very ripe and have a well-freckled skin. It can be simply mashed or blended with a little milk. Watermelon goes over big: babies just suck the juice out and then paint their faces with the pulp. Peaches, pears, apricots, plums, berries, what-have-you—dried fruits can be rehydrated and puréed.

Cereals are usually recommended as baby's first food, but feeding cereals too early may be a burden on baby's immature digestive system. Start 4-8 weeks after adding fruit. Whole grains are fine, cooked and blended with some water or milk to the consistency baby likes. They may also be mixed with some fruit for better acceptance.

Then, at about the same time as cereals: vegetables. It's fine to use food you have prepared for everyone else, but before excessive salt or spices have been added. As soon as baby is interested in picking things up, offer slivers of whatever vegetable you're having. It may not be too far afield to suggest that the American child's well-known aversion to vegetables other than peas and carrots might be traceable to the narrow selection of commercially prepared baby food vegetables: have you ever seen cauliflower, asparagus, or zucchini in jars?

Somewhere between six months and one year, eggs, cottage cheese and other cheeses, yoghurt, puréed beans, and other high-protein foods can be introduced. Until that time, baby is getting enough protein from breast milk (or formula). There is controversy about babies' need for iron. Egg yolk, whole grains, beans, nuts, and some green vegetables have respectable amounts of iron. On the other hand, the form of iron used to "enrich" commercial baby cereals is practically unassimilable. Babies don't need more iron than mother's milk supplies—their own store of it should provide enough until they can get it from food.

There are many infants' vitamin and mineral supplements available, although they share the drawback of any vitamin and mineral formulations (see Chapter VII). Brewer's yeast is not only chock-full of trace elements, it's impressively high in iron and protein. Why not add it to orange juice from the beginning before baby knows what orange juice is *supposed* to taste like?

Aside from other considerations, homemade baby food saves lots of money. Most fruits, for example, come in jars that hold between 3 and 4 ounces at an average cost of 14¢. Frequently, water is the first ingredient on the label—which means the jar contains at most 2 ounces of fruit. A pound of baby food banana comes out to more than $1.00 per pound.

MSG, nitrates, and modified food starch (modified so that the jar of baby food won't get "watery"—also modified so that it resists normal digestion!) have all been in baby food at one time or another.

NITRITES

In laboratory tests, nitrosamines are among the most potent carcinogens. Nitrosamines are formed from the combination of nitrites or nitrates and amines, which are naturally present in "everything from antihistamines to beer to cigarette smoke"[19] to many prescription drugs. Some water supplies have high levels of nitrates and some vegetables that have been heavily fertilized tend to concentrate nitrates in their leafy portions.

Since it is difficult to prove that nitrosamines are actually formed in the intestine of someone eating nitrates and amines at the same time, the FDA has been reluctant to enforce the Delaney Clause, which prohibits carcinogens in foods. However, already formed nitrosamines have been found in a few samples of bacon, frankfurters, dried beef, smoked fish, and ham. Bacon seems to be the worst offender because the process of cooking accelerates nitrosamine formation.[19] As Michael Jacobson has suggested, "Don't bring home the bacon," or for that matter, the baby food.

There is certainly no problem feeding a child adequately on the whole foods vegetarian diet. It is our contention that

229

if a child's palate is not jaded by excessive sweets, he or she will eat adequate quantities of the healthful foods offered (assuming no physiological problems affecting appetite). If you are providing a well-balanced diet, you can be sure your child is consuming the amounts his or her body needs *providing* that empty calories are not around to be substituted. The handful of peanuts eaten for an afternoon snack contains iron, protein, vitamins, and minerals. The fruit for dessert contains potassium, fiber, natural sugars, and Vitamins A and C. The glass of milk provides large amounts of calcium, protein, and riboflavin. If each calorie carries some necessary component of a healthful diet—as it must with whole foods —only excessively restricted food choices would lead to malnutrition. (All peanuts, all bananas, or all milk obviously would not make a well-rounded diet.)

HYPERKINETIC CHILDREN

A serious indictment of the effects of chemical additives on children has been made by Dr. Ben Feingold, Chief Emeritus of the Kaiser-Permanente Medical Center. Dr. Feingold has shown that certain hyperkinetic children can be "cured" by removing all artificial flavorings and additives from their diet. He hypothesizes that these children have genetic variations which predispose them to adverse responses to additives found in most cheap "kid's" foods. His patients change from jumpy, inattentive children (who have often been prescribed stimulants and tranquilizers) to ordinary kids who do better in school and can sit still for normal periods of time. When someone relapses, it can almost always be linked to a forbidden food that has found its way back into the diet. After refusing to consider his evidence for three years, the FDA has finally said it will "look into the matter."

"RETIRED" APPETITES

Ask anyone; they'll tell you the life expectancy has increased enormously in this century. That's true in the raw sense: the life expectancy of the whole population has jumped from about 47 years in 1900 to about 65-70 years today. But that figure reflects advances in combatting the illnesses of children and young adults. The life expectancy at age 65 has hardly increased at all since the turn of the century.

230

There are many places in the world with a higher proportion of septuagenarians. It is hard to make a generalization about the life styles of people in areas ranging from the Andes to the Caucasus to the Himalayas. Many of the societies with healthy *active* old people consume little meat. In most of them the calories consumed per person are limited but of high quality.

It has long been known that in rats, restriction of calories to about half of what they would freely eat can increase their life expectancy by roughly 50%. But it is also an accepted theory that life span is genetically determined and environmental factors such as diets have limited influence.

Senate testimony has indicated that the 20 million elderly might be the most malnourished part of our population, despite governmental programs. For the aged, caloric requirements fall but basic nutrient needs stay about the same. Combined with the poorer absorption of some nutrients, this leaves even less room for "empty calories." "Quick" and "single-serving" foods contain fewer nutrients and far more additives than are needed in the diet—particularly if caloric needs are declining. The malnutrition most prevalent in America—too few nutrients and too many calories—is due to the highly-processed products that have become the Modern Four. The average American spends almost half his or her calories on these "staples": white flour, white rice, sugar, and salad oil;[21] where then, is the *wide variety?* Regardless of which subpopulation you represent—nursing mother, hungry adolescent, dieter, older American—the basic diet pattern should be the same. Learn to eat right and have the times of your life.

Epilogue

Almost daily, newspaper stories about food and food additives cause increased consumer concern. But preliminary research findings often conflict, and as the list of suspected carcinogens grows to include many common foods as well as widely used chemicals, the bewildered consumer can be seen standing glassy-eyed in the supermarket aisle wondering what's left to eat. This book has tried to provide the answer; there are still good, safe, nutritious foods on which to base a satisfying, tasty diet. We have combined these foods in a diet pattern we like, but these same food choices could form an entirely different, though equally nutritious, diet based on different taste or combination principles. In other words, the diet described in this book is not *the* answer, it is *one* answer.

The recent controversy over the safety of food colorings, centered on Red-2, gives an idea of the problems in evaluating food additives and processes. The political and economic forces involved are enormous.

Although Red-2 has recently been banned, the history of the FDA and coal-tar dyes makes it hard to feel much elation. When the 1958 law which required prior safety testing was enacted, the food color industry was immediately in trouble. Within a year, seven colors had been de-listed and seventeen more were proposed for de-listing. Hearings on new legislation spoke of consumer protection, but most major industry demands were met. An anti-cancer clause similar to the Delaney clause was deleted and the FDA was given considerable leeway in determining safety *"as used."* The Color Additives Amendment of 1960 solved the problem by redefinition: dyes were no longer "food additives"; they became "color additives" and as such the provisions of the 1958 law were inapplicable. Most importantly, dyes were given "provisional listing" until safety tests could be completed. When, in 1972, consumer groups protested the continued use of Violet-1—the dye used by the USDA to stamp meat grades—it was discovered that in every instance the 2½ year period had been extended as it expired. Twelve years after the law designed to determine the safety of food color had been passed, only one color has been permanently, as opposed to provisionally, listed.

The safety of various colors has been repeatedly questioned by the international scientific community. Although Russian tests, which showed that Red-2 was carcinogenic, have been discounted for poor design in tests conducted by the FDA itself, Red-2 proved to be highly toxic to chick embryos. It also produced thalidomide-like deformities in the chicks which lived to hatch. In rats it caused fetal resorptions—similar to a miscarriage—at a dose equivalent to only two bottles of cherry soda. Even so, the banning of Red-2, the *most widely used* food color, took three years.*

Most colors are still provisionally listed. The question of safety is still unresolved. In no other category of additive is the risk-benefit ratio so clear: the industry reaps the benefits; the consumer assumes the risk.

One observer noted: "We may now be sowing the seeds for a cancer epidemic in the 1980's and 1990's"—according to the latest cancer statistics, that epidemic has arrived. The jump in cancer incidence has been astounding and alarming. It cannot be accounted for, as some have claimed, by the increased number of people who are living longer. In fact, some cancers are developing earlier than had been the case. According to most cancer research specialists, 80% of all carcinogens are environmental. Most, like ultraviolet light and naturally occurring carcinogens in water and some foods, are largely unavoidable. It seems clear, therefore that any *added burden* must be severely restricted.

Given the enormous pressure exerted by industry, and the often ambivalent attitude of the FDA, more and more pressure to intelligently evaluate food choices has come to rest on the consumer. It's not an easy job: it takes some practical knowledge, a willingness to change old patterns and try new ones. We have tried to provide tools which can both help the consumer choose more wisely, and make those choices palatable. Although it may be awkward at first to alter something so basic as food habits, we believe that nutrition survival may depend on it.

---

*For details on the FDA's handling of Red-2, read Dr. J. Verret's *Eating May Be Hazardous to Your Health*.

Appendix

I. CHD: OTHER RISK FACTORS

It's not enough that they've taken away your favorite foods, now they're going to start attacking all your other vices. Besides diet, there are several other medically accepted risk factors associated with CHD: hypertension, cigarette smoking, stress, lack of exercise, obesity, mineralization of drinking water, diabetes mellitus, and hyperuricemia (a precursor of gout). Age, sex, and heredity, which you can do nothing about, also play a part. These risk factors cannot be listed in order of prominence, though there is a statistical relationship between them. For example, the presence of a single risk factor may double the chance of getting heart disease. If two are present (such as elevated serum cholesterol and hypertension) the likelihood of getting CHD is more than tripled. If three risk factors are included (add smoking more than one pack a day), the chance of heart disease is increased tenfold. Some small consolation —except for post-attack victims who cannot walk up a flight of stairs without their pulse rate climbing over 100—sex is good for the heart. (Maybe there's something that can substitute for smoking after all.)

II. GENERAL SUBSTITUTION RULES: Whole Wheat for White Flour

• *White sauce* (béchamel, velouté): use about half again the amount of white flour called for in the recipes: i.e., if the recipe says use 3 Tb white flour, use 4 to 5 Tb wholewheat flour. If necessary, increasing the fat slightly will make cooking the flour easier.

• *"Tea cakes"* (baking powder cakes): Use finely ground (pastry) flour, if available; use 1 Tb less wholewheat than white flour per cup of flour. Obviously, in a recipe which calls for only one or two cups of flour, this adjustment is not essential. Or you may wish to *add* a tablespoon or so of milk, instead.

• *Dessert cakes* (the kind usually frosted): use 2 tablespoons less wholewheat than white flour per cup (⅞ cup per cup called for). It is not necessary to sift unless the flour is *very* full of large particles. To measure, stir flour to lighten and then scoop *gently* into measuring cup and level.

• *Bread* (yeast): it is not necessary to make adjustments since all bread recipes are approximate anyway. Using gluten flour in the ratio of one-quarter to one-sixth the amount of wholewheat flour will make a lighter, higher protein loaf, but this is optional.

• *Noodles:* use about 1 tablespoon less wholewheat than white flour per cup. Wholewheat noodles (indeed, any home-made noodles, unless you have a noodle-rolling machine) tend to be thicker and 'doughier' than the commercial product. But they taste great!

234

• *Pie and pastry:* use pastry flour if possible. Do *not* use gluten (this will not lighten the dough, only make it tougher). No other adjustment is necessary.

• *Cookies:* it is not necessary to make adjustments: just moisten the dough with an additional tablespoon or two of milk, if this seems necessary. In very delicate butter-type cookies, you may wish to use finely ground (or even sifted) wholewheat flour. Measure after sifting.

III. PROTEIN NEEDS

The first protein requirements were set by extrapolating average intakes of heavy meat-eating groups. Old texts still carry this outmoded information. When nitrogen-balance studies were subsequently carried out, it developed that the initial values were unnecessarily inflated. Nitrogen-balance studies determine the amount of dietary protein actually needed to avoid depleting the body of protein. The body does not *store* protein in the same way that it does fat or glucose: both these energy storehouses are designed to be used when intake is lower than optimal. But there is no repository of excess amino acids: if sufficient protein is not eaten, tissues must be broken down.

In adult males consuming enough calories, the amount of high quality protein necessary for nitrogen-balance is calculated to be a little less than one-half gram per kilogram of body weight, (.47 gm) or about 33 grams for a 150 lb. person. This figure is increased (30%) to allow for individual variability, and it is increased (25%) again to allow for the differences in useable protein in a mixed diet (75%). The figure used by the NAS/NRC in setting the RDA for protein therefore becomes about .8 gram/kg. But this figure is meant to be used with food composition tables listing *total* protein. We have used the figures for *available*, NPU-adjusted, protein, because it is more accurate.

To figure out how much available protein you need, multiply your weight in pounds times .28 (that's the NAS/NRC base nitrogen-balance figure adjusted for individual variability and translated into pounds. It does *not* take increases for "mixed diet" into account, since this is already deducted by figuring actual, instead of total, protein).

Pregnant women need about one-third more protein; lactating women need about one-half again the usual need.

To get the actual (available) protein of a food for which you have the total analyses, use the NPU as a percent. A food with 10 grams total protein and an NPU of 80, will give 8 grams of available protein.

Having told you all of this, we're now going to tell you: it doesn't matter. "It is difficult to obtain a mixed vegetable diet which will produce an appreciable loss of body protein without resorting to high levels of sugar, jams, and jellies, and other essentially protein-free foods."*

---

*Mervyn Hardinge and Hulda Crooks, "Non-Flesh Dietaries III, Adequate and Inadequate," *Journal of the American Dietetic Association* 45 (1964).

Reasons for inadequate vegetarian diets largely fall into one of four categories:

1. pure vegetarian (vegan) diets have produced B-12 deficiency in some persons;

2. grossly unbalanced near-vegetarian diets in which 95% of the calories were provided by starchy foods extremely low in protein, such as cassava root;

3. diets dependent too largely on refined cereals, such as cornmeal or white rice, even with small amounts of animal foods;

4. intake of total calories insufficient for maintenance requirements.*

"It is most unlikely that a protein deficiency will develop . . . on a diet in which cereal and vegetables supply adequate calories."**

The essence of the situation is this: eat enough calories (provided they're not "empty") and the protein will take care of itself. (We are assuming you haven't decided to eat only bananas.) Eat enough calories and protein *from a variety of whole food sources* and the chances are excellent that the nutrients will take care of themselves also.

IV. *Bran Test*

Since everyone has a different requirement for fiber, it is useful to have a simple test which can help you determine whether your diet is providing enough for intestinal health. Dr. Denis Burkitt has provided one. If your stool has segments and fissures, or if it is compact and pebbly, you are not getting enough fiber (even though you may evacuate daily.) According to Dr. Burkitt's studies, people who live on unrefined grains (and who never get bowel cancer) have large, soft, moist and bulky stool.

---

*Ibid.
**D. Mark Hegsted

References

Chapter I—POLITICS IN THE KITCHEN

1. "Dietary Levels of Households in the U.S.: Spring 1965," Preliminary Report ARS 62-17, Consumer and Food Economics Research Division, Agriculture Research Service, U.S. Department of Agriculture.
2. Michael Jacobson, *Nutrition Scoreboard—Your Guide to Better Eating* (Washington D.C.: Center for Science in the Public Interest, 1973).
3. Ted Greiner, *The Promotion of Bottle Feeding by Multinational Corporations: How Advertising and the Health Professions Have Contributed*, Cornell International Nutrition Monograph Series, Number 2 (Ithaca, New York: Cornell University, 1975).
4. James S. Turner, *The Chemical Feast* (New York: Grossman Publishers, 1970).
5. "Feed Statistics", Supplement for 1971 to Statistical Bulletin #410, U.S. Department of Agriculture.
6. Lester Brown, *By Bread Alone* (New York: Praeger Publishers, 1974).

Chapter III—START YOUR DAY A LOT BETTER

1. Rachmiel Levine, "Role of Carbohydrates in the Diet," in *Modern Nutrition in Health and Disease*, 4th edition, edited by Michael G. Wohl and Robert S. Goodhart (Philadelphia: Lea and Febiger, 1970), p. 162.
2. S. Wapnick, A.C.B. Wicks, E. Kanengoni and J. J. Jones "Can Diet Be Responsible for the Initial Lesion in Diabetes?" *The Lancet*, August 12, 1972, p. 300.
3. Corrine Robinson, *Normal and Therapeutic Nutrition*, 14th Edition (New York: The Macmillan Company, 1972), p. 231.
4. J.A. Campbell and D.C. Chapman, "Evaluation of Protein in Foods —Criteria for Describing Protein Value," *Journal of the Canadian Dietetic Association*, 21, (1959), p. 159.
5. Michael Jacobson, "The Sugar Content of Fabricated Foods," Center For Science in the Public Interest (1973).
6. Michael Jacobson, *Eater's Digest* (New York: Doubleday and Company, 1972), p. 56.
7. Eva Wilson, Katherine Fisher and Mary Fuqua, *Principle of Nutrition*, 2nd Edition, (New York: John Wiley and Sons, 1967) p. 438-446.
8. Charlotte R. Gallagher, Ann L. Molleson and James H. Caldwell, "Lactose Intolerance and Fermented Dairy Products," *Journal of the American Dietetic Association*, 65, October, 1974, p. 418.
9. Shepard Shapiro, "Control of Antibiotic-Induced Gastrointestinal Symtoms With Yoghurt," *Clinical Medicine*, 7, February, 1960.

Additional References:

1. D. Mark Hegsted "Food and Nutrition Policy—Now and in the Future" *Journal of the American Dietetic Association*, 64, April, 1975.
2. "Nutrition Content and Advertising for Dry Breakfast Cereals," Hearing Before the Consumer Subcommittee of the Committee on Commerce, 92nd Congress, 2nd Session, March 2, 1972.

Chapter V—BE TRUE TO YOUR HEART OR IT WILL ATTACK YOU

1. Mayer Friedman and Ray H. Rosenman, *Type A Behavior and Your Heart*, (Alfred A. Knopf, 1974).
2. Ancel Keys, *National Research Council Publication #338*, (1954).
3. Norman Joliffe and Morton Archer, "Statistical Association Between International Coronary Heart Disease Rates and Certain Environmental Factors," *Journal of Chronic Diseases*, 9, June, 1959.
4. S. L. Malhotra, "Serum Lipids, Dietary Factors and Ischemic Heart Disease," *American Journal of Clinical Nutrition*, 20, May, 1967, p. 462.
5. John Yudkin, "Diet and Coronary Thrombosis: Hypothesis and Fact," *The Lancet*, July 27, 1957.
6. L. Michaels, "Aetiology of Coronary Heart Disease: An Historical Approach," *British Heart Journal*, 28, (1966), p. 258.
7. Mohamed A. Antar, Margaret Olson and Robert E. Hodges, "Changes in Retail Market Food Supplies in the U.S. in the Last 70 Years in Relation to the Incidence of Coronary Heart Disease with Special Reference to Dietary Carbohydrate and Essential Fatty Acids," *American Journal of Clinical Nutrition*, 14, March, 1964.
8. Roger J. Williams, *Nutrition Against Disease* (New York: Pitman Publishing Corp., 1971).
9. Henry A. Schroeder, "The Role of Trace Elements in Cardiovascular Diseases," *Medical Clinics of North America*, 58, March, 1974, p.381.
10. Henry A. Schroeder, "Chromium Deficiency as a Factor in Atherosclerosis," *Journal of Chronic Diseases*, 23, (1970), p. 123.
11. Mervyn Hardinge and Frederick J. Stare, "Nutrition Studies of Vegetarians—Dietary and Serum Levels of Cholesterol," *American Journal of Clinical Nutrition*, 2, March-April, 1954.
12. George Kromer, "Symposium on Fats and Carbohydrates in Processed Foods," reported in News Digest of *Journal of the American Dietetic Association* (1973), p. 668.
13. Beatrice Trum Hunter, *Consumer Beware!* (Bantam Books, 1972), p. 228.
14. C. Bruce Taylor, Dorothy Patton, Nelson Yogi and George E. Cox, "Diet as a Source of Serum Cholesterol in Man," *Proceedings of the Society for Experimental Biological Medicine*, 103, (1960), p. 768.
15. Ernest L. Wynder, Frank R. Lemon and Irwin J. Bross, "Cancer and Coronary Artery Disease Among Seventh-Day Adventists," *Cancer*, September-October, 1959.

16. Title XXI, Food and Drug Administration, 19.755-19.778.
17. Hugh Trowell, "Ischemic Heart Disease and Dietary Fiber," *American Journal of Clinical Nutrition*, (1972), p. 926.
18. Hugh Trowell, "Epidemiology of Digestive Diseases and Ischemic Heart Disease," *Digestive Diseases*, (1972).
19. Hugh Trowell "Dietary Fibre, Ischemic Heart Disease and Diabetes Mellitus," *Proceedings of the Nutrition Society*, 32, (1973), p. 151.
20. A. Antonis and I. Bersohn "The Influence of Diet on Fecal Lipids in South African White and Bantu Prisoners," *American Journal of Clinical Nutrition*, 10, (1962).
21. K. S. Mathur, M. A. Kahn and R. D. Sharma, "Hypocholestremic Effect of Bengal Gram: A Long Term Study in Man," *British Medical Journal*, (1968).
22. Jacqueline Verrett and Jean Carper, *Eating May Be Hazardous to Your Health*, (Simon and Schuster, 1974).

Chapter VI—YOU COULD END UP WITH A SEMI-COLON

1. "The Hard Facts About Constipation," *Moneysworth: the Consumer Newsletter*, 4, July 22, 1974.
2. "Diet and Cancer of the Colon," *Nutrition Reviews*, 31, April 1, 1973.
3. T. G. Parks, "The Role of Dietary Fibre in the Prevention and Treatment of Diseases of the Colon," *Proceedings of the Royal Society of Medicine*, 66, July 1973.
4. Denis P. Burkitt, "Epidemiology of Cancer of the Colon and Rectum," *Cancer*, 28, July 1971.
5. Hugh Trowell, "Epidemiology of Diverticular Disease and Ischemic Heart Disease," *Digestive Diseases*, 19, September 1974.
6. P. F. Plumley and B. Francis, "Dietary Management of Diverticular Disease," *Journal of the American Dietetic Association*, 63, (1973).
7. C. Noel Williams, "Diet and Diseases of the Gastrointestinal Tract," *The Nova Scotia Medical Bulletin*, October 1973.
8. John G. Reinhold, "Phytate Destruction by Yeast Fermentation in Whole Wheat Meals," *Journal of the American Dietetic Association*, 66, January 1975.
9. Sydney M. Feingold, et. al., "Effect of Diet on Human Fecal Flora—Comparison of Japanese and American Diets," *American Journal of Clinical Nutrition*, 27, December 1974.
10. Denis Burkitt, A. R. P. Walker and N. S. Painter, "Dietary Fibre and Disease," *Journal of the American Medical Association*, 229, August 19, 1974.
11. Denis P. Burkitt, "Epidemiology of Large Bowel Disease: the Role of Fiber," *The Proceedings of the Nutrition Society*, 32, December 1973.
12. B. R. Maier, et. al., "Effects of a High-Beef Diet on Bowel Flora: A Preliminary Report," *American Journal of Clinical Nutrition*, December 1973.
13. M. A. Antar, M. Ohlson and R. E. Hodges, "Changes in Retail Market Food Supplies in the U.S. in the Last 70 Years in Relation to

the Incidence of Coronary Heart Disease with Special Reference to Dietary Carbohydrate and Essential Fatty Acids," *American Journal of Clinical Nutrition*, 14, March 1964.

14. E. W. Pomare and K. W. Heaton, "Alteration to Bile Salt Metabolism by Dietary Fiber (Bran)," *British Medical Journal*, November 3, 1973.
15. "Diet, Intestinal Flora and Colon Cancer," *Nutrition Reviews*, 33, No. 5, (1974).
16. M. H. Hill, et. al., "Bacteria and Aetiology of Cancer of the Large Bowel," *The Lancet*, 16, January 1971.
17. J. W. Berg, M. A. Howell and S. J. Silverman, "Dietary Hypothesis and Diet-Related Research in the Etiology of Colon Cancer," *Health Services Reports*, 88, December 1974.
18. R. A. Malt, and L. W. Ottinger, "Carcinoma of the Colon and Rectum," *The New England Journal of Medicine*, 288, April 19, 1973.
19. L. V. Ackerman, "Some Thoughts on Food and Cancer," *Nutrition Today*, January-February 1972.

Chapter VII—WHERE HAVE ALL THE NUTRIENTS GONE

1. *Proposed Fortification Policy for Cereal Grain Products*, National Academy of Sciences, Washington, D.C., 1974.
2. Aaron M. Altschul, "The Revered Legume," *Nutrition Today*, March-April 1973, p. 28.
3. *Recommended Dietary Allowances Eighth Revised Edition*, National Academy of Sciences, Washington, D.C., 1974.
4. "Read the Label, Set a Better Table: A Guide to Nutrition Labeling From the Food and Drug Administration," U.S. Department of Health, Education and Welfare, DHEW Pub. No. (FDA) 75-4001.
5. *Ten-State Nutrition Survey*, 1968-1970, U.S. Dept. of Health Education and Welfare, Washington, D.C., 1972.
6. Colin Norman, "Iron Enrichment," *Nutrition Today*, November-December 1973.
7. Roman J. Lutsky, *Handbook of Vitamins and Hormones* (New York: Van Nostrand Reinhold, 1973).
8. R. E. Hughes and P. R. Jones, "Natural and Synthetic Sources of Vitamin C," *Journal of Science of Food and Agriculture*, 22, (1971).
9. R. P. Nikolav, K. L. Povolotskaya and N. A. Vodolazskaya, "The Biological Value of Different Concentrates and Preparations of Vitamin C," *Biokhimiya*, 18, (1953).
10. D. Mark Hegsted, "Food and Nutrition Policy—Now and in the Future," *Journal of the American Dietetic Association*, 64, April 1974.
11. Ruth M. Leverton, "The RDAs are Not for Amateurs," *Journal of the American Dietetic Association*, 66, January 1975.
12. "Vitamin B-12," *Life and Health*, July 1974.
13. Dorothy Fisher, "Gangrene Decubitus and Stonal Ulcers Treated with Alpha Tocopherol," in *The Summary*, Shute Institute for Clinical and Laboratory Medicine, 26, December 1974.

14. A. L. Tappel, "Where Old Age Begins," *Nutrition Today*, December 1967.
15. B. K. Armstrong, R. E. David, D. J. Nicol, A. J. van Merwyck and C. J. Larwood, "Hematological, Vitamin B-12, and Folate Studies on Seventh-Day Adventist Vegetarians," *American Journal of Clinical Nutrition*, 27, July 1974.
16. Miguel Layrisse, Carlos Martinez-Torres, and Marcel Roche, "Effect on Interaction of Various Foods on Iron Absorption," *American Journal of Clinical Nutrition*, 21, October 1968.
17. D. Mark Hegsted, "Dietary Standards," *Journal of the American Dietetic Association*, 66, January 1975.
18. Henry A. Schroeder, "Losses of Vitamins and Trace Minerals Resulting From Processing and Preserving of Foods," *American Journal of Clinical Nutrition*, 24, May 1971.
19. Henry A. Schroeder, "Is Atherosclerosis a Conditioned Pyridoxal Deficiency?" *Journal of Chronic Diseases*, 2, (1955).
20. Henry A. Schroeder, Alexis P. Nason and Isabel H. Tipton "Chromium Deficiency as a Factor in Atherosclerosis," *Journal of Chronic Diseases*, 23, (1970).
21. Henry A. Schroeder, "The Role of Trace Elements in Cardiovascular Diseases," *Medical Clinics of North America*, 58, March 1974.
22. Henry A. Schroeder, "The Role of Chromium in Mammalian Nutrition," *American Journal of Clinical Nutrition*, 21, March 1968.
23. K. Michael Hambridge "Chromium Nutrition in Man," *American Journal of Clinical Nutrition*, 27, May 1974.
24. I. Szelnyi, "Magnesium and Its Significance in Cardiovascular and Gastro-Intestinal Disorders," *World Review of Nutrition and Dietetics*, 17, (1973).
25. Willard Krehl, "Magnesium," *Nutrition Today*, September 1967.
26. Henry A. Schroeder, Alexis P. Nason and Isabel H. Tipton "Essential Metals in Man: Magnesium," *Journal of Chronic Diseases*, 21, (1969).
27. Henry A. Schroeder, Joseph J. Balassa and Isabel H. Tipton, "Essential Trace Metals in Man: Manganese, A Study in Homeostasis," *Journal of Chronic Diseases*, (1966).
28. Harold H. Sandstead, "Zinc Nutrition in the United States," *American Journal of Clinical Nutrition*, 26, November 1973.
29. Clara R. Bunn and Gennard Matrone, "In Vivo Interactions of Cadmium, Copper, Zinc and Iron in the Mouse and Rat," *Journal of Nutrition* 90, (1966).
30. Henry A. Schroeder, Alexis P. Nason, Isabel P. Tipton and Joseph J. Balassa, "Essential Trace Metals in Man: Zinc. Relation to Environmental Cadmium," *Journal of Chronic Diseases*, 20, (1967).
31. Roger J. Williams, "We Abnormal Normals," *Nutrition Today*, December 1967.

Chapter VIII—MEAT IS BEAN REPLACED

1. A. L. Herbst, D. C. Peskanzer and H. Ulfelder, "Adenocarcinoma of the Vagina: Association of Maternal Stilbesterol Therapy With Tumor Appearance in Young Women," *New England Journal of Medicine*, 284, (1971), p. 878.
2. P. Greenwald, J. J. Barlow, P. C. Masca, et. al., "Vaginal Cancer After Maternal Treatment with Synthetic Estrogens," *New England Journal of Medicine*, 285, (1971), p. 390.
3. Hearing Before the Subcommittee on Health of the Committee on Labor and Public Welfare (Regulation of DES) on S. 2812, July 20, 1972.
4. Hearing Before the Committee on Public Welfare, "Food, Drug and Cosmetic Amendments of 1975," S. 973, July 3, 1975.
5. "Death Due to Penicillin Anaphylactic Reaction," *The Lancet*, March 12, 1956.
6. Lester R. Brown, *By Bread Alone*, (New York: Praeger Publishers, Inc., 1974).
7. M. Narayana Rao and M. Swaminathan, "Plant Proteins in the Amelioration of Protein Deficiency States," *World Review of Nutrition and Dietetics*, Vol. 11, (1969).
8. Allan R. Magie and Elmer A. Widmer, "The Real Energy Crisis is a Cow," *Life and Health*, September 1973.
9. Alan Berg, *The Nutrition Factor*, (Washington, D.C.: The Brookings Institution Publications, 1973).
10. "Feed Statistics," *Supplement for 1971 to Statistical Bulletin No. 410*, United States Department of Agriculture.
11. "New Sources of Protein," *The Lancet*, 2, (1959), p. 956.
12. E. B. Hart, "Abuse of Data on the Biological Value of Protein," *Nutrition Review*, 10, (1952), p. 130.
13. D. M. Hegsted, et. al., "Lysine and Methionine Supplementation of All-Vegetable Diets For Human Adults," *Journal of Nutrition*, 56, (1955).
14. Aaron Altschul, *Proteins: Their Chemistry and Politics*, (New York: Basic Books, 1965), p. 264.
15. Mervyn G. Hardinge, Alma C. Chambers, Hulda Crooks and F. J. Stare, "Nutritional Studies of Vegetarians III — Dietary Levels of Fiber," *American Journal of Clinical Nutrition*, 6, Sept.-Oct. 1958.
16. M. G. Harding, et. al., "Nutritional Studies of Vegetarians—Dietary Fatty Acids and Serum Cholesterol Levels," *American Journal of Clinical Nutrition*, 10, June 1962.
17. Margaret Dana, syndicated article in Gainesville *Sun*, January 1976.
18. M. G. Hardinge, et. al., "Nutritional Studies of Vegetarians I—Nutritional, Physical, and Laboratory Studies," *American Journal of Clinical Nutrition*, 2, March-April, 1954, p. 73.
19. F. R. Ellis and P. Mumford, "The Nutritional Status of Vegans and Vegetarians," *Proceedings of the Nutrition Society*, 26, (1967).
20. B. K. Armstrong, R. E. Davis, D. J. Nico, A. J. vanMerwyck and C. J. Larwood, "Hematological, Vitamin B-12, and Folate Studies on

Seventh-Day Adventist Vegetarians," *American Journal of Clinical Nutrition*, 27, July 1974.

21. F. R. Lemon and R. T. Walden, "Death From Respiratory System Disease Among Seventh-Day Adventist Men," *Journal of the American Medical Association*, 198, (1966).

22. M. G. Hardinge, et. al., "Non Flesh Dietaries—Adequate and Inadequate," *Journal of the American Dietetic Association*, 43, Dec. 1963.

23. R. O. West and O. B. Hayes, "Diet and Serum Cholesterol Levels: A Comparison Between Vegetarians and Non-Vegetarians in a Seventh-Day Adventist Group," *American Journal of Clinical Nutrition*, 21, August 1968.

24. Frank M. Sacks, William P. Castelli, Allen Donner and Edward Kass, "Plasma Lipids and Lipoproteins in Vegetarians and Controls," *New England Journal of Medicine*, 202, May 1975.

25. Frey R. Ellis and John W. Ellis, "Incidence of Osteoporosis in Vegetarians and Omnivores," *American Journal of Clinical Nutrition*, 25, June 1972.

26. Per-Olof Astrand, "Something Old and Something New . . . Very New," *Nutrition Today*, June 1968.

27. J. Bergstrom, L. Hermanson, E. Hultman and B. Saltin, "Diet, Muscle Glycogen, and Physical Performance," *Acta Physiologica Scandia*, 71, (1967).

Chapter X—THE WAISTLAND

1. "The Role of Sugar in Diet, Diabetes and Heart Disease," Hearings before the Senate Select Committee on Nutrition and Human Needs, April, 1973, 93rd Congress, 1st Session.

2. Henry A. Schroeder, "The Role of Trace Elements in Cardiovascular Disease," *Medical Clinics of North America* 58, March 1974, p 381.

3. Henry A. Schroeder, et. al., "Chromium Deficiency as a Factor in Atherosclerosis," *Journal of Chronic Diseases*, 23, (1970), p 123.

4. Hugh Trowell, "Epidemiology of Digestive Diseases and Ischemic Heart Disease," *Digestive Diseases*, 19, September 1974.

5. Hugh Trowell, "Dietary Fibre, Ischemic Heart Disease and Diabetes Mellitus," *Proceedings of the Nutrition Society*, 32, (1973), p 151.

6. Denis P. Burkitt, "Epidemiology of Cancer of the Colon and Rectum," *Cancer*, July 1971.

7. Henry A. Schroeder, "Serum Cholesterol and Glucose Levels in Rats Fed Refined and Less Refined Sugars and Chromium," *Journal of Nutrition*, 97, (1969), p 237.

8. James L. McDonald and George K. Stookey, "Influence of Whole Grain Products, Phosphates and Tin Upon Dental Caries in the Rat," *Journal of Nutrition* 103, November 1973, p. 1528.

9. S. Wapnick, E. Kanengoni, A. C. B. Wicks and J. J. Jones, "Can Diet Be Responsible for the Initial Lesion in Diabetes?", *The Lancet*, August 12, 1972, p. 300.

10. A. M. Cohen, S. Bavly and R. Poznanski, "Change of Diet of Yem-

enite Jews in Relation to Diabetes and Ischematic Heart Disease," *The Lancet*, (1961), p. 1399.

11. A. M. Cohen, "Fats and Carbohydrates in Atherosclerosis and Diabetes in Yemenite Jews," *American Heart Journal*, 19:46, (1966).
12. Michael Jacobson, "The Sugar Content of Fabricated Foods," Center for Science in the Public Interest, (1973).
13. Humphrey F. Sassoon, "Time Factors in Obesity, *The American Journal of Clinical Nutrition*, 26, July 1973.
14. A. K. Adatia, "Diseases Associated with Refined Carbohydrate: Dental Caries and Periodontal Disease," *Plant Foods for Man*, Spring, 1974.
15. Howard M. Ausherman, personal communication, December 1975.

Chapter XI—TIMES OF YOUR LIFE

1. Jacqueline Verrett and Jean Carper, *Eating May Be Hazardous to Your Health* (Simon and Schuster, 1974).
2. James Turner, *The Chemical Feast: the Nader Summer Study Group Report on the FDA* (Grossman Publishing, 1970).
3. Michael Jacobson, *Eater's Digest* (Doubleday, 1972).
4. Senate Select Committee Hearings, *Nutrition and Human Needs: Food Additives*, 92nd Congress, September 1972.
5. Roger J. Williams, *Nutrition Against Disease* (New York: Pitman Publishing Company, 1971).
6. Corrine Robinson, *Normal and Therapeutic Nutrition*, 14th Edition, (Macmillan Company, 1972).
7. "Maternal Nutrition and the Course of Pregnancy: Summary Report" NAS/NRC Commission on Maternal Nutrition, the Food and Nutrition Board, 1970.
8. La Leche League, *The Womanly Art of Breastfeeding*, 2nd Edition (Interstate Printers and Publishers, 1970).
9. J. H. Ritchie, M. B. Fish, M. Grossman and V. McMasters, "Edema and Hemolytic Anemia in Premature Infants: A Vitamin E Deficiency Syndrome," *New England Journal of Medicine*, 279, (1968), p. 1185.
10. A.D. Hunt Jr., et. al., "Pyrodoxine Dependency: Report of a Case of Intractible Convulsions in an Infant Controlled by Pyrodoxine," *Pediatrics*, 13, (1954), p. 140.
11. John W. Gerrard, "Breast-feeding: Second Thoughts," *Pediatrics*, 54, (1974).
12. Jerome Glazer, "The Dietary Prophylaxis of Allergic Disease in Infancy," *The Journal of Asthma Research*, 3, March 1966.
13. Jean Mayer, "Hypertension, Salt Intake and the Infant," *Postgraduate Medicine*, January 1969.
14. L. S. Taitz, "Overfeeding in Infancy," *The Proceedings of the Nutrition Society*, 33, September 1974.
15. D. B. Jeliffe and E. P. F. Jeliffe, "Fat Babies: Prevalence, Perils and Prevention," *The Journal of Tropical Pediatrics and Environmental Child Health*, 21, June 1975.
16. Helen A. Guthrie, "Infant Feeding Practices—a Predisposing Factor

in Hypertension?" *American Journal of Clinical Nutrition*, 21, August 1968.
17. Samuel J. Fomon, "Commentaries on Infant and Child Nutrition," *Journal of the American Medical Association*, 231, March 1975.
18. "Are Baby Foods Good Enough For Babies?", *Consumer Reports*, September 1975.
19. Michael F. Jacobson, "Don't Bring Home the Bacon: How Sodium Nitrate Can Affect Your Health," Center for Science in the Public Interest, (1973).
20. J. D. Gussow, "Improving the American Diet," *Journal of Home Economics*, 65, November 1973.
21. George Kromer, "Symposium on Fats and Carbohydrates in Processed Foods," reported in *Journal of the American Dietetic Association*, (1973), p. 668.

Index

(All recipes are in *italics.*)